Three False Convictions, Many Lessons

The Psychopathology of Unjust Prosecutions

David C Anderson and Nigel P Scott

 WATERSIDE PRESS

Three False Convictions, Many Lessons: The Psychopathology of Unjust Prosecutions
David C Anderson and Nigel P Scott

ISBN 978-1-909976-35-1 (Paperback)
ISBN 978-1-910979-14-3 (Epub ebook)
ISBN 978-1-910979-15-0 (Adobe ebook)

Main UK distributor Gardners Books, 1 Whittle Drive, Eastbourne, East Sussex, BN23 6QH. Tel: +44 (0)1323 521777; sales@gardners.com; www.gardners.com

North American distribution Ingram Book Company, One Ingram Blvd, La Vergne, TN 37086, USA. Tel: (+1) 615 793 5000; inquiry@ingramcontent.com

Cataloguing-In-Publication Data A catalogue record for this book can be obtained from the British Library.

Printed by Lightning Source.

e-book *Three False Convictions, Many Lessons* is available as an ebook and also to subscribers of Myilibrary, Dawsonera, ebrary, and Ebscohost.

Published 2016 by
Waterside Press Ltd.
Sherfield Gables
Sherfield-on-Loddon
Hook, Hampshire
United Kingdom RG27 0JG

Telephone +44(0)1256 882250
E-mail enquiries@watersidepress.co.uk
Online catalogue WatersidePress.co.uk

Table of Contents

About the authors

David Anderson is a retired British physician, endocrinologist and former Professor of Medicine in Manchester and Hong Kong. He is the author of 128 original scientific papers and a 60 film medical education teaching film series, *MediVision*. David Anderson first awoke to miscarriages of justice in connection with a former patient of his, Stefan Ivan Kiszko, who in 1976 was wrongly convicted of the murder of eleven-year-old Lesley Molseed. He lives in Umbria, Italy.

Nigel Scott is a British writer and researcher who (along with David Anderson) has written extensively on the murder of Meredith Kercher and the improbable case brought against Amanda Knox and Raffaele Sollecito for their supposed involvement. He has been Head of Information at the Herpes Viruses Association for 19 years and advised on several legal cases and potential cases involving herpes simplex transmission. He has also served as an Opposition councillor in Haringey, North London.

Acknowledgements

Neither of us trained as psychologists and those excellent scientists, whose relevant work we draw on, are acknowledged in the text. Their work was critical for our analysis of the psychopathological faults in justice systems, as viewed through the prism of the falsely convicted.

This book is the culmination of two separate journeys that led to our meeting in July 2012 in Seattle at a (distinctly premature) supporters' celebration of the release from prison of Amanda Knox and Raffaele Sollecito. We acknowledge with gratitude the many members of the two families and their friends who we came to know following our own involvements, which both started at the end of 2009. That was two years after Meredith Kercher's horrific and tragic murder by Rudy Guede, which followed when a simple break-in went horribly wrong. The subsequent trials and tribulations of Amanda and Raffaele also brought us contact and friendship with many fighting for justice in Italy, including Frank Sfarzo and the crime journalists Mario Spezi and Francesco Mura. Many others have helped in our book's gestation during the various stages in the long fight for justice for two young people who had been convicted of a crime they had nothing to do with. We specifically would like to thank Candace Dempsey, Bruce Fisher (both authors of excellent books on the subject), Sarah Snyder, Karen Pruett, Michelle Moore, Avrom Brendzel and Paul Smyth. Our friends the late Joseph Bishop and Joe Starr tirelessly and generously each played a major role in fighting for justice from the early stages.

Our project has become more than a criticism of Italy's highly faulted criminal justice system, which is so well illustrated by the Kercher murder and its aftermath. David Anderson was involved in the belated release of Stefan Kiszko, whose 1976 conviction for the murder of Lesley Molseed remains a blot on English criminal justice; so it was eminently logical to include this as the UK case considered in depth in this book. He is particularly indebted for discussions with Kiszko's tireless solicitor Campbell Malone, and to Michael O'Connell, another expert on the Kiszko case and a staunch campaigner for criminal justice reform. The two have provided much insight into this case. David is also grateful to Darlie Routier's mother Darlie Kee, for discussions over the torment of her daughter, who has been held on Death Row in Texas for 20 years for the supposed murder of her two young sons. Her case epitomises all the worst about the USA's highly faulted criminal justice system. We have only recently become aware of the tireless work of former cold case detective John A Cameron in his single-handed pursuit of America's most prolific serial killer, the late Edward Wayne Edwards. The murder of the two young Routier boys and the attempted murder of Darlie on 6/6/1996, have the stamp of this highly intelligent psychopath, who with his diabolical *modus operandi* single-handedly perverted the course of justice across the USA for two thirds of a century. This discovery has implications that will extend far into the future and far beyond the Routier case. Meanwhile we sincerely hope that Darlie will soon be released, fully exonerated, and able for the first time to embrace her remaining much-loved son, Drake.

The authors would like to acknowledge the encouragement, diligence, patience, legal expertise and editing skills of Bryan Gibson, without whose efforts this book would not be in your hands.

Finally we acknowledge with gratitude the encouragement and comments of others too numerous to mention by name, including our many friends and family members; and especially the support of our wives Jenny and Annie.

David Anderson and Nigel Scott,
June 2016

This book is dedicated to the many innocent people who have been convicted and punished for crimes perpetrated by others, in the hope that it provides insight to improve justice systems, and so help prevent such errors in the future.

Publisher's note

The views and opinions expressed in this book are those of the authors entirely and are not necessarily shared by the publisher. Readers should draw their own conclusions about all claims made or any facts or opinions stated in the book concerning which the possibility of alternative interpretations, narratives, terminology or descriptions should be kept in mind.

Glossary of relevant terms

Aggression (secondary/reactive) Normal aggression in response to provocation.

Aggression (primary/targeted/instrumental) A form of aggression unique to individuals with defective neurotransmission in the amygdala.

Aggression inhibition mechanism A mechanism for inhibiting aggression in normal people with a normal empathy circuit who see in distress in others a mirror of their own distress.

Amygdala A pair of almond-shaped structures at the base of the brain, part of the empathy circuit, that is necessary for socialisation and the inhibition of instrumental aggression.

Asperger's syndrome Condition of mild autism mainly seen in boys, in which cognitive empathy is lacking, but emotional empathy is intact.

Capanne Prison Large prison just outside Perugia, Italy.

Confirmation bias Predisposition to selectively seek information supporting a belief already held, while ignoring contrary evidence.

Constitutional negative empath (CNE) An individual with a genetic defect in the amygdala function that impairs ability to socialise. Implies high risk of developing psychopathy/sociopathy.

Dietrologia The tendency to see the simplest solution as too obvious, and prefer one that is more complicated. The opposite of Occam's Razor (below). Suggested by the authors as a feature of the Italian mindset/ culture when faced with conflicting ways to deal with a problem.

Empathy The capacity to see in another human being's distress a reflection of one's own distress; depends on the brain's normal empathy system of which a central station is the amygdala. **Empathy (emotional)** Subjective response to another's distress as if it was one's own. **Empathy (cognitive)** Objective recognition that another is distressed. **Empathy circuit** Complex brain circuit in which the amygdala is central, that functions to make normal people care for others.

Imprinting Fixation of beliefs that have formed under conditions of great stress.

Innocence Project Organization in the USA dedicated to freeing innocent people through DNA (see http//www.innocenceproject.org).

Jail-house snitch Prisoner who 'spies' on other prisoners and testifies against them for favours from investigators, prison governers, etc.

Occam's Razor The principle attributed to the medieval friar-philosopher William of Occam that in solving a problem one should not multiply basic necessities; the simplest explanation that fits the facts is probably the most likely to be correct.

Oggi Italian glossy weekly magazine (see http://www.oggi.it) that was pro-innocence of Amanda Knox and Rafaelle Sollecito.

PCR technique The polymerase chain reaction technique that allows minute traces of DNA to be amplified up to a million-fold; essential for forensic DNA-testing, especially from small samples, but that carries risks of contamination.

Polizio-judicial Appertaining to the work and interactions of the police, judiciary and those parts of the criminal justice system in which they operate.

Polizia Scientifica Rome-based forensic laboratory run by the police.

Psychopath or sociopath An individual with a genetic defect in amygdala function, poor socialisation, lack of conscience and pathological behaviour targeting others.

Reid technique An evidence gathering technique used extensively by police in which interrogation is an accusatory process where the interrogator opens by telling the suspect that there is no doubt about their guilt. See for example https://www.reid.com/educational_info/critictechnique.html

Schadenfreude Fascination in and comfort from the distress of others; a normal human reaction.

Stringer Freelance journalist, often working for several titles.

WYSIWYG 'What you see is what you get.'

WYSIJAC 'What you see is just a con.'

Dramatis Personae

Case 1. The murder of Meredith Kercher

Alessi, Mario	Convicted murderer who shared a room with Rudy Guede and gave evidence.
Aviello, Luciano	Male to female transsexual, with a criminal record, who said brother Antonio had killed Meredith Kercher and given him keys and a knife to hide.
Battistelli, Michele	Officer from the postal police, first on crime scene with a colleague.
Benedetti, Giacomo	Rudy Guede's best friend who confided in him via Skype from Germany.
Bongiorno, Giulia	High profile lawyer and politician, who represented Raffaele Sollecito and also stoutly defended Amanda Knox.
Brocchi, Paolo	Lawyer whose office was broken into on the night of October 13th 2007, by Rudy Guede.
Burleigh, Nina	Author and champion for innocence.
Caporali, Paolo	Head of the Caporali family, director of Liomatic Company, Perugia. Adopted Rudy Guede aged 16. Reported to have disowned him two years later.
Capezzali, Nara	Elderly lady living opposite 7 *Via de la Pergola* (murder location) who heard a scream on the night in question.
Carlizzi, Gabriela	Satanic theorist blogger in contact with Prosecutor Mignini (See *The Monster of Florence* referred to in the text and Bibliography, written by Preston and Spezi).

Ciolino, Paul	Innocence Project criminal investigator who spoke of a 'railroad job from hell.'
Comodi, Manuela	Assistant prosecutor, Hellmann appeal.
Conti, Stefano	Professor and forensic expert who testified with Carla Vecchiotti (below).
Curatolo, Antonio ('Toto')	A tramp whose testimony was used against Amanda Knox and Raffaele Sollecito. Curatolo slept on a bench in *Piazza Grimana*, near *Via de la Pergola*.
Della Vedova, Carlo	English-speaking lawyer from Rome who represented Amanda Knox.
Del Prato, Maria	Head mistress of an infants school in Milan where Rudy Guede was found on the morning of 27th October 2007 with stolen goods from the 'Brocchi break-in' and a lady's gold watch.
Dempsey, Candace	Author and champion for innocence.
Ficara, Rita	*Poliziotta* (police officer) who Amanda alleges slapped her during interrogation (though this is denied).
Fisher, Bruce	Author and champion for innocence.
Follain, John	Journalist and author of *Death in Perugia*. The present authors consider that Follain may have been 'used' by prosecutors as a media outlet for their pro-guilt views.
Ghirga, Luciano	Perugia lawyer who represented Amanda Knox, with Carlo Della Vedova (above).
Gill, Peter	Pioneer of the use of DNA in forensics.
Guede, Rudy	An Ivorian man brought to Perugia at age five by his father; adopted by the Caporalis at age 16, later disowned. History of break-ins. DNA, hand and foot prints at crime scene. Serving 16 year sentence for 'involvement with others' in Merdith Kercher's murder.

Hampikian, Greg	Molecular biologist and innocence campaigner.
Harry Rag	Anonymous pro-guilt blogger, also uses the name 'The Machine.' True identity insufficiently certain for publication at the present time.
Heavey, Michael	Seattle judge (now retired) whose daughter was a schoolfriend of Amanda. Founder of Judges for Justice.
Hellmann, Claudio Pratillo	President of the court for the appeal against the Massei verdict.
Kercher, Arline	Meredith Kercher's mother.
Kercher, John (Snr)	Meredith's father. As distinct from her older brother John Kercher Jnr.
Kercher, Lyle	Meredith's second brother.
Kercher, Meredith	Twenty-one-year-old English Erasmus student, murdered in 7 *Via De La Pergola,* Nov 1st 2007.
Kercher, Stephanie	Meredith's older sister.
Knox, Amanda	Twenty-year-old student from Seattle living with Meredith, Filomena and Laura at 7 *Via de la Pergola*.
Knox, Curt	Amanda and Deanna Knox's father, remarried with two further daughters.
Knox, Deanna	Amanda's younger sister.
Kokomani, Hekuran	Albanian drug dealer called as (it is supposed by the present authors an unreliable) witness before Micheli.
Lalli, Luca	Forensic pathologist who carried out the *post mortem* examination on the victim; but was 'prevented' from measuring the cadaver's core temperature for 12 hours.
Lumumba, Patrick	The bar owner who Amanda Knox worked for. Initially arrested alongside Amanda and Raffaele.

Maori, Luca   Local Perugia lawyer who with Giulia Bongiorno (above) represented Raffaele Sollecito.

Marasca, Gennaro   Head of the Fifth Section of the Supreme Court that finally and completely exonerated Amanda and Raffaele.

Maresca, Francesco   Lawyer for the Kercher family; seemingly, claim the present authors, taking a lead from the prosecution.

Massei, Giancarlo   Chief trial judge in the first trial of Amanda Knox and Raffaele Sollecito.

Matteini, Claudia   Judge in Perugia who committed Amanda and Raffaele to 'precautionary imprisonment' pending their trial.

Mellas, Edda   Mother of Amanda and Deanna Knox.

Mellas, Chris   Amanda's stepfather.

Mezzetti, Laura   Trainee lawyer and co-habitant at 7, *Via de la Pergola*.

Micheli, Paolo   Judge who dealt with the pre-trial hearings, and also the judge for Rudy Guede's eventual 'fast track' trial.

Mignini, Giuliano   Lead investigator and public prosecutor in the case against Amanda and Raffaele.

Mura, Francesco   Journalist and producer of periodical and TV series *Delitti e Misteri*.

Nadeau, Barbie   Freelance journalist; author of a book, *Angel Face*.

Napoleoni, Monica   Head of Perugia police's *Squadra Mobile*.

Nencini, Alessandro   President of the second appeal in Florence, 2013-14. Amanda and Raffaele reconvicted.

Paccelli, Carlo   Lawyer representing Patrick Lumumba in a civil case against Amanda Knox. Critical in court of Knox.

Patumi, Walter   Forensic witness for Amanda Knox.

Penna, Alessandro   Journalist for *Oggi* magazine.

Pisa, Nick Journalist (originally pro-guilt): author of the moniker 'Foxy Knoxy.' Changed his stance after meeting present co-author, David Anderson, Nov 2010.

Popham, Peter Author and journalist for *The Independent*.

Popovic, Jovanna A Serbian friend of Raffaele Sollecito.

Pruett, Karen Champion for innocence from Seattle.

Quintavalle, Marco A witness who 'saw' Knox in his shop buying bleach early on Nov 2nd. 'Found' one year after the murder.

Romanelli, Filomena Trainee lawyer and co-habitant at 7 *Via de la Pergola*.

Sfarzo, Frank Freelance journalist and *innocentisti* blogger. Accused of *calunnia* (defamation) by Giuliano Mignini (above).

Silenzi, Giacomo One of the four boys 'living downstairs', and lately Meredith's lover

Sollecito, Francesco Raffaele's urologist father, and staunch fighter for him to be exonerated.

Sollecito, Raffaele Boyfriend of Amanda Knox for five days before the murder, from Puglia, studying Informatics.

Sollecito, Vanessa Raffaele's sister, seven years older, working for Rome's *Carabinieri* in November 2007.

Spezi, Mario Veteran Italian crime journalist and co-author of *The Monster of Florence*. Arrested and imprisoned in 2006.

Spezi, Miriam Mario Spezi's wife.

Stefanoni, Patrizia DNA expert for the *Polizia Scientifica,* Rome.

Sulas, Gianavino Journalist for *Oggi* magazine, consistently pro-innocence.

TJMK True Justice for Meredith Kercher website. See: http://truejustice.org/ee/index.php

Tramontano, Christian	A bar owner whose house was broken into in early-September by Rudy Guede.
Vecchiotti, Carla	DNA expert from Sapienza University who testified at the Perugia appeal.
Vogt, Andrea	Freelance journalist; pro-prosecution.
Waterbury, Mark	Author of *The Monster of Perugia: The Framing of Amanda Knox*.
Zanetti, Massimo	Second judge in the Hellmann appeal, 2010-11.

Case 2. The murder of Lesley Molseed

Akeroyd, John	One of the investigating police officers.
Anderson, Freddy	Lesley Molseed's natural father.
Bilton, Michael	Author *Wicked Beyond Belief,* on the Yorkshire Ripper.
Castree, Ronald	Taxi driver convicted after 30 years of Lesley Molseed's murder.
Cooper, Detective Inspector	Police officer who interviewed the present co-author, David Anderson, on December 23rd 1975.
Coverdale, Christopher	Witness to the moment when Lesley Molseed was led up a slope by her killer. Evidence ignored by the police.
Greenwell, David	A joiner from Nottingham, who found Lesley's body above a lay-by.
Helm, Maurice	Milkman who was seen by young girls relieving himself on October 3rd 1975.
Hewlett, Raymond	A man with a record as a paedophile who was suspected by Trevor Wilkinson of being Lesley's killer.

Holland, Dick	Detective inspector who was in charge of investigating the murder of Lesley Molseed. Later part of the team investigating the Yorkshire Ripper murders.
Humble, John Samuel	The 'Geordie hoaxer' who took in the police and obstructed finding the real Yorkshire Ripper.
Kiszko, Charlotte	Stefan Kiszko's mother.
Kiszko, Stefan Ivan	Rochdale tax clerk wrongly convicted of Lesley Molseed's murder. Later wholly exonerated.
Malone, Campbell	Solicitor who took up the fight to clear Stefan's name.
Mawson, D S John	Detective sergeant who interviewed Kiszko on Nov 7th and 10th 1975.
McFadzean, DC	Police officer who interviewed Kiszko on December 21st 1975.
Molseed, April	Lesley's mother.
Molseed, Danny	Lesley's stepfather.
Molseed, Freddie	Lesley's older brother, whose turn it was to run the fatal errand that Lesley went on instead.
Molseed, Lesley Susan (formerly Anderson)	Eleven-year-old who was murdered on October 5th 1975.
O'Connell, Michael	Barrister and author of a forthcoming book on the Kiszko case, *Delusions of Innocence*.
Oldfield, George	Head of the Yorkshire Ripper investigation, until replaced by Dick Holland (above).
Oliver, PC	Police officer, with Woman Police Constable Shaw (below).
Outteridge, Ronald	Home Office forensic scientist.
Park, Hugh, Mr Justice	The judge at Kiszko's trial.

Russell, Colin	Detective constable who interviewed Kiszko Nov 7th and 10th 1975.
Shaw, Woman Police Constable	Police officer who interviewed Kiszko about possible indecent exposure.
Sutcliffe, Peter	Serial killer also known as 'The Yorkshire Ripper.'
Tarsh, Michael	Psychiatrist who testified at Kiszko's trial.
Taylor, Peter	Prosecuting barrister at Kiszko's trial, who later became Lord Chief Justice during the Thatcher years.
Tong, Emma	A witness who saw Lesley Molseed sitting in a white car driven by her killer, and a man getting into the vehicle. Evidence ignored by police.
Waddington, David QC	Barrister leading Kiszko's defence. Tory MP at the time, and later Home Secretary; became Lord Waddington.
Whittle, DC Anthony Melvyn	Detective constable who interviewed Kiszko on December 21st 1975.
Wilkinson, Trevor	Detective Inspector who ran the investigation that finally cleared and freed Kiszko.

Case 3. The murders of Damon and Devon Routier

Bevel, Tom	'Expert' on blood spatter analysis, who gave evidence in the Routier (and other) trials. The present authors claim that this method of identifying offenders is discredited: see the official reports referred to in the text.
Brown, Christopher	Author of *Media Tried, Justice Denied: The Darlie Lynn Routier Murder Case* (Ad Vice Marketing Inc., 1999).
Cameron, John A	Cold case detective investigating Edward Wayne Edwards and his life of crime and murder.

Camm, David   Another innocent victim who was convicted on evidence which included that of blood splatter analysis.

Claubour, Ben   A man who with Barry Fife was suspected of involvement in an insurance scam.

Cron, James   Retired crime scene investigator who testified that within minutes of arrival at the murder scene he thought it was an 'inside job.'

Cruz, Kathy   Author of a book on Routier murders, *Dateline Purgatory*.

Echols, Damien   One of the so-called West Memphis Three, falsely convicted and for many years on Death Row. Author of *Life After Death; Eighteen Years on Death Row* (Atlantic Books, 2014). The actual convicted murderer of three young boys in a ritual killing, on May 5th 1993, was serial killer Edward Wayne Edwards (who is also suspected by the authors of the Routier killings).

Davis, Barbara   Author of *Precious Angels* (Dutton/Signet, 1999) a pro-guilt book that painted Darlie as a killer, something the author later retracted.

Davis, Greg   Prosecutor in the Routier case.

Edwards, Edward Wayne   Prolific serial killer, active across USA 1946–2009. Now suspected of Routier killings due to his *modus operandi*.

Fife, Barry   Petty criminal who had organized a car insurance scam for Darin Routier.

Frosch, Chris   Police inspector, who with James (Jimmy) Patterson (below), was allowed to plead the Fifth Amendment.

Horinek, Warren   A man falsely convicted based on evidence that included blood spatter analysis (by Tom Bevel, above), of the murder of his wife Bonnie, who committed suicide.

Kee, Darlie   Darlie Routier's mother.

Kerrville	Ultra-conservative small town where Darlie Routier was tried and convicted.
Lobato, Kirstin 'Blaise'	Notorious case of a woman who was falsely accused and convicted of involuntary manslaughter on what was effectively zero evidence and despite a watertight alibi.
Milke, Debra	A mother, released in 2015, after having spent 22 years on Death Row in Arizona, wrongly convicted of complicity in the murder of her son Christopher.
Mulder, Doug	Former prosecutor, now defence attorney who defended Darlie Routier.
Myers, Christine	Mother of Edward Wayne Edwards, who died of gunshot wounds when Edwards was aged five.
Neal, Karen	Neighbour of Darlie, who reported suspicious black car.
Patterson, James (Jimmy)	Inspector in charge of the Routier murders investigation, who was allowed to plead the Fifth Amendment.
Ramsay, Jon-Benét	Six-year-old beauty queen brutally murdered on Christmas Day 1996 by Edward Wayne Edwards.
Routier, Devon	The oldest Routier son, aged six, stabbed to death in a downstairs room.
Routier, Damon	Second Routier son, aged five, murdered with brother.
Routier, Darlie Lynn	The defendant who was convicted of the murder of her son Damon (only) and sentenced to death. Wife of Darin, mother also of Devon (also killed) and Drake.
Routier, Drake	Youngest Routier son, aged six months at the time of the murders.
Routier, Darin	Darlie Routier's husband, since divorced.
Tolle, Judge Mark	Trial judge; his last case before retirement.

Wade, Henry   'Tough on crime' former Dallas prosecutor, under whom Greg Davis (above) worked, and on whom Davis may well have modelled himself.

Zodiac Killer   Serial killer active in the San Francisco Bay area of the USA in the 1960s and 1970s, for whom John A Cameron (above) has strong evidence that this was in fact Edward Wayne Edwards.

Introduction

This book is for anyone who cares about justice. It is principally about the workings of the criminal law, and specifically false allegations and charges that were compounded by defects in justice systems. It is meant to stir-up thought and action by politicians, pressure groups and individuals of conscience who may suspect that the law, being riddled with complex rules, has for far too long been left entirely in the hands of lawyers. All too often it appears to be obsessed with process, procedure and legalities, and to have ignored its primary purpose of delivering justice.

In the book we look at man as a social mammal, albeit a quite unusual one with a complex brain and unusual psychology. This view lies uneasily with the origins of our legal systems that came about when science was in its infancy, superstition prevailed and juries, as they emerged, were seen as the infallible instruments of God. It is written by two *non-lawyers*, and examines unjust prosecutions both generally and through the prism of three high profile cases from separate countries — Italy, the UK and the USA — in which one or more arms of 'The Law' seems to have broken the law, and where the powers that be failed to intervene.

Amanda Knox and Raffaele Sollecito

In November 2007, Amanda and Raffaele had been lovers for less than a week when they were accused of the murder of Amanda's flat-mate, Meredith Kercher. There can have been few modern-day trials in which public opinion became so visible or polarised, as the case played out in the courts of Perugia, Italy and the international press. As we note in *Chapter 10* it became a modern-day 'witch-trial' played out in slow motion. More than 20 books have been written on the case, from all angles, including three by the former defendants and one by the victim's father. So far, however, we believe that none has explored the deep undercurrents of this injustice. We believe that like the other cases featured in the book

29

it derives from forms of individual or collective psychopathology that extend to all police and judicial systems, and the communities they supposedly serve. To use a medical analogy, other books have looked with varying degrees of impartiality at the *symptoms*, rather than the *fundamental causes*. This book seeks to correct that and draw lessons for reform (see particularly the closing chapter).

In the course of becoming involved in the Kercher case it became clear to both of us that something had gone seriously wrong, but what exactly was it? Was it unique to Perugia or something more profound in Italy's justice system, and what were its characteristics?

In early-2013, after a trial and a successful appeal, the highest court in Italy closed legal ranks, and sent this case back for re-trial in Florence with instructions to find an innocent couple guilty, instructions that were faithfully obeyed. This verdict was then again appealed to the Supreme Court. With tortuous logic (arguably peculiarly Italian logic), the review of a review of a review has now been re-reviewed by a section of the same Supreme Court that sent the first review for review! The final result, arrived at in late-March 2015, is that Knox and Sollecito were found definitively *innocent*. But you might not know that. We hope to demonstrate in the book that any lingering view that they were 'really guilty' and somehow 'got away with it' has no substance whatsoever, though such a view continues to blight the lives of those involved.

The Kercher case (in Italy *Caso Meredith*) raises questions about just how deep-seated some faults lie. It also shows that common sense and truth may finally prevail, but at enormous cost and intolerable suffering. In clinical medicine it is well-accepted that individual case histories are highly instructive. So we also look at two further examples. Arguably, these resulted in even greater officially-dispensed injustice than was visited on Amanda and Raffaele.

Stefan Kiszko

Stefan Kiszko was a 23-year-old tax clerk of Ukrainian/Slovenian parentage who served 16 years in prison after being wrongly convicted of the sexual assault and murder of a young girl, eleven-year-old Lesley Molseed, in West Yorkshire. He was released in 1992 after forensic evidence showed *conclusively* that he could not have been the perpetrator. He died a year later. Ronald Castree was found guilty of Lesley's murder in 2007. One of us (David Anderson) was Stefan's endocrinologist and so well-placed to write about this case. We argue that Kiszko should never have even been a suspect. Ultimately he was totally vindicated by hard scientific evidence, and decades later by the conviction of the real perpetrator who had been inexplicably ignored.

Darlie Routier

Darlie Routier is an American from Rowlett, Texas, USA who was convicted of murdering her five-year-old son, Damon. Two of her sons, both Damon and six-year-old Devon, were killed in the attack, but she was only tried for the murder of Damon. Twenty years later she remains on Death Row, and we will argue that she is the victim of an obvious and extreme miscarriage of justice, the origins of which are still unfolding.

The Kiszko and Routier cases further demonstrate the tendency of justice systems towards a form of psychopathology — or 'lock down' — in which questions concerning the correctness of prosecutions, convictions or punishment are avoided on the basis that the system or its practitioners could not have got things so wrong. There are many other such examples from history in which supposed infallibility prevailed over plain common sense, getting at the truth and putting wrongs right.

A reluctance to acknowledge mistakes

Once someone stands convicted at law there is generally a strong and sometimes immovable *de facto* presumption (and official momentum), backed by the court's legally binding decision, against innocence being allowed to emerge, even though there may have been a complete mistake. It can be difficult to dislodge the idea that the police would not have made an arrest unless the individual was guilty, especially given elements of psychopathy or sociopathy which exist in all societies including or maybe especially within the kind of professions to which certain personality types may be drawn (*Chapter 1*). We explore how all three injustices came about, and try to draw some general lessons by exploring differences as well as similarities between them.

Human psychology, superstition and belief

As human beings we are all different, each with our unique genetics (identical twins aside), upbringing, intellect, personalities, prejudices and failings, which together have formed our adult psyche. We are each flawed to some degree by our own special character and psychology. Most of us are reasonably caring, but amongst us are those whose mentality lies on a different scale. Of these, at least one person in 100 has a permanent defect in the brain's empathy system, and is termed a 'psychopath' or 'sociopath'. In this book, because early nurture doubtless modifies the impact of such a genetic defect on an individual's later behaviour, we mainly use the less loaded term 'constitutional negative empath/empathy' (CNE).

We examine what modern research has defined as the characteristics of such people, who lie hidden among us, concealed behind a mask of normality. One of the most important lessons of history is that such people can be expert at exploring and exploiting the weaknesses of others. They can therefore easily create and exploit systems, recasting them in their own image to achieve control.

Legal systems in mainland Europe have their origins in medieval times, and take many of their traditions from the Catholic Church and its Holy Inquisition. At that time guilt was divined by a process of trial by stress, and not based on evidence, let alone on a presumption of innocence. Modern-day processes hold that an individual is innocent until found guilty, but in the hands of many law professionals you might not know it. In the book we describe why we think the Kercher case in particular is a clear, indeed flagrant, one in which 'The Law' broke the law, not once but repeatedly. It seems that in a country where face and *La bella figura* take pride of place, and superstition is still prevalent, that medieval beliefs may yet provide a screen behind which people and systems can conveniently hide.

We also look at defects in other supposedly civilised countries. Their systems too have their origins in medieval times, when the philosophy of the law derived from Christian beliefs in God and justice on the one hand and the workings of the Devil or anti-Christ on the other. Arguably, this was and is compounded by teachings of original sin, heresy and confession, which can have the effect of putting normal people with normal urges (especially universal ones of sexuality) under the control of those in power. Scandals relating to paedophile priests amply illustrate the risks of dogma in the name of religion, while the laws of evidence and forensic science are relative newcomers to the justice scene. So we try to explore which defects are shared amongst Western countries.

The internet age and mass media

The Perugia murder case and its drawn-out legal processes have taken place at a time of rapid change in press and communication systems, and these have had a major effect on judicial processes. From the start, Amanda Knox communicated with friends on MySpace and by email, probably thinking her thoughts were in the private domain. However, it was open to the police to cherry-pick statements to use against her whilst unjustly neglecting any that didn't fit their theories.

Another twist to unravel is the extent to which such communications have been abused, for example in the Kercher case by pro-guilt bloggers or internet trolls hiding behind anonymity to try and influence public opinion and the outcome of judicial processes (*Chapter 5*). And how, in all three cases (Kiszko's case pre-dates the internet age proper) and to an extent, the emotions of the victims' families seem to have been toyed with and even we would like to suggest exploited.

Facebook, Twitter, Wikipedia and other social media are theoretically commendable innovations. We explore how they have become susceptible to manipulation in the context of justice and especially injustice. We argue that because of this some form of national and international regulation is needed to stop abuse. Without such controls it is inevitable that, to suit their own ends, individuals, some of whom may be lacking in normal empathy, will exploit weaknesses in the system.

Avoiding mistakes

Finally, the book asks how the mistakes illustrated by such cases might be avoided, and urges evolution towards a process of real fairness and reason in the pursuit of justice. The law is too important to be left to lawyers, judges, prosecutors and police if we are not ultimately to sink to the levels described by Franz Kafka in *The Trial*. There the victim, Josef K, discovers at first-hand just what can happen when lawyers decide that their role is to earn a living at the expense of the accused, and where things cannot be questioned. In Kafka's Prague, a surreal underground psychopathological judicial system exists solely to support the interests of those in legal power. They in turn select and mould other individuals who further distort the system to suit their own image. In discovering this as a victim trying to fight the system alone, Josef K is himself destroyed.

We believe it is incumbent upon men and women of goodwill to act, for in the words of Edmund Burke, '[A]ll that is necessary for the triumph of evil is that good men do nothing.' We argue that psychopathy (with its constituent lack of empathy), and other attendant forms of psycho-pathology, are what lies behind this famous adage.

Human beings are highly variable thinking and social animals with extraordinarily complex brains, so in this quest against injustice we start by looking at this aspect (*Chapter 1*). We explore first the role of empathy in normal socialisation and the nature of the absent empathy that makes the primary psychopath or sociopath so dangerous to others. The book then raises questions that go to the core of what so often turn out to be *injustice* systems.

At first glance it may seem presumptuous that such a book should be written by two lay people — one a retired doctor and medical academic scientist, the other a writer, local politician and head of a healthcare pressure group. What business do lay people have trespassing onto the hallowed ground of trial by one's peers and robed lawyers and judges? But then, how did the small child in the fairy tale fail to see the emper-or's new clothes? Maybe it is time for some straightforward questions to be asked of those who make their living from what has been described as a 'justice industry', questions may be so obvious that those who have pupated and now fly within the existing system are likely not to ask them.

David Anderson and Nigel Scott
September 2016

CHAPTER ONE

The Law, The Human Brain and Psychopathy

The law is notionally there to protect the innocent against the transgressor and is therefore everyone's business. In terms of personnel it comprises individuals working within a structured group of professions and organizations—police, lawyers, prosecutors, judges—with interconnected and sometimes overlapping responsibilities. Their combined function is to protect law-abiding citizens and their communities from 'nasty' people (that is, those who abuse the rights of individuals or threaten society with violence or in other criminally-defined ways) and their actions. However these are human structures and it is a truism that things left to themselves generally go from bad to worse.

Most people have an innate understanding of right and wrong, and live their lives accordingly; but regrettably not everyone is made like that, and some people are very good at concealing their true nature. The worst of these are called 'psychopaths' or 'sociopaths'; and their nature is of great relevance to the rest of us. We have to work on the assumption that in all walks of life some intrinsically nasty people somewhere are going to abuse their authority. In recent decades there have been many important scientific studies using modern psychological and brain-imaging techniques that throw light on how such people function.

It also seems obvious that no legal system is perfect, but they all should at least aspire to perfection. In order for it to do so, those in power first need to acknowledge this and then try to understand their own vulnerabilities. The best way to do that is to learn from past mistakes, through lessons from individual examples. In medicine a well-worn saying is *primum non nocere*—first do no harm. This is something all medical students have ingrained into them at medical school and surely the law should apply a similar dictum? There are plenty of examples in history where injurious laws have been a cornerstone of tyranny; and tyrannies generally start on a small scale and grow until at a critical point they run completely out of control. So this is also a book about the *tyranny of the law*, which is perhaps an image that those nurtured within the justice system would prefer to paper out of existence. So maybe, again, it is a type of book that only *non-lawyers* can write.

We wish to focus on criminal law through the prism of three high profile cases, one from Italy, one from Britain, and one from the USA, in each of which the law failed miserably. In each case, one or more of its elements appears to have broken the law with impunity, exploited its defects, and thereby secured the unjust conviction of one or more innocent people. Our purpose is to explore how and why this happened rather than to directly criticise the individuals involved and who are after all caught-up in a system that tends to encourage, even demand, aspects of CNE in the sense, chiefly, that emotions must be set aside.

We are principally concerned here with murder, that most serious of crimes, but there are also many innocent people who have been falsely convicted of rape, fraud and other serious offences. Arguably, in each of these cases instead of doing their jobs as they should have done them, one or more people abused and/or neglected their positions of responsibility and trust, and 'got away with it' in the sense that no proceedings appear to have been brought concerning their actions.

So an important starting point is to look at any aspects of human brain function (and malfunction) that are relevant to causing ordinary (in the context of this book) violent crime. It hardly needs to be emphasised that as well as being unfair to individuals falsely convicted, any abuse of power and responsibility within the justice system also endangers other citizens who are thereby put at risk of future attacks by the real perpetrator, who remains free. Professional arrogance and self-interest have often insisted that public officials, by virtue of their office and training, are above such mortal considerations, but the cases examined in this book question whether this is a dangerous assumption.

Medicine and law: How both need to be controlled

In western medicine, the days are long gone when patients accepted that a doctor might simply appeal to his or her own authority as if he or she were omnipotent. As patients we now expect and demand explanations, and as a result medical accountability has improved. Nevertheless individuals such as the medical mass-murderer Dr Harold Shipman still slip through the net, even though safeguards are supposed to be in place to prevent and detect malpractice. Concerning the law, can it really be right for example that, in Italy today, the word of a policeman is still considered to be worth that of two lay people? And is it fair and just that the charge of *calunnia* (slander) is often levelled against individuals who claim that they have been abused by officers of the law or interrogators, even when they claim so in court? And how can we stand idly by when it has been officially estimated that as many as five million people in Italy have been wrongfully imprisoned over the past 50 years?[1]

One conclusion from this book is that since we are *all* flawed humans, within the law there should be safeguards against officials hiding in the shadows of their own inflated authority. Everyone should be accountable for his or her actions, and no professional should, as the law itself requires, be above the law — or to be allowed to think they are above the law — just because they work within it. We must have systems in place that detect the danger signs, and that lead to tests when red lights start to flash. And these need to recognize the universal tendency for groups to be self-interested and to close ranks when the actions of one member threatens to damage 'face' and therefore the profession's reputation.

The science of empathy, psychopathy, and modern concepts of evil

But what has science taught us of the nature of evil, long held to be the role of religion to explain? Man is a social animal, and most of us at least aspire to the aim, extensively annunciated in the *New Testament*, that we should treat others as we would have them treat ourselves. That is what we widely believe is moral and regard as a basic human virtue.

---

1. Antonio Giangrande, https://infosannio.wordpress.com/2016/04/26/
    antonio-giangrande-parliamo-un-po-della-giustizia-italiana-la-giustizia-dei-paradossi/

An increasingly scientific approach to studying the human brain has been made possible by a wide range of psychological tests and dynamic brain-imaging techniques, using the non-invasive technique Functional Magnetic Resonance Imaging (FMRI). So the mechanisms behind normal and abnormal human behaviour have become much better understood, in ways unimaginable only a generation ago. Specifically, with the work of Robert Hare, James Blair, Simon Baron-Cohen and others we are beginning to understand the neurological basis behind good and evil. These studies point to intrinsic basic abnormalities in the brain function of people who have a particularly high innate potential for evil, and this cannot be dismissed solely as the product of upbringing.

We know that 'good' brains (ones that care for others) have already started to develop in most of us as toddlers. Thus a normal three-year-old child distinguishes between a technical transgression (talking to Mary when Mummy said, 'Be quiet!') and a moral one (pinching Mary to make her cry). The development of this process of *empathising* is inherent, and depends on complex brain circuitry, whereby from an early age we see in the distress of others a reflection of our own potential distress. As a result we develop an *aggression inhibition mechanism* that makes us averse to inflicting deliberate harm on other beings (primarily humans, but also animals). When we see others in distress, or images of it, the empathy circuit of our brain literally 'lights up' as if we ourselves were being hurt. In other words, we actually *feel* their pain mirrored in our own nervous system. This mechanism is at the core of our being as social creatures. Individuals who completely lack it become extremely difficult and potentially dangerous adults. However, the extent to which this empathising happens varies, and some of us are better at it than others. And even in those who are normally empathic, the system may at times be switched-off or greatly reduced.

Professor Simon Baron-Cohen has devised tests that yield an adult 'empathy quotient' score, and as with most measurements in science this quantification has a bell-shaped 'normal' distribution curve. Most of us lie somewhere in the middle, while at the two extremes are high and low empathisers. The former are those extremely caring people who see only good in others. Baron-Cohen singles out Bishop Desmond Tutu as a striking example of someone in public life who is extremely empathic. Those at the opposite extreme include occasional individuals who are set apart by a total lack of empathy. This is now known to be due to defective neurotransmitter function in a crucial deep brain relay station, the *amygdala*;[2] and such people are predisposed to become what are variously termed *psychopaths* or *sociopaths*. Of course their personality and behaviour will be forged also by experiences in childhood and adolescence, but in many such individuals there is nevertheless a qualitative difference from normal. As they mature they learn to imitate normal human social behaviour, and ruthlessly use what they have learned to exploit others. If unrecognised and unchecked, individuals with CNE become very dangerous. It should be said at this stage that many psychiatrists have been unwilling to embrace the concept of psychopathy or sociopathy, something that is encapsulated in the American Psychiatric Association's *Diagnostic and Statistical Manual for Mental Disorders*, which uses the term 'anti-social personality disorder.' Baron-Cohen's classification[3] and its relation to our capacity to empathise and systemise, however, seems intrinsically more helpful in the context of this book, although it is certainly not the last word on the matter.

For those of us who fall somewhere in the middle of the empathy spectrum, we do not always express the same *level* of empathy; our empathy circuit may be temporarily switched-off when we are concentrating on something. It may be drummed into neutral through military training, or in other situations where we are constrained to separate people into 'us' and 'them'. This applies in certain professions (neurosurgeons, for example) in which it is important to divorce emotion from the task in hand. So here we see selection for particular traits suited to that specialty, which are then further amplified by training. You cannot do a delicate operation on a critical part of someone's brain while thinking of the emotional consequences should it go wrong. And you also need

---

2. See for example Blair, Mitchell and Blair, *The Psychopath, Emotion and the Brain*, 2005, pp. 133-4.
3. In *Zero Degrees of Empathy* Baron-Cohen classifies lack of empathy into zero degrees positive (encompassing autism and Asperger's) and zero degrees negative, encompassing types p (psychopathy), n (narcissism) and b (borderline). Type p individuals often have additional features of types n and b; they lack emotional but possess cognitive empathy, the opposite is seen in autism.

to be both confident and highly competent; and where things do go wrong, hard-skinned enough that it does not affect future performance. The fictional figure of James Bond stands for a dashing and athletic psychopath harnessed to fight evil with ruthlessness; in other words the archetypical SAS operative.

It is also important to understand that there are two components to empathy, namely its *cognitive* and *emotional* aspects. Through cognitive empathy I understand that you are distressed. Through emotional empathy I feel your distress as if it were my own. These two elements are quite distinct. Both are required in socialisation, but only emotional empathy involves the amygdala. To be an effective doctor I principally need cognitive empathy, but emotional empathy may be what attracted me to the profession in the first place.

Gender differences in empathy and systemising

It is well-established that the normal distribution curve for empathy is overall shifted somewhat to the left (i.e. towards less empathising) in boys and men relative to girls and women. There is of course considerable overlap, but on average women are somewhat better empathisers than men. We have long had a good understanding that physical differences in body structure of the two sexes are determined by the presence or absence of testes. These in turn act through at least two types of chemical hormones: the androgenic steroid hormone testosterone; and a locally active substance, operative early in the male fetus, called Mullerian inhibiting hormone (which wipes out the uterus and fallopian tubes).

The structural and functional differences in brain function between the two sexes depend on high levels of *testosterone on the male fetus and neonate*, which imprints a male pattern of development. Baron-Cohen, in his book *The Essential Difference* (2003, p. 119 et seq), argues that this has been important during evolution, to prepare adults of the two sexes for their respective roles as men (hunter-gatherer-warriors) and women (home-builder-child-rearers). The differences are not absolute, and vary greatly between individuals. They probably also influence sexual preference, which in most people is towards the opposite sex.

There is a further complementary difference also imposed by testosterone, and that concerns *systemising*. By this is meant the compulsion to see order in things. Again, as with empathy there is a bell-shaped normal distribution curve, whose position also shows a global gender difference. The male brain is shifted to the right — towards better systemising — relative to the female. It is argued also that this capacity was especially important for the male of our hunter-gathering human species. It is well established (see for example books by Jared Diamond[4]) that *homo sapiens* evolved, and lived until relatively recently, as a hunter-gatherer.

In male fetuses, testicular hormones impose maleness on our physical body structure, such that male primary sexual characteristics are imposed on the (neutral) female form. So it should come to us as no surprise that sex-determined differences in brain function also involve a similar mechanism. Modern work shows that statistical differences can be seen as early as the first day after birth; given a choice of a face or a mechanical object to look at, Baron-Cohen's team have shown that new born girls overall show a greater preference for a face, and boys for a mechanical object. This difference is clearly inborn. Later there are obvious general differences in how little girls and boys play — dolls, animals and make-believe being a feature of play in small girls; and machines, cars, inanimate objects and systems being of more interest to boys. As a result for the most part small boys tend to choose to play with other boys, and girls with girls.[5]

Later there are well-established overall differences in how men and women navigate, with map-reading being a more natural function of the male brain. These differences are also reflected in specialisation in the structure of parts of the two cerebral hemispheres. Speech, for example, involves areas on both sides of the parietal cortex in women, but only the left side in men; equivalent areas on the right side are involved in spatial recognition, which is better developed in men. Overall, speech develops earlier in baby girls than boys. Of course, these generalisations refer to groups, not to differences between specific individuals of different gender. But they undoubtedly also influence how we select life partners;

---

4. See, e.g. *Guns, Germs, and Steel: The Fates of Human Societies*, 1997, Norton & Co., New York and *The World Until Yesterday*, 2012, Viking.
5. See Baron-Cohen *The Essential Difference* pp. 31-32 and 57-58.

a degree of common thinking, matched also by complementary physical and behavioural differences, usually including those necessary for reproduction of our species, and child rearing.

Testosterone effects on the brain/specific syndromes

Such sex differences in brain development are now recognised to be relevant to the development of the syndromes of autism and Asperger's, which are ten times more common in males than females, and may be regarded as extremes of the male brain. In Asperger's, the individual is often highly talented in areas involving systemising, such as mathematics and music. Such individuals do respond emotionally to distress in others, as if it was happening to them, but they do not *understand* it cognitively. This is classified by Baron-Cohen in his book *Zero Degrees of Empathy* as zero degrees *positive*.

Broadly, therefore, we can consider empathy as having these two components, respectively *cognitive* and *emotional*. In his book (above) Baron-Cohen describes three overlapping extremes of what he refers to as zero degrees of empathy *negative*. Here, cognitive empathy is intact, but emotional empathy is missing. These are *Type p (psychopath), Type n (narcissist)* and *Type b (borderline) personality disorders*. Together these may account for around five per cent of a normal population. Of course these descriptions do not take into account all the other ways in which we differ. But individuals within these three groups, which overlap substantially, are set apart by a dysfunction of that basic part of the brain called the amygdala, which is integral to the brain's complex empathy circuit. They are individuals born with what we less pejoratively term CNE.

The most socially destructive of these personalties is the primary psychopath, who lacks emotional but has intact cognitive empathy. The full-blown psychopath develops a range of other features discussed below. That is the opposite of the individual with Asperger's. The primary psychopath (or CNE) recognises and cognitively ('reads') emotional distress in others, but does not respond to it in the normal aversive way (i.e. as an image of his or her own distress: above).

Obviously, the ability to 'read' distress and emotion in others without seeing in it our own distress inhibits our capacity to socialise. It brings with it a lack of true conscience, but it may also put such people, in certain situations, at a great advantage. For this to work well enough to get away with it in everyday adult life, such individuals need to learn to *simulate* normal social behaviour with what the psychiatrist Hervey Cleckley called *The Mask of Sanity*. Once they have achieved a position of power they may be increasingly able to take off the mask, revealing their real persona, but they are adept at using it whenever on guard.[6]

The Psychopathy Checklist

One problem when considering psychopaths is that most studies have been done on prison populations, for whom the so Psychopathy Checklist (Revised) (PCL-R) has been developed and widely applied by Professor Robert Hare in Vancouver.[7] The elements that go into this tool, as assessed in prison populations, fall into two categories, which do not necessarily go together, but form elements of anti-social behaviour disorders.

- *Group 1* features concern lack of emotion, and include *superficial charm, emotional poverty, pathological lying, callousness, lack of conscience, fearlessness and lack of anxiety.*
- *Group 2* features encompass violent and reactive aggressive *anti-social behaviour*. Anti-social behaviour is often under less conscious control, and so is what most obviously gets individuals into trouble, and into prison in the first place. And it is essentially a feature of disturbed teenage males and young men, as they adapt to the resurgence of male hormones that accompanies puberty.

In general, as they advance through adulthood, men who have Group 2 but not Group 1 features have a good prognosis, and can be helped to socialise. This is not the case with individuals high on the scale with Group 1 psychopathic features of the check-list.

Some 20 per cent of men in prison populations score in the psychopath range for Group 1 features, and these men commit 50 per cent of crimes.

---

6. *The Mask of Sanity. An Attempt to Clarify Some Issues About the So-Called Psychopathic Personality*, first published 1941 by C V Mosby, St Louis; the edition we have read is the third, 1955.
7. See Robert D. Hare and Craig S Neumann, 'The PCL-R Assessment of Psychopathy. Development, Structural Properties and New Directions', Chapter 4 in *Handbook of Psychopathy*, Christopher J Patrick (ed.), 2007, Guilford Press.

They are the ones who never stop committing offences, suggesting that they never change in the light of experience. In fact there is considerable evidence that such primary psychopaths with social and behavioural training, simply become better at *simulating normal behaviour*.[8] They may therefore just learn to target and exploit others more effectively, with less likelihood of getting caught. The lessons they gain from social education are summed up by the so-called eleventh commandment — 'Thou shalt not get found out'!

High functioning (non-criminal) psychopaths

In the context of abuse of power, we are also concerned with *non-criminal psychopaths*. They score highly in Group 1, but low in Group 2 features. They are generally superficially successful in their careers, and when they misbehave are seldom caught. They appear to be charming, but this is skin deep. They are likewise completely lacking in conscience, are persistent and flagrant liars, and often come to believe their own lies. They are cruel and ruthless and engage in what is known as targeted aggression, often getting others whom they control to do their dirty work. They are often sexually promiscuous. Psychopaths lack friends, and as children they were bullies and often cruel to animals.[9]

Overall there are two types of aggression, *instrumental* and *reactive*. Many things determine an individual's propensity to engage in reactive aggression. It depends on the level of his or her threshold for aggression, and the particular stimulus. A disordered childhood, and problems with parental bonding, as well as examples from adults, will often lower the threshold for aggression, which is triggered by frontal lobe activation in the threat response. Normally a low level of threat leads to freezing; a higher level to flight; and the highest level to aggressive fighting. This threshold is, for example, also affected by hormonal surges, such as the

---

8. There is no evidence that any treatments yet applied to psychopaths have been shown to be effective in reducing violence or crime. In fact some treatments that are effective for other offenders are actually harmful for psychopaths in that they appear to promote recidivism. Grant T Harris and Marnie Rice, p. 568 in 'Treatment of Psychopathy', Chapter 28 in *Handbook of Psychopathy*, 2007, Christopher J Fitzpatrick (ed.), Guilford Press.

9. There is an excellent summary of the types of aggression seen in normal individuals and offenders, in 'Psychopathy and Aggression', Chapter 24 by Stephen Porter and Michael Woodworth, in *Handbook of Psychopathy*, Christopher J Fitzpatrick (ed.), 2007, Guilford Press.

dramatic rise in testosterone levels with puberty. There is a condition of impulsive aggressive disorder, in which particular triggers may set off an inappropriate level of aggression. Depressed individuals may also have a lower threshold for aggression. All such conditions, which lie at the base of much criminal activity seen in late adolescents and young adult males are, generally, subject to psychological and other treatment.

The second main type is called *instrumental aggression*; that is to say aggression directed towards a particular goal. This is a special feature of psychopaths because they lack the normal aversive mechanism that should inhibit them from such violence. If I steal your handbag in the street, or stab you and rob you, this involves goal-directed, instrumental aggression. The easiest ones to spot are those that are physically violent; and most of those that end up as criminals in prison do so because of a combination of the two types of physical aggression. However many studies have shown that there are in every community, and in all walks of life, higher func-tioning individuals with CNE who engage in selective targeted aggression whereby they abuse the facilities and responsibilities of their profession. They have learnt to avoid as far as possible reactive aggression, because it is easily detected and causes them immediate trouble. But they have a strong tendency towards targeted, goal-driven, instrumental aggres-sion. This is the type of aggression espoused in Sun Tsu's famous book on the art of war.[10] This book on instrumental psychopathy is compulsory reading in military academies worldwide, and scaled-up can be assumed to be the type of aggression which is responsible for global warfare.

Are there psychopaths within the justice system?

Yes, quite obviously we would maintain. Such people are found in all walks of life, all professions, where they function with variable degrees of success under Cleckley's Mask of Sanity above. What is especially relevant when considering the law and adversarial trial systems, is to ask where people with the characteristics of extreme CNE might best fit in? One does not have to be a genius to spot that public prosecutors are expected by the very nature of the system to be selective with the

---

10. Written in the 6th century BC, Sun Tzu's *The Art of War* remains the ultimate guide to military combat strategy, and is also used extensively to train in the arts of deception.

truth. They need to be sufficiently and superficially charming in order to impress the jury, but to lack any real empathy towards the person in the dock if they are to secure a conviction. Thus their institutional role has elements that are essentially and intrinsically psychopathic. It is logical to assume that successful prosecutions and the destruction of a defence become that much easier if the prosecutor actually is a CNE, rather than simply acting that way! The same goes for police officers, especially interrogators or if they are, e.g. under great pressure to 'solve' crimes or hit targets for arrests.

In her Confessions of a Sociopath, M E Thomas (a pseudonym) the author gives what appears to be an honest account of how life is for a female psychopath.[11] She trained as a lawyer, and describes how well-suited she was to fulfil the role of public prosecutor. She writes:

> 'I'm cool under pressure. I charm and manipulate. I feel no guilt or compunction, which is a handy thing to have in such a dirty business ... [and] ... the thing with sociopaths is that we are largely unaffected by fear. It's not that I am certain I'll do a terrific job, although historically that has been true ... The stereotypes about the bloodlessness of lawyers are true, at least about the good ones. Sympathy makes for bad lawyering, bad advocacy, and bad rule making ... The prosecution and defence would both benefit from a little hard-hearted sociopathic lawyering.'

Is it possible that our confrontational justice system actually selects people with psychopathic traits, or at least a form of zero degrees of empathy, to fulfil the qualities needed in a public prosecutor? This possibility will crop up repeatedly as we consider real life examples. And perhaps the system under certain circumstances actually trains people who are biologically at the low-empathy end of the scale to become even more overtly unempathic in their official role.

Many top prosecution lawyers are doubtless decent people in their everyday lives (but then Adolf Hitler was kind to his dog). Some people are good at compartmentalising their lives and emotions. The infamous

---

11. Pan Macmillan, 2013.

Auschwitz doctor Josef Mengele had no problem de-humanising Jewish children on whom he experimented. He was doubtless a primary psychopath working within a psychopathic system under the overall control of psychopaths in politics. A convergence of forces, of which the First World War and the Versailles Treaty in its aftermath were important features, allowed a breakdown in civilised life in what was once an advanced democracy. And the system was allowed to degenerate because others failed to act in confronting the perpetrators early enough to prevent it.

One further issue we try to address in this book is the nature of the press, and how it panders to our natural inclination towards excitement and *schadenfreude*. Sensationalism gives us a kick, makes for more interesting reading, and sells newspapers and TV time. The press and other media outlets are also *corporations*, set up by law and with the legal rights of an individual, but constrained *by law* to be solely concerned with the profits of their shareholders. Professor Joel Bakan, in his *The Corporation* concludes that this legal responsibility towards one's corporate self means they are legally bound to act like psychopaths. They may be constituted by perfectly normal caring empathic individuals, but when push comes to shove, collectively, *limited companies are forced to act as corporate psychopaths.* They are only constrained to act responsibly if they are harmed if they do otherwise. Their default position is always to act only in their own immediate interests and those of their shareholders. What happens when companies are put in the charge of a true psychopath is well described in *The Psychopath Test* by Jon Ronson, in which the psychopathic company director Al Dunlap engineered and oversaw the destruction of the Sunbeam Toaster Company.

In the context of the legal system we would expect real problems if someone with a vested interest in a particular outcome in a case (such as a public prosecutor who in some jurisdictions in the USA is judged by the number of people he or she convicts, in effect regardless of guilt or innocence) were to exploit the press to help secure a conviction. We can easily think of ways (for example failure to sequester a jury and keep it away from outside influences) where such forces might be subtly brought into play in a trial. After all, the audience (ourselves) is being fed with and thriving on sensationalism, and we have a strong propensity to form opinions on the basis of horror and disgust. Furthermore, there is a well-known phenomenon and a powerful force in both individual and collective psychology, and this is *confirmation bias.*[12] Many people, once they have made up their minds, show a great reluctance to change their opinions even in the face of overwhelming evidence to the contrary. And this reluctance can in turn be amplified if we for some reason come to derive personal benefit from holding or sustaining a particular position. In the context of the cases examined in this book we examine confirmation bias and in particular its reinforcement in relation to blogs and the abuse of the internet. We also examine whether, in the light of abuses of *polizio-judicial* systems and legal loopholes, legislation is needed to avert such abuses.

The danger of relying on confessions

Another commonly held and strong belief is that confessions are a reliable index of guilt—after all, who on Earth would confess to a crime they have not committed? In fact, nothing could be further from the truth; false confessions are commonly elicited using specific psychological methods which border on torture, like the Reid technique (A method of questioning suspects to try to assess their credibility. Supporters argue it is useful in extracting information from otherwise unwilling suspects, while critics claim it can elicit false confessions from innocent persons, especially children. Whilst widely used it has been criticised for eliciting false confessions). And juries, that is to say people like us, tend to believe such confessions. So we need to examine why people confess to crimes they did not do, and why juries believe such confessions, even if their reliability has been countered or even disproved by other hard evidence. And what safeguards are needed to prevent abuse of the confession, or supposed confession. Thus, as we shall see, one of the cases considered in this book involves a palpably false confession and a second case a statement that was interpreted as a confession by investigators. Both of these are perfectly understandable once the circumstances are explained.

---

12. For full discussion, see e.g., Raymond S Nickerson's article in the *Review of General Psychology*, 1998, 2, 175-220, http://landman-psychology.com/ConfirmationBias.pdf

Trust and exploitation in unjust prosecutions

Another important issue concerns trust and its potential abuse. Normal empathic people make friends easily, and this is something that depends on developing mutual trust. You feel attracted to someone, maybe because of a shared interest, and as friendship develops there is an exchange of confidences. This in turn leads to the development of further trust. In fact a first step in making friends is that one or other party confides to the other something about themselves, which is then reciprocated in kind. Concerning friendship between individuals of the same sex, on a personal level, women are better at emotional confidences; while the more systemising males will generally instead discuss and share their interests and hobbies.

Such capacity to trust another, often on the slenderest of evidence, is endearing, and provides a powerful bonding force in normal society. It can also be dangerous if one of a pair is not playing by the same rules. If the person being confided in completely lacks empathy, and is simply imitating it, the relationship becomes highly imbalanced. He or she will become extremely effective at controlling the other by abusing that trust (i.e. that of a highly empathic individual), and will not hesitate to capitalise on this later, especially if the empathic party starts to get insight and to assert their rights.

The importance and dangers of trust

Kieran O'Hara's book *Trust: From Socrates to Spin,* is concerned with the development of complex modern societies. Each day there are thousands of ways in which we implicitly trust others. We buy an electrical item, and we trust that it has been manufactured to function to a high enough standard of quality and safety. To secure this we have a range of certifying and standard-setting organizations that we also trust are doing their job. We trust that our doctor has been educated to a reasonable standard, and that the licensing authorities have vetted him or her, and minimised the risk that he or she is dangerous. And we trust that people paid to keep us safe from potential burglars and murderers, are themselves trustworthy. So we act as if we expect others to treat us as they would wish us to treat them. And we trust that organizations are trustworthy. When it becomes clear that they have slipped-up, we trust that they will correct the fault, and not simply paper over the cracks. We shall see in this book, however, that this is not necessarily the case.

On WYSIWYGs and WYSIJACs

One problem is that out there in the big wide world there will always be some very nasty CNEs, whose *modus operandi* is exploitation rather than trust. Psychopaths do not distinguish, as normal people do, between objects and beings. And the people they find easiest to exploit are those who seem weak because they are too trusting. When we were children our parents and other adult friends shielded us from such dark truths. Children will find out soon enough, and we don't want them to develop an overly pessimistic and untrusting attitude to others; nor for the most part do we need to. After all, 19 out of 20 people who they meet will be exactly as they seem to be—if not necessarily their cup of tea, or someone they have much in common with. To use computing terminology, they are 'What-you-see-is-what-you-get' sort of people, WYSIWYGs. That leaves one in 20 who are not quite what they at first seem to be. But it may only take one to get someone into long-term trouble from which there may be no easy escape.

So what happens if you meet a person, an adult in a position of responsibility who is what we can label a 'What-you-see-is-just-a-con', WYSIJAC? The most dangerous to children are of course paedophiles who exploit their innocence for sexual gratification; one of the cases we will look at, that of Stefan Kiszko, concerns a horrific paedophile murder, but one for which the wrong man was convicted. However, many such WYSIJACs do not engage in devious sexual exploitation, but instead cause selective harm in their own specific professional sphere of action. Any normal adult who has lived long enough will recall with embarrassment how they fell hook, line and sinker into the trap set by one or more such individuals. And our natural inclination is to pretend it did not happen—to cover up, partly to protect ourselves from the reality of our own naïvety.

The way in which WYSIJACs trap us depends on how and where they are plying their trade; if the person happens to be the pyramid scam operator Bernie Madoff, then he or she will make off with your money, in the nicest possible way of course. You will not know about it until it is too late, and often you will then keep quiet, unable to admit that you have been a fool. This will be especially tempting if the amounts are small. And we see repeatedly, e.g. in news reports how such people thrive in the field of finance of all levels. We may even have been taken in by whole WYSIJAC companies, as was the case with Enron, because as we have already seen limited companies are constituted *by law* to constrain them to behave as corporate psychopaths. How much more effective are they going to be if actually run by a CNE or a team of them?!

The cancer of collective psychopathy

The cases we examine in this book show, so we argue, how all too easily institutions can be infected with the cancer of collective psychopathy. The analogy is apt, because it is now well-established that mutant cancer cells are arising in our bodies all the time, and that we have systems for recognising and eliminating them; a cancerous tumour arises when these mechanisms fail. These mutant cells also exploit normal tissues (such as the vascular system that will bring them oxygen and nutrition). Only if we are unlucky enough, or our detection systems themselves are defective, and allow a particularly nasty nascent cancer cell past our protective radar will we find, long down the line, that we are dying of cancer. Cancers are known to vary enormously in their degree of malignancy, and this is often due to multiple mutations, each one of which may not be fatal in its own right.

Pursuing this social cancer analogy further may also be worthwhile, by looking at the individual 'mutations'. First, as we have considered, there may be serious institutional problems with a legal system, so maybe we have a *corporate body that is already predisposed to malignancy*. This allows people with CNE to 'clone' themselves; and once a really severely affected CNE has crawled up the legal ladder, if there are no in-built defence mechanisms, he or she can control the appointment of people in key positions. By then the cancer is well-established, but the body corporate feels the need to appear to be functioning normally, so it tries to adopt increasingly illegal or suspect techniques. One of these goes badly wrong, so much so that even the defective immune control system of the whole body politic may fail. At this point the cancer 'metastasises' (in cancer terminology), spreading itself wherever it deems it is necessary in order to keep itself alive. Such mechanisms led to the rise of Nazism and the consequent Holocaust.

Witch-burning and exploitation of sympathy and horror

In order to understand the multi-dimensional nature of such a social disease, we need also to examine how this cancer interacts with other social mutations out there in the big wide world. We will see in the cases to be examined the dangers for the accused, if the system plays on the emotional and financial heartstrings of the family of the deceased. In unguarded minds this can strengthen the case for guilt (and possibly make people 'pro-guilt' regardless of the evidence) and weaken the case for innocence of the accused. Just as in the days of burning witches, there is little to distinguish between the accused and the accursed. We consider the history of witch-hunts in *Chapter 10*.

Here we need to be aware of one abuse of the press, whose primary object is to sell newspapers (or secure on-line 'hits'), which it can do by printing lies, as long as they come from untouchable sources. Then there is increasing abuse of the internet, and what has come to be the blogosphere which we consider in *Chapter 5*.

Some provisional thoughts

It must be for the reader to decide whether or not what we describe in the book points to any deliberate (possibly even criminal) miscarriages of justice. But the cases we feature should at least alert the reader to flashing red lights, especially at critical early stages in any investigation. We need to be sensitive to the possibility that power can be abused, even if we can see no obvious reason why it should be.

CNEs live by targeting others. Unlike the rest of us, they do not need specific, logical reasons for what they do, because they aren't made that way. We need to ask a number of questions, for example of the police, the legal and judicial systems and about career selection. And we need to be particularly aware of specific structural weaknesses that can lead to high risk and possibly dangerous concentrations of power, that can then be usurped to influence investigations, arrests, prosecutions or outcomes.

History is replete with examples of how critical failure to detect and check CNEs early in their path to power led ultimately to the development of full-blown psychopathic systems. Witness, for example the rise of Nazism in Italy and Germany after the First World War; and the dictatorial regimes of Idi Amin in Uganda, Pol Pot in Cambodia, Mao Tse Tung in China and Kim Il Sung in North Korea (and his son and now his grandson). We will argue that *the law* may be especially vulnerable to takeover by such people. And it behoves the rest of us, and the body politic, to constrain them before it becomes too late, and before we are dragged further towards a new Dark Age.

CHAPTER TWO

Murder in Perugia: An Improbable Conviction

On the night of November 1ˢᵗ 2007 in the medieval city of Perugia in Central Italy, a young English woman was assaulted in her flat, stabbed in the neck in three places and left to die. Undoubtedly in her last moments the victim, Meredith Kercher, tried to fight off her killer, a man who at some stage also masturbated over her body. We know this because he left his seminal blueprint on the cushion on which her body lay. Bizarrely, we cannot be sure of its source, because the police and courts repeatedly rejected requests to have its DNA-profile examined. That is surely strange, since the sperm in semen are virtually pure male DNA, and crimes of violence are almost always carried out by a lone man, and often involve orgasm and ejaculation.

This deliberate error of omission alone is a sure sign that aspects of Perugia's *polizio-judicial* system may have been dysfunctional. And the fact that other courts failed to pick-up on this glaring error points to something systemically and systematically wrong.

The Kercher case

Many books have been written about *Caso Meredith*. What follows first below is a synthesis of what, according to available evidence, actually happened—who killed Meredith, how, and why. In our view it is quite straightforward; the killer was a disturbed but well-connected young man of Ivorian African extraction called Rudy Guede, who acted alone and on impulse on the evening after Halloween. He was by then a relatively accomplished burglar, and under cover of dark at around 8.30 pm had just illegally broken into the house through an upstairs window, probably to look for money. What he would not have known, when he was disturbed by Meredith's unexpected early return home at around 9 pm, as he sat on the toilet, was that he could not escape without a key. The latch on the front door was defective. To close it Meredith had to lock it from the inside, and then remove the key, so her flatmates could also get in if they needed to. The only thing that would point to another man as the killer, something Guede initially claimed in his first SODDI defence, might be a tell-tale DNA-profile (SODDI is a popular American police term: 'I was there but Some Other Dude Done It.') Unfortunately, the judicial authorities, including the lawyers acting for the murdered girl, deemed this essential test to be superfluous.

Occam's Razor versus *dietrologia*

William of Occam was a 14th-century English friar-philosopher, and our reconstruction follows his basic philosophical principle known as Occam's Razor. Like *primum non nocere* (first do no harm: *Chapter 1*), it is something that 50 years ago every student had drummed into him or her at medical school. It goes back at least as far as Ptolemy (2nd-century AD) who stated, 'We consider it a good principle to explain phenomena by the simplest hypothesis possible'. Or in the words of Bertrand Russell, a later exponent, 'One should always opt for an explanation in terms of the fewest possible causes, factors, or variables.' It is an expression of reasoned logic and common sense; the simplest solution is usually correct.

Unfortunately, a preferred approach in Italy is known as *dietrologia*, in which the simplest explanation is deemed to be too obvious, and the more complex is preferred. *Dietrologia* deliberately 'multiplies entities beyond necessity.' It may appeal to Italian character because it is more exciting and glamorous, and it fits with the Catholic tradition of obsessive ritual; but it is dangerous for those at the receiving end of justice, because it seeks evidence to support decisions already made and thrives on confirmation bias. It is perfect for any policeman or prosecutor who has divined what happened 'by a wiggle of the hips' or chat with a dead priest, and needs only to dress-up his or her theory under a cloak of respectability.

We are not denying that conspiracies do occur, in fact we will suggest a hypothetical one that would explain the outcome of this case, but *dietrologia* can all too easily provide a smokescreen behind which evidence is selected to fit a pre-existing theory. *Dietrologia* adjusts the facts and is the enemy of science, including forensic science, which works the other way round. As we shall see later in this book, it is not unique to Italy; it was also seen in particular forms in the other two main cases we analyse in this book. It may be much commoner than we dare suspect.

Inspector Occam's reconstruction of Meredith's murder

Let us first look at the Kercher murder as William of Occam might have done, working back from observation and facts towards the simplest explanation. We will then examine the *dietrologia* that placed Meredith's American flatmate Amanda Knox and her boyfriend Raffaele Sollecito, at the centre of a convoluted murder conspiracy. We will see that this dietrological mountain was monstrous even by Italian standards, and suggest that it was attended by destruction of potentially exculpatory evidence, and by flagrant abuse of professional privileges. We can also then try to apply Occam's Razor to deduce the simplest explanation as to why a person or persons in authority needed to go to such lengths to obscure the truth. In all of this we need to retain a modern understanding of the functioning of the brains of CNEs as outlined in *Chapter 1*.

In Italy, public prosecutors are in the privileged and protected position (amply shown by actions in this case) of being able to sue anyone who suggests that they or the police might be less than perfect, a position which by definition seems to set them above the law. So we may need to engage in some inter-linear writing, mindful of the risks of being taken to court as so many others in this case have been. We stress that everything you read in this book about the Kercher case (and others) should be taken as our personal suggestions, as explanations and interpretations, of which there may be more than one.

The simplest explanation for Meredith's murder is that Guede killed her in the course of a break-in and robbery that all of a sudden went spectacularly wrong. First, he was seemingly a disturbed young man, with a history of break-ins of this type. Second, he is the only person other than Meredith for whom there is any scientific evidence of a physical presence at the murder scene — that is, in the room in which the murder occurred and the body was found. He was identified on the basis of a handprint in blood on her pillow. His prints were on file because he was an immigrant and five days before Meredith's murder had been caught after breaking into a Nursery School in Milan; the police, intending at first to charge him, had then released him apparently on instruction from authorities in Perugia.[1] His DNA was found in the victim's vagina, and on her handbag from which her rent money had been stolen. Nike shoe prints in blood at the murder scene were of the same brand and size as those worn by Guede. Close to one such shoeprint was a small shard of glass from the shattered window. The right footprint in Meredith's blood found on the mat in the bathroom she shared with Amanda Knox, matched Guede's. His DNA was found on toilet paper left in the other unflushed toilet.

No investigator, however *dietrological* by inclination, could deny that Guede had been present in the flat and room at the time when Meredith was murdered. He even admitted he was there, in what he believed to be a private Skype conversation to a trusted friend, Giacomo Benedetti, when he was in Germany after fleeing Perugia. At that time he also said that Amanda Knox was not there (On TV in January 2016 on the other hand he said he was 101 per cent sure Amanda was there!) He had a cut on his right hand, not fully-healed when he was arrested two weeks after the murder, which is explicable if it was he that had climbed in through a broken window and left blood on the frame, or if it was inflicted when Meredith tried to fight him off, as the knife he used to threaten and then stab her slipped from his grasp (On TV he said it was caused by fighting off a mysterious man accompanying Amanda as she slew Meredith).

Guede's behaviour after the murder was also incriminating. After returning home he went to a night club. He returned there the following night and conspicuously continued dancing when the bar owner called for a minute's silence for Meredith. That struck people as very strange. In the early hours of the same morning he caught a train to Milan and thence to Germany, where he was caught travelling without a ticket two weeks later.

---

1. See Nina Burleigh, 2011, *The Fatal Gift of Beauty*, p.129.

Rudy Guede's troubled past

From the point of view of psychopathology we know that he was a highly disturbed young man. He had been wrenched by his father Roger from his mother in the Ivory Coast at the age of five years, and later, at the age of 15 abandoned by his father. He is athletic, and played basketball for Perugia Juniors in 2004–5. He knew the four boys downstairs (one of whom, Giacomo Silenzi, had recently become Meredith's lover) because they played basketball together in the nearby Piazza Grimana. As a teenager, after receiving help from his teachers and a priest, he was adopted at age 16 by the Caporalis, a wealthy Perugian family, who own Perugia's basketball team as well as the vending machine company Liomatic. As part of that family, he travelled with them on skiing holidays. They helped with his education and gave him work. However he repeatedly dropped out of courses and was finally and formally disowned by the head of the family for indiscipline and unreliability in mid-summer 2007. He went to stay with his aunt near Milan, and worked there for a short time in a bar before returning to Perugia. He was a perennial sleepwalker. There is a strong suspicion that he was on and dealing in hard drugs, such as cocaine and crack cocaine. His nickname was 'The Baron'.

Rudy Guede's troubled present

He was also a known burglar, and being unemployed with rent to pay it seems pretty certain he would have needed money. Anyway, he stole 300 Euros from Meredith's purse.[2] On the night of September 27th 2007, he broke into the home of a Perugian bar owner Christian Tramontano, and produced a jackknife when confronted by the occupant. Tramontano testified in court during his trial hearings that he had recognised Guede in his nightclub later that day, and tried to report him to the police, but gave up after three attempts because of the wait at the police station. On 4th October someone broke into Maria del Prato's nursery school in Milan and stole €2,000. On the night of 8th October someone broke into the house of Guede's elderly neighbour, stole a jewel box and a lady's gold watch, left clothes on a lit lamp, setting fire to the flat and

---

2.   Allegedly. He was never found guilty of this. See http://www.amandaknoxcase.com/rudy-guede/

killing the cat. Then on the night of 13-14 October, someone broke into lawyer Paolo Brocchi's office in Perugia, climbing-up using an outside grill protecting the first floor window below and entering through a second-story window after having thrown in a 'rather large stone'. A computer belonging to Brocchi's colleague, and a mobile phone were stolen; clothes from a cupboard were deliberately strewn on top of the glass from the broken window.

Two weeks later, on 27 October 2007, five days before Meredith's murder, Rudy Guede was arrested in Milan after breaking into the above-mentioned nursery school. The school owner, Maria del Prato testified that she had stopped by her school on Saturday Oct. 27, and found Guede in her office. 'I asked him who he was,' she testified in court, 'and he replied perfectly calmly, even though I had caught him red-handed.' He told her he was 'a kid from Perugia' who had arrived the night before and had nowhere to sleep. He said that someone at the railway station had told him about the school and he had paid €50 to stay there. Del Prato found her locker had been opened, and believed Rudy was looking for something to steal. Some small change was missing, and she noticed Rudy had a laptop computer. He said it was his, but it was later traced to the lawyer's office in Perugia.

When police arrived at the school, they searched Rudy's backpack and found in addition to the laptop, a mobile phone, a small hammer, a knife with a ten inch blade that had been taken from the school kitchen, and a lady's gold watch. Rudy was later booked at Milan Police Station and accused of theft, receiving stolen goods and being in possession of a weapon. He was released after they had contacted Perugia police. Two days later Rudy Guede went and apologised to Paolo Brocchi, claiming he had purchased the computer legitimately in Milan, but had somehow discovered it was stolen from the lawyer's office! This is all written in Judge Giancarlo Massei's motivation report after the first trial of Amanda and Raffaele. The computer, strangely, was never returned to its owner. We have not been able to interview Brocchi as he has since died.

Maria del Prato testified that Guede had *replied calmly even though he had been caught red-handed*. Such brazenness and superficial charm are features strongly suggestive of CNE, even of primary psychopathy. Mark

Waterbury in his book *Monster of Perugia; The Framing of Amanda Knox* suggests that perhaps this property of Guede was useful to someone in high places. He argues that instructions from one police force to another to release him without charge could only have come from the highest level, almost certainly with clearance from Perugia's public prosecutor. Inspector Occam would surely have raised an eyebrow at such a sign of apparent protection for Guede. And obviously by releasing him the police left at large a loose cannon, a man who turned out to be even more dangerous than common sense should anyway have dictated. After all, he had been caught in possession of objects stolen during other break-ins, as well as a knife stolen from the school kitchen. And he had shown himself willing to use knives when he threatened Tramontano. The message read by Guede would surely also have been that he had *carte blanche* to get away with anything. (Interviewed on TV in January 2016 he said he had unwittingly bought the computer in a Milan market; he was not asked about Brocchi's cellphone or the lady's gold watch!).

Criminal profiling

In forensic work it is well recognised that criminals tend to use the same *modus operandi* in repeated crimes. This is the basis of *criminal profiling*, something which is thoroughly described and explained by John Douglas, former FBI criminal profiler, in his 2013 book *Law and Disorder*. So let us look at the Perugia murder crime scene further. The four girls lived upstairs in No. 7 *Via de la Pergola*. The building was well-known to Guede through his sporting contacts with the four young men who lived downstairs. The latch for one of the shutters in Filomena Romanelli's room, which is one floor up from the ground floor and level with the driveway, was broken as could doubtless be seen from outside including by a man wanting to break in. Guede knew the property well and would have confirmed the broken latch on an exploratory foray climbing-up on the downstairs window grill. The Brocchi break-in had provided a nice dress rehearsal. Unfortunately, the fact that the girl's front door could only be secured by re-locking again with a key on the inside meant that anyone returning home had to lock it, and then remove the key so that flat-mates might then also use their own keys to enter. That meant Guede would not have then been able to slip out of the flat unnoticed. The presence of glass on top of Romanelli's clothes was claimed to indicate that the break-in had been staged, yet the room was in some disarray and there is no evidence that all the clothes had been neatly stored prior to the crime. The 'fake break-in' canard was used by the prosecution to shut down critical comment of their crime theory, because their whole case rested on this hypothesis. There was no forensic investigation of the glass shatter pattern, the window, or the ground outside, but the location of the rock and the broken glass is suggestive of it having been thrown from outside, as would be expected.

It was obvious when Amanda and Raffaele first looked critically at 7 *Via de la Pergola*, late on the morning of November 2nd, and then reported to the police, around midday, that an intruder had broken and entered through Filomena Romanelli's window. This involved climbing up the metal grill over a ground-floor window, and hoisting himself (presumably him) up onto the window ledge. This was shown by the defence team, and later on a British Channel 5 TV programme, to be easily possible, using the grill below for handholds and footholds. This is precisely the sort of commonplace process that burglars use to break and enter, and similar to the method used to enter Brocchi's office. Guede could have done this having first climbed up to open the broken shutter; descended; waited to see no-one was coming; and have thrown the rock in from the driveway which was at the same level. There was indeed a large stone on the floor of the room, and fragments of the glass from the shattered window directed inside the flat and spread across the floor, as well as being impaled on the outer face of the inner shutter. There were no shards reportedly found on the ground outside.

As indicated, Guede was an athletic young man: he was certainly capable of climbing-up using the grill below, and perhaps a nail in the wall, and climbing through the window, albeit with the risk of cutting his hand on glass shards in the process (Some blood was in fact noticed on the window ledge, but never analysed for its DNA-profile). Guede, as we have seen, also seemed to be abnormally fearless, something that would be enhanced by such drugs as crack cocaine or dexamphetamine. We do not have to look far for a motive. The date was predictably when money was collected together by Filomena from the four girls to pay the month's rent.

So Guede is after money it seems. He searches drawers and surfaces in Romanelli's room, but doesn't find any; takes a drink from the fridge and goes into the toilet in the large bathroom next to the kitchen for a bowel movement. He is sitting there when he hears Meredith come in through the front door and close and lock it with her key. He doesn't want to make a noise and alert Meredith, so leaves the toilet unflushed. He needs to escape, but discovers a major problem getting out through the locked front door. Now in a heightened state he goes into Meredith's room, assaults her from behind, and threatens her with the knife he had used to threaten Tarantino. Of course, she recognises him, tries to fight him off (she had some martial arts training) and in the process she jerks her neck onto the knife that he is holding pressed against her. This causes a lot of bleeding but she fights hard. He decides then to finish her off with two more stabs in the neck. If not already bleeding from the glass shards he is cut in the palm of his right hand when the knife slips. At some point, sexually aroused, he interferes with her digitally and masturbates over her, in a final act of sexual defiance. He covers the body with a duvet (an action not unusual in the first murder of psychopathic killers), and cleans up as best he can. His right foot is soaked in blood so he washes it, and leaves a diluted imprint in blood on the bath mat in the nearby small bathroom.

Before leaving, Guede takes the rent money from Meredith's purse, removes her two phones and her keys, locks her bedroom door, and exits through the front door which he leaves pulled to. We will leave for the moment the downstairs flat, but Guede clearly went in there, as there was a great deal of blood in that flat, improbably attributed to a cat that was bleeding. But we do not know how much of that blood was Rudy's, how much Meredith's, and how much a mixture from both. It is unlikely any came from the cat, as DNA in the blood was replicated by the police using forensic methodology specific to humans.

Guede, soaked in blood, may well have gone out and down through the undergrowth in the ravine immediately below the cottage, avoiding the route that might have taken him past people. He doubtless throws away the knife and keys in the dense undergrowth. He tries to switch off Meredith's English phone, activating the first number on the list, the Abbey Bank (this we know happened at 10 pm). On the way home he discards both phones over a wall and into the garden belonging to Elizabetta Lana and her family, which he may have thought was over a ravine. Half an hour later (10.30 pm) someone phones the house, where the phones have been thrown, saying there is a bomb in the toilet. Elizabetta Lana was concerned because there had recently been an attempted burglary there. The police came and found no bomb. But that phone call is another extraordinary coincidence, on which I think William of Occam would also have commented, bearing in mind the evidence discussed above of Guede's apparently 'protected' status by Perugia police.

So the 21st-century Chief Inspector Occam would be working on the assumption that an athletic adult male burglar had broken in to 7 *Via de la Pergola* via the window of Romanelli's room on a dark winter's night, with the intention of taking the thing he most needed — money for drugs and rent. Since, as already described, Guede left copious evidence of his presence and since he was a known and fearless burglar with a past history of intolerable behaviour, and at least one previous crime with the same *modus operandi*, the above would constitute the simplest and there-fore the most probable theory. And the one thing Occam in 2007 would have examined and tested before all else, would have been the putative semen stains on the cushion on which Meredith Kercher's body lay, to verify it was semen and determine its unique DNA profile. He would have confirmed by microscopy at least, that it contained sperm heads. The DNA-analysis would have told him whether the sperm sample came from the suspect who had already been identified from the hand print, or whether a second assailant was present. Later on, he might also have asked how and why the police believed a black man to be involved, and why they arrested the wrong one, before they had to admit that Patrick Lumumba had an incontrovertible alibi. Occam might also have asked why, when the forensic test results implicated only Guede, the police insisted on clinging to the belief that a woman was also involved.

Dietrologia: An improbable case is constructed

In November 2007, 20-year-old American student Amanda Knox had been in Perugia for six weeks, fulfilling a long-held ambition to study abroad. By all accounts from her native Seattle, she was an empathic, industrious and ebullient young woman in the full flush of youth. Nobody has accused her of not being beautiful. And she was a good athlete who had earned the moniker 'Foxy Knoxy' for her soccer skills at the age of 13. In September that year, on a joint foray to Perugia her younger sister Deanna had found 7 *Via de la Pergola* by chance when one of the Italian girls was posting an advertisement on the University for Foreigners' notice board. Amanda was delighted with her find, and when she moved in two weeks later after a trip to visit relatives in Germany, a fourth girl, English Erasmus student Meredith Kercher, had taken the last place. They soon settled in, and there was nothing to suggest anything unusual or hostile in the relationship. Unfortunately, shortly after the murder the postal police 'inadvertently' destroyed much potentially important objective evidence of her friendship with Meredith. Amanda's camera, containing photographs and short movies of her and Meredith, was seized and was never seen again. The hard drives of both Amanda's and Meredith Kercher's computers, which doubtless also contained photographs, plus one of Raffaele's and Filomena Romanelli's, had their hard drives 'accidentally' destroyed by police operators. As far as we know, no-one has even been reprimanded for this. This we are asked to accept as just another unfortunate happening.

Two other pieces of background information about Amanda are worth placing on the record. She is among the most empathic of women, something I have formally confirmed using the questionnaire in Professor Baron-Cohen's book *Zero Degrees of Empathy*. Her empathy is illustrated by a schoolfriend, Washington State Judge Michael Heavey's daughter, who remembers being in a car with her at the age of eight, when Amanda insisted that the driver stop so that she could open the door and let a spider out. As a child she literally would not hurt a fly. 'She was way too trusting,' says her mother Edda. Second, and even more obviously, crimes of violence by women are exceptionally rare and such crimes by women against other women are virtually unheard of. It is probable that many of the crimes of violence in Italy ascribed to women against their children, and for which they have been convicted, have also been wrongly attributed. This is considered in a later chapter.

Romance and classical music

A week before the murder, on October 25th 2007, Amanda and Meredith went to a classical music concert in Perugia. Meredith left at the interval but Amanda stayed on, and fell into conversation with a shy, good looking, and equally empathic young Italian man three years her senior, computer student Raffaele Sollecito. He is the son of a respected urological surgeon, Francesco Sollecito, from Puglia in the south of Italy (and so, by Perugia standards, also a foreigner). The two young people, clearly star-struck, began a whirlwind romance of the type many of us can doubtless remember from our early adulthood. Raffaele, like Amanda, had an impeccable upbringing, and was close although rather subservient to his father; his mother, to whom he had been especially attached since his parents divorce, had died 18 months before from a heart attack.

As this romance took off, Amanda was working in the evenings at a bar run by a Congolese man called Patrick Lumumba, for which she was paid €5 an hour. On October 31st, Halloween presented an occasion for students to party and drink too much. Meredith went dressed as Dracula with a group of her English friends, while Amanda went to work with cat's whiskers drawn on her face, in Patrick's bar on one of its busiest nights of the year. The day after Halloween is All Saints Day (also known as the Day of the Dead), and not surprisingly was exceptionally quiet. In the afternoon Raffaele went with Amanda for lunch at the girls' flat and also met Meredith. Amanda had been expecting to work in the bar that night, but at 8.20 pm received a text from Lumumba saying it was quiet and she wasn't needed. Furthermore, Raffaele had agreed to take a Serbian friend Jovanna Popovic to the station, to pick up a bag due to arrive by train, but this too was cancelled. So the two young lovebirds were free to spend an unplanned evening together. They ate, drank, watched the film *Amelie*, downloaded via the internet, shared a joint of hashish together, and of course made love. It is highly unlikely they were bored with one another's company.

Nevertheless, the prosecution theory of the crime requires us to believe that two attractive youngsters with no past history of any violence, and clearly swept off their feet, went out on a dark November night to look for something more exciting than their private company and pleasure. The construct created by the public prosecutor is that, bored, they left Raffaele's flat for 7 *Via de la Pergola* and a more exciting sex game, with Amanda's flat-mate and an Ivorian burglar whom Raffaele had never met. Amanda was Raffaele's first true passion or love, and we are expected to believe that this shy young computer whizz-kid, who was due to graduate in a week, would have been bored with her in six days.

Yet this fable was bought by literally millions of tabloid readers and is the theory on which the pair were convicted of murder two years later. It is surely reasonable to conclude that it was the construct of one or more CNEs, themselves hiding behind a mask of sanity, that was then amplified by a press that thrives on salacious fantasies. In Italy, such stories coming from the prosecutor or police can be published with impunity. The equally startling thing about this misleading, seemingly fabricated account is that there is no evidence, direct or circumstantial, to suggest either was capable of such an act. Yet in court the prosecutor was allowed to hypothesise at will, with no reference to anything except what seems to be speculation.

Amanda first on the crime scene

On the next morning, November 2nd, also a public holiday, the couple had planned to drive to the town of Gubbio in Raffaele's car. Amanda, not surprisingly, wanted a change of clothes so she went back to her flat. Raffaele's sink had been leaking the night before, and she had offered to pick up a mop. These are the little commonplace things that happen to normal people every day, but were to be worked into an improbable suspect-centric framework in a *dietrological* prosecutorial context. Amanda went to her house at around 11 am, and noticed a few things that were unusual. First, the door was open, so she thought Meredith or one of the others had just gone out. She knew that there were problems with the lock, which had been reported to the owner (with no response). No-one was in. She went into her room, next to Meredith's, undressed, and went for a shower. She noticed a few drops of blood in the bidet, and thought that maybe Meredith must have a period. She herself had had multiple ear piercings a few days before, so that was another possible source. She later noticed a weakly bloodstained partial footprint on the bath mat. After showering and dressing she knocked on Meredith's door, which she found was locked.

Amanda writes in her own book, *Waiting to be Heard: A Memoir*,[3] that the thing that really alarmed her, when she went into the second bathroom that was shared with the Italian girls, to use the communal hairdryer, was the sight of unflushed faeces in the toilet. Neither of the older girls would have left the toilet unflushed, so she realised a stranger had been there. She grabbed her coat and purse, somehow managed to remember the mop, and rushed out in a panic, just managing to lock the front door as she left. She records that as she went back to Raffaele's flat her anxiety started to diminish.

Forgetting, or not caring about, the nine hour time difference she phoned her mother on the way home, and asked for her advice, which was to call her room mates, go to Raffaele, and call her back. She called Filomena first, and told her she had found a few drops of blood in one bathroom and shit in the other. The much older Italian girl sounded worried that something might have been stolen and told her to phone Meredith. Amanda then tried to do so, first calling Meredith's British phone, which a recording said was out of service. Then she phoned her Italian phone (which was in Filomena's name) and got no reply. Back at Raffaele's, he had just come out of the shower; she told him of her concerns and he agreed it sounded weird and they needed to go back. They snatched a quick breakfast — 'maybe the toilet is just broken' said Raffaele. They were still sipping coffee when Filomena phoned, her panic further triggering Amanda's concern.

The strange case of the missing phones

Of course *we* know that all this time Meredith was dead, but Amanda didn't — and it is not the sort of thing a normal 20-year-old girl is going

---

3.   Harper Collins, 2013.

to imagine even in her worst nightmare. We know that Meredith's Italian phone had already been picked up by Elisabetta Lana, and taken to the postal police. It was Amanda's attempted call that led her daughter to find Meredith's English phone in the garden, in the undergrowth close to where the first had been found. This is hardly something she would have done if she and Raffaele had thrown the phones there. Unless, that is, you invoke double *dietrologia* and argue it was to put people off the scent.

After breakfast Raffaele and Amanda went back to 7 *Via de la Pergola*, where Amanda discovered that Filomena's room had been broken into, and was in complete disorder with glass everywhere, clothes heaped over the bed and floor, drawers and cupboards open. 'Oh my God, someone broke in,' she called to Raffaele. She spotted the laptop and camera on the desk and writes, 'I couldn't get my head round it.'

Filomena phoned her again, and said she was just coming round. Meredith's door was locked, and there was no sound from her room. Amanda was more concerned about the broken window, and ran outside to see if the guys downstairs were at home. She ran back upstairs and knocked increasingly hard on Meredith's door. She couldn't figure it out, tried to look under the door, and went outside to climb over the wrought iron railing and lean out to try and peer in. Raffaele told her to stop as she could fall. He tried to kick Meredith's door down, and then to ram it hard with his shoulder; nothing gave way. Amanda phoned her mother again, and she told her to phone the police, while her stepfather told her to 'get the hell out of that house, this instant.' Meanwhile Raffaele called his sister, a police officer in Rome, and then 112 for Italy's *Carabinieri* (state police). The two went outside and waited.

Amanda also phoned Filomena, who sounded panic stricken; the Italian trainee lawyer promptly contacted a lawyer herself. Shortly afterwards, Michele Battistelli and a colleague from the postal police (technical people concerned with theft of phones) arrived, though the official timeline was changed later, which made it sound as if Raffaele had only phoned the *Carabinieri after* the postal police had arrived. This was done by referring to the time code on the CCTV of the car park opposite the flat, which was ten minutes fast, and instead claiming it was ten minutes slow. While talking to the postal police Filomena's boyfriend Marco arrived with a friend Luca in one car, and two minutes later Filomena with Luca's girlfriend Paola; Filomena stormed into her room, saying 'my room is a disaster. There's glass everywhere and a rock underneath the desk, but it seems like everything is there.' The postal police, intent solely on identifying the phones, were satisfied there had been a break-in. They were told Meredith's door was locked; Amanda said this was unusual though she locked it sometimes when changing clothes or going away for the weekend; while Filomena said, 'She *never* locks her door.' Again, great significance was later attached to this. Filomena told the postal police to break down the door, which they said was not within their authority.

Meredith's body discovered

There were now six people crammed into a tiny hallway, all talking at the same time loudly in Italian, while Amanda and Raffaele were further away. At around 1 pm Paola's boyfriend, Luca broke down the door of Meredith's room with several thundering kicks to dislodge the lock; this revealed the full horror of what had happened. Filomena screamed 'A foot! A foot!' One of the guys shouted, 'Blood! Oh my god!' Filomena screamed, hysterically. Amanda heard someone exclaim '*Armadio*' — closet, and '*Corpo*' — body. And she tried to reconstruct a scene she and Raffaele never saw.

So the net began to close on the two young lovers. About 90 hours later, and after 43 hours of interrogation, culminating in an overnight inquisition with changing tag teams of interrogators sent up from Rome, without a lawyer or a proper translator, with apparently no recording, a near-confession was extracted from Amanda, in which she closed her eyes and 'imagined' Patrick Lumumba killing Meredith. The name of the black man Lumumba was suggested to the police by a text on Amanda's phone saying business was slow so she did not need to come in. And by a mistranslated message back from Amanda, '*Buona notte. Ci vediamo piu tardi*' (meaning 'Good night. See you later'). The 'confession' was promptly retracted in her '*memoriale*' (meaning 'memoir'), once Amanda had had a few hours sleep.

But this was enough to have Patrick Lumumba arrested at 6 am from his home, in front of his terrified wife and small child. Meanwhile, unbeknown to Amanda and Raffaele until it was too late, it was being decided that they (and especially Amanda) were guilty, and on November 6th, in front of a mass of police it was announced '*Caso chiuso*' — 'We have them, case closed.' The world heard that three people (none of them from Perugia) had killed Meredith in a 'sex game gone wrong'.

Two weeks later, when the evidence against Rudy Guede proved inescapable, and the police finally checked Patrick's watertight alibi, all that happened was that one black man was substituted for another, and the confusion from then on was pinned on Amanda for naming Lumumba. Meanwhile newspaper sales soared and shocking details were revealed as to supposed inappropriate behaviour by Raffaele and especially Amanda, who hardly spoke any Italian, and for whom there had been absolutely no support system apart from her newfound boyfriend whom she hardly knew. The global confirmation bias was fed by stories of the two going out and buying sexy underwear, when Amanda literally had no change of clothes, and of a conversation in English heard by the shop owner who didn't speak the language. There were also stories of imagined cartwheels by Amanda in the police station.

Occam applied to Perugia's *polizio-judicial* system

One would think it should be accepted that public officials are susceptible to the same faults and foibles as the rest of us. This does not just concern illnesses, but personality problems that derive from a disordered empathy system as considered in *Chapter 1*. This will also apply to the organizations within which they work. Later in the book we examine specific problems to which police and judicial systems are vulnerable worldwide, but it is reasonable to presume that among police and public prosecutors at least the expected average of one per cent will have the intrinsic condition of brain function with CNE, that we have seen defined by Professor Baron-Cohen as zero degrees of empathy, *Type P*, and who therefore qualify as primary psychopaths. They have a major defect in the development and function of the amygdala, and so have never socialised. And as with the rest of the population *at least* a further four per cent will be seriously deficient in empathy of the narcissistic (n) or borderline (b) types, or various mixtures of all three.

Psychopathy and the justice system

But that may well be a gross underestimate, since it ignores two additional factors. *The first* is the nature of the judicial process, which is confrontational. It is therefore one in which it is the public prosecutor's job to paint a picture of the accused that is especially bad; and it is the job of the defence to try to counter this. The appointment process for prosecutors is likely to select people who can easily see the accused person in the dock as an object to be despised; and to eliminate those who feel empathy and would respond easily to genuine distress in another.

But just as surgeons are probably selected (mainly by other surgeons), from the less empathic and more systemising end of the spectrum of freshly qualified doctors, this is equally likely to apply to prosecutors in the legal profession. The defence (which attracts lawyers of the more empathic variety) answers with its own particular refutation, which may or may not lead the truth to emerge. The jury represents God, the infallible umpire, and the decision is placed thereon; except that in Italy the otherwise lay jury of eight is led by two judges, who themselves may lean towards a prosecutorial type of low empathy. In Italy public prosecutors and judges have the same training, and an individual will often move back and forth between the two roles. The six lay members of the jury are unlikely to go against the recommendations of the two judges on the same panel. It is especially risky, as happened in this case, when the public prosecutor is the person who oversees key elements of the investigation, and is in a position where he or she has been able to build a network that controls the system. In this case Giuliano Mignini has been quoted as saying that he keeps lists of his enemies and, 'If you are my enemy I shall investigate you.'[4]

The second factor is that within any dysfunctional system, natural selection often operates to make it more extreme. Appointment committees are influenced especially by their most senior and powerful members; and

---

4.   Silvio del Vigo, *Panorama* magazine, 11 February 2010, p.80; *'Sei mio nemico? Vai indagato.'*

CNEs are good at identifying and eliminating people who will oppose them. Remember, their lives have to function entirely through control and so without real friends. This intrinsic bias is especially so if the system lacks adequate supervision from above designed to detect and weed out 'bad eggs'. In Italy, the public prosecutor is all-powerful, and his or her role applies to all stages of the investigative process, as well as to the interrogation of suspects. He or she also has an unhealthy level of control over junior lawyers, who after leaving law school may be desperately short of work and often depend on court work paid for by the state. These individuals may well see the omnipotent senior prosecutor as having a vital say in their next pay cheque and in their career advancement. Absolute power corrupts absolutely, and in court one observes that even defence lawyers defer obsequiously to the public prosecutor.

So the process of selection of law students and then legal training is likely to concentrate individuals leaning towards the low end of the empathy spectrum. A CNE, because of an intrinsic defect in amygdala function, does not see and respond to the distress in the accused. Such function, you will recall, is necessary (though not sufficient) for normal socialisation in childhood. Psychopaths will not respond to genuine emotions, and have no conscience, and if in other ways normal this must make them more 'effective' as prosecuting lawyers in a confrontational process. And then procedure tends to harden these hearts even further, as the trial is fought as a gladiatorial war game conducted against the accused. As with opponents in jousting contests, between sessions lawyers of opposing parties can be seen chatting amicably together. For the accused it is a matter of life and death, for lawyers all too often a game.

We will see later that this is not unique to Italy. Indeed under Italian law the prosecutor is supposed to give equal consideration to the rights of the accused. The trouble is that that is not how the brains of CNEs operate. Instead they have a propensity to engage in targeted aggression, and such aggression tends to be directed against the weak and vulnerable. As a child such a person will have bullied 'sissies', that is to say nice children high on the empathy scale. This process can easily mature into forming an effective 'hanging judge' such as England's Judge George Jeffreys, notorious for his role in serving the monarch and liberally handing out death sentences following the Monmouth Rebellion of 1685. We all have to earn a living, and this would surely be a rather refined way for an intelligent and ruthless psychopath to do so.

The Monster of Florence

So what might William of Occam have observed about Italian judicial processes? That they are flawed or open to abuse? There is, he might well have pointed out, nothing in Italy to stop someone subject to claims or investigations concerning their day-to-day role from continuing to work. At the time of Meredith's murder, allegations had been brought against prosecutor Mignini and a senior police officer, Michele Giuttari, concerning their investigation into serial murders of seven couples while they were engaged in sex in their cars, from 1975 to 1984. The allegations (wholly denied) were of abuse of office and illegal investigation for supposed conspiracy of 21 individuals in Perugia who they alleged had been part of a secret group that in October 1985 had murdered Dr Francesco Narducci. They held this group to be involved in the Monster of Florence murders. Giuttari had been temporarily suspended on full pay, but Mignini was allowed to continue working as a public prosecutor. Only charges of abuse of office were sustained in 2010 by the first court[5] and on appeal in November 2011 the cases were sent back on technical grounds to the court in Turin. Whatever the final result of those proceedings, Occam might have hinted that a successful outcome against Knox and Sollecito would restore confidence, and reinforce the decision to release Rudy Guede from police custody in Milan five days before Meredith's murder.

In fact it was the satanic theorist blogger Gabriella Carlizzi, who had introduced the notion of a conspiracy conducted by the so-called Order of the Red Rose in Narducci's death. She it was who we believe also suggested to Mignini that the murder of Meredith Kercher, the night after Halloween, might have the same satanic root cause. This information had come to Carlizzi (now deceased) by a claimed communication

---

5. See http://www.corriere.it/cronache/10_gennaio_22/mostro-firenze-giuttari-mignini_8d07606e-075a-11df-8946-00144f02aabe.shtml?refresh_ce-cp

with a long dead priest! In 2007, this could surely only happen amongst the unusually superstitious!

Prejudicial effect of the civil case in Italian law

A second feature of the Italian system that is intrinsically inimical and prejudicial to true justice is that the civil case is heard at the same time and in the same court as the criminal case. The relatives of the deceased within any criminal case almost invariably side with the prosecution, from whom they get their first semi-coherent reconstruction of events. When the loss of a loved one is still fresh, their minds are likely to become imprinted with the first story they hear; and of course they are desperately keen to see those responsible brought to justice. In Italy, however, the civil case runs as a supplementary arm of the criminal one and therefore acts as an extra emotional force for criminal conviction of the accused. This initial emotional reason is then supplemented by a potential financial motive at the promise of monetary damages, possibly large, against the families of the accused (provided they are solvent). Many people still say to me, 'What about the poor Kerchers?' Well, their nearest and dearest was murdered, which is of course tragic and they have our most sincere sympathy and condolences; but the bereaved in any murder case are looking for certain and hopefully quick answers, and are perhaps the least likely people to be able to look at the facts objectively.

Within less than five days of the murder, the police had made a high profile declaration of a 'sex game gone wrong,' and this theory, however misleading, seems to have become embedded in the psyche of many people. Even today it is perhaps the one thing they recall when the case is mentioned, however wrong or distorted.

Four-and-a-half days passed between the discovery of Meredith's body and the fanfare announcement of 'Case closed,' and more than seven years later all concerned were still left with no judicial, let alone factual certainty. Our sympathy for the Kerchers, however, should not be stretched to the point of avoiding the simple truth that Amanda and Raffaele were not involved. Eight years later, and after the definitive Supreme Court pronouncement of their absolute innocence, we think some relatives of the victim still found it hard to abandon a lingering belief in their guilt, e.g. by requesting them not to visit Meredith's grave. Why not if they are innocent?

The involvement of families of the deceased is apparently the rule in Italy. A similar approach was adopted in the case of Albert Stasi, accused (and now after four trials and retrials definitively declared guilty) of murdering his girlfriend Barbara Poggi, also in 2007. Two courts found him innocent, but then a third, on orders from the Supreme Court, found him guilty, a judgement that was upheld by the Supreme Court, despite the prosecutor himself arguing it was unsafe and that a new trial was needed. Pressure for this has come from Poggi's relatives (who have been awarded €1 million in compensation).

A further important element was the allegation of *calunnia* (slander) by Amanda Knox against Patrick Lumumba, which was 'milked' by the prosecution and press for all it was worth. Strangely, on that fateful night of November 5th/6th nothing of her interrogation was recorded, ostensibly for lack of funds. So we have no idea how much pressure Knox was put under to 'see' Lumumba kill Meredith. A sad element of this case is that after initially blaming the police on his release for the mix-up and for abuse, Lumumba then turned on Amanda. Supported by his lawyer Carlo Pacelli, he appears to have exaggerated and distorted the role she had in his own unpleasant but brief two weeks of incarceration.

Forensic shortcomings

The motivation report from the Marasca final Supreme Court is scathing in its criticism of the initial forensic investigation. It is hard to identify what failings may have been deliberate and what accidental. But throughout the investigation, only lip-service was paid to rules of procedure. As in many criminal cases in Italy, the alleged 'truth' was divined first and the supporting 'evidence' found (or created) later. A quick look at types of police uniform in Italy is maybe symbolic of perfect appearance trumping content. So it comes as no surprise that the investigation of the crime scene was bungled from the start, with the independent DNA experts Stefano Conti and Carla Vecchiotti at the appeal in 2011 cataloguing no less than 52 pieces of inadequate or downright bad forensic procedure shown on the official police film alone. These things should have been obvious to the judges and jury in the first trial, but were ignored or glossed over. Only the word of the *Polizia Scientifica* from Rome was given credence, yet on the basis of employees not rocking the boat it was intrinsically probable this was biased towards the prosecution.

Who can seriously test a knife that was clearly *plucked at random* from a drawer in the kitchen of one of the accused, then unprofessionally packaged in a cardboard box, and treat it as the murder weapon? And who can believe that finding Sollecito's DNA on a bra clasp recovered from the floor 46 days later meant anything? Laboratory analyst Patrizia Stefanoni herself during cross-examination in 2009 would neither confirm nor deny that she'd touched the bra-clasp with obviously dirty forensic-gloves. In any case, to rip off a bra in a frenzied attack you would pull on the bra, not on the bra clasp; the force of this ripping was evidenced by the fact that the clasp itself was bent. Guede's DNA, you will recall, was found on Meredith's bra itself, which had been picked up on the day after the murder. The bra was negative for Sollecito's DNA.

Abuse of DNA evidence

There is an informative work on the science of DNA[6] and its use in forensic work, by a world leader in the use of DNA in forensics for nearly a third of a century. Professor Peter Gill was lead author in a seminal paper published in the prestigious journal *Nature* in December 1985 (with Professor Alec Jeffreys) and has been at the forefront of the field ever since. He has become increasingly concerned, as the techniques become more widely used and more sensitive, at their potential abuse (innocent or malicious). In the last chapter of his book he examines the Kercher murder, and specifically the fallacies and abuses by which the judge in the first trial, Giancarlo Massei, convicted Amanda and Raffaele using DNA evidence. He founds his arguments firmly on science, and is scathing of so-called expert opinion from specialists paid to support state-funded prosecution.

In a dry environment, DNA, which is shed from skin cells, saliva and other body fluids, is quite stable. It is literally all around us. The

---

6. Peter Gill, 2014, *Misleading DNA Evidence: Reasons for Miscarriages of Justice.*

finding of mixtures of DNA from two flatmates (as in this case) is to be expected in a bathroom they share. Blood from Meredith Kercher, the victim of a crime, mixed with DNA from Amanda Knox on surfaces in the bathroom *had no probative value.* Gill explains that contamination can occur at each and every stage. Just because it can be said that there is a billion to one chance that a person's unique DNA is on an object when it is finally subjected to a polymerase chain reaction (PCR) and chromatography (for example the notorious bra clasp above used against Raffaele), does not mean it got there as a result of the crime under investigation. Miscarriages of justice occur when the boundaries of knowledge are exceeded. Gill goes on to cite a host of ways in which errors become compounded from the 'association fallacy', 'hidden perpetrator effect', 'naïve investigator effect' and 'swamping effect'.

Gill's conclusions are that there is *no scientific basis that gives any credibility to the DNA evidence against Amanda and Raffaele*; the DNA was innocent, irrelevant, or the result of contamination at one of a number of stages from collection at a poorly regulated crime scene onwards. And the onus is always on the investigators to rigorously minimise the chances of contamination, and to run appropriate controls.

Errors of omission and the time of Meredith's death

Another elementary and arguably flagrant early error of omission in this case was that on police or prosecutorial insistence, the pathologist, Dr Luca Lalli, was prevented from taking one of the most elementary of measurements, the deceased girl's core body temperature. This, along with ambient temperature, and body weight of the victim, is essential to allow calculation of the likely time limits between which death occurred. It has to be done for the first time as soon as possible after the body is found, then serially as the temperature of the body falls to ambient levels. But Lalli was not allowed to make this measurement until 12 hours after Meredith's body was found. This greatly extended the possible time of death, providing the prosecution with a means to implicate Amanda and Raffaele by extending it into the hours when they had no alibi. Fortunately the pathologist was good, and did the *post mortem* in a way that allowed some timing estimate to be made from studying food in the stomach (he put a ligature around the pyloric exit and the duodenum before examining the contents of the stomach and intestine). But still, temperature readings were also needed and this it seems was expressly forbidden.

The necessity that the break-in was simulated not real

It appears that from the very moment he arrived at the crime scene prosecutor Mignini concurred with the first postal policeman and concluded that the break-in into Filomena Romanelli's room had been simulated. He has repeatedly argued that if the break-in was real, Amanda and Raffaele would be innocent.[7] This issue is further explored in relation to the Nencini Report in *Chapter 3*.

False and contrived witnesses

Then there was the question of witnesses who claimed to have seen Amanda and Raffaele outside the villa at critical times, when they claimed to be at his apartment and in bed. In a process reminiscent of the contrived 'alphabetical witnesses' in the Monster of Florence murders, they were to a person the most improbable bunch. Witnesses with little credibility who would not even have been entertained in Britain or the USA. The first was Hekuran Kokomani, an unreliable Albanian drug dealer who claimed to have been threatened by a menacing Knox emerging from a black plastic bag on the road late that night!

There was Antonio ('Toto') Curatolo (now deceased), a self-confessed born again Christian anarchist heroin addict who slept on a bench on the Piazza Grimana, and who was a 'convenient' serial murder witness. This case is the third in which his evidence has been used to secure a conviction. It is something that the supplementary public prosecutor Crini, in Florence, regarded as a plus for reliability, but which most observers would surely view with suspicion; something shared by the final Supreme

---

7. Recorded presentation 24 November 2014 https://www.youtube.com/watch?v=b8EzR6uNpAE &feature=youtu.be He says, '... *Io ho capito subito, e un staging c'e una mesa in scena*'. '...I understood immediately that this was a staging, a simulation of a break-in. The fake break-in was necessary for those who needed to distance suspicion from themselves ... because a stranger did not need to simulate ... During that time there was only Amanda, and Meredith. This is the first point, and it seems to me most important.'

Court ruling. Curatolo was 'found' about seven months after the murder, by an enthusiastic young newspaper reporter. He managed to get the day wrong, by linking it to buses that took students to discotheques out of town, which had happened the night before (Halloween). The same journalist also tracked down another 'important' witness, Quintavalle, who claimed to have seen Amanda in his shop the following morning buying bleach. And there was a distant opposite neighbour who heard a scream and then footsteps running away, through double glazed windows. These witnesses, even had they been reliable, were 'found' months after the murder.

Two jailhouse snitches were rejected, but allowed at the appeal. The more reliable of these, Mario Alessi, said Guede had told him that a man he was with had masturbated over Meredith's body. Jailhouse snitches are often unreliable, but this testimony surely provideed another reason for testing the DNA of the putative semen stain on the cushion that was found beneath Meredith's body.

Destruction of important evidence

There were no less than four computers (Amanda's, Meredith's, one of Raffaele's, and Filomena Romanelli's) that were destroyed by the postal police; in most countries destroying one evidential computer would be a matter for enquiry and disciplinary action, let alone four. Why has no-one been disciplined for this? Why were the defence not allowed access to the computers so they could be sent to real experts at the manufacturers or elsewhere to see what could be retrieved?

The unfortunate case of the shoe prints

The sole reason for Judge Claudia Matteini, a female magistrate who acted early in the preliminary stages, arraigning Raffaele, was a supposed match based on his shoe prints being found in blood in Meredith's bedroom. Yet four months later it was the defence who were the ones to show that these in fact matched shoes owned by Guede (which he had disposed of, but which were identified from the box in which the shoes were purchased found in Guede's flat), and were incompatible with Raffaele's.

Human rights issues

Inspector Occam would surely have been disturbed at the coercive way in which Amanda and Raffaele were treated. Two facts of many come to mind. *First*, even before he had been charged, Raffaele was placed in solitary confinement for no less than six months. This is completely counter to the European Convention on Human Rights, and at least 25 per cent of young adults treated in this way will suffer irreparable psychological damage. In many jurisdictions, imprisonment, already of dubious value in fighting crime, has over the past three decades got completely out of control. This is especially so in the USA, with a *per capita* imprisonment five to ten times higher than in similarly 'civilised' European countries. But the extensive use of preventive incarceration, on the whim of a judge, is a curiously Italian speciality, and what was done to Raffaele before he was even officially indicted shows a particularly concerning and unjust aspect of this case. Combined with a judicial system that proceeds at snail's pace it becomes cruel beyond belief.

Second, there is evidence of sexual harassment in prison of Amanda. Heads should have rolled immediately concerning whoever confronted her dressed as a doctor and it seems told her she was HIV positive, thereby extracting a list of her lifetime sexual encounters, which (including Raffaele) amounted to seven in all. These were then promptly 'leaked' to the press and presented as if they had all happened since she came to Italy. This illegally extracted information was used in the British press and elsewhere to further sully her name, a process known as 'slut-shaming.'

Willing exploitation of the press

From the beginning a picture was systematically fed to and painted in the press of Amanda as a person capable of doing things no normal woman would do — of behaving like a satanic-she-devil-witch. Just think of it — the 'making out' outside the flat (which was just a tender kiss of consolation from the only person she could turn to, her boyfriend). This was repeatedly played in slow motion in every television news item about the case and a still photograph was placed in most newspaper articles and misconstrued as evidence of callous behaviour.

We will see also in *Chapter 7* in the case of Darlie Routier that repeated playing of the same highly selective clip out of context can do irreparable damage by prejudicing a jury, and the same applies to public opinion. There was the 'Foxy Knoxy' childhood footballing moniker; the supposed cartwheels in the police station witnessed by Monica Napoleoni and Rita Ficara. The latter was the *polizziotta* ('policewoman') who Amanda claims beat her around the head (a claim denied), for which accusation she faced a *calunnia* charge, heroically dismissed by a judge in Florence as late as January 2016! And the supposed 'sexy underwear' purchased when the house was sealed-off, and she had no clothes (under or other) to access.

Everything was distorted to paint the worst possible picture, especially in the British press, which operated as it must (being run by commercial companies) to flout reporting restrictions that would have applied had the case been brought in the UK. As already stated, much of the British press was throughout this case the focus for sympathy for the Kercher family, with its undisguised belief in Amanda's guilt in particular.

A crime within a crime?

It is hard not to believe that Inspector Occam would have concluded that the litany of problems catalogued above suggest a considerable and arguably systematic abuse of power, intended to mislead the world at the expense of two innocent youngsters. He might even have used the term 'malicious' though as we have said earlier we must make every allowance and perhaps say simply that the scenario demands some kind of explanation at the very least. A central puzzle, seeing that the straightforward explanation is so obvious, would be this; why was everyone so keen to obscure the role in Meredith's murder of a disturbed burglar, Rudy Guede, a man with a known criminal history? We believe Meredith's family initially played down his obvious guilt (and conviction) though seem to have made no related comments lately. So what was someone keen to hide? Is it going too far to say that by pure coincidence Guede had recently been kicked out by the head of one of the wealthiest families in Perugia, who at the age of 16 had formally adopted him?

Taking the investigation completely out of the hands of the Perugia authorities, Inspector Occam would have opened a simple inquiry into the movements of Guede: asking who spoke to whom in Milan on October 27th, and what happened to the goods stolen from the lawyer Brocchi. He would have wanted to know whether the lady's watch was indeed the one stolen earlier that month from Guede's elderly female neighbour. He would surely have had to conclude that the catalogue of events suggests that somehow the Perugian *polizio-judicial* process has over the years morphed into a CNE-based system, which has so it must be argued been used to frame the most gullible and unprotected innocent targets it could find. This is also expounded in Mark Waterbury's book on the case.[8]

The curious appeal of *dietrologia*, doubtless inculcated by its religious past, plus a tradition of inherent misogyny, makes attractive to many the very improbability of a beautiful 20-year-old girl directing the murder of her flatmate. Further, because it could not be denied for fear of *calumny* charges, it had to be published and amplified. And all of that sold papers: a game in which, in the short-term at least, everyone was a winner, except the innocent young lovers, but then who cares about witches?

Inspector Occam would be most disquieted to see that the obviously fair appeal, conducted by judges (Hellman and Zanetti) and a jury who were outside the control of the inner Perugian circle, was quite irrationally overturned by the Court of Cassation, which Judge Hellmann himself has said is strongly influenced by the 'Party of the Prosecutors'. He would have had lots of questions about an obvious crime within a crime, and set up an inquiry into what had actually gone wrong in a civilised country. In 2015 we had the amazing reinstatement of the Hellmann decision (see further *Chapter 3*), and declaration that Amanda and Raffaele were innocent because they did not commit the crime. And nearly six months later the reasoning, which is devastating in its criticism of the investigation! It is now time to examine the strange case of Italy's dysfunctional legal system, in the light of this and other recent cases and to ask why no one is willing or able to do anything about it. We start with a personal experience of the law in relation to the Knox/Sollecito case, as viewed from no-man's land.

---

8. Mark Waterbury, *The Monster of Perugia*, Ibid.

CHAPTER THREE

Italians in Court: One Man's View
From No Man's Land

In Italy the police and the justice system for the most part operate as one. I (David Anderson) only fully awoke to the Kafkaesque nature of Italy's *polizio-judicial* system at the start of the Appeal Court sessions in late 2010. During the preceding year I had, however, brought myself up to speed with the evidence, thanks mainly to Greg Hampikian and supporters in the USA. I had been in direct contact throughout that time with Amanda's family, especially her stepfather, Chris Mellas.

I got a foretaste of what I was later to see in court at first hand. My first shock was to hear that Meredith Kercher's family had accepted the prosecution line and that their personal lawyer Francesco Maresca was able, perfectly legally and within his rights I must stress, to tug both in and out of court on the heartstrings of sentiment towards them. Sympathy for the victim and her family have throughout been inseparable from the question of the guilt or innocence of those charged. It slowly became clear how great an effect the family's confirmation bias was having.

In the UK and America there are rules against involving the family of a victim in criminal proceedings, at least until a guilty verdict is reached. I believe this is because they are likely to be ruled by emotion. Yet in Italy, criminal and civil cases concerning the same matter often run side-by-side, and both are heard in front of the same judge and jury, who are expected to divide their minds/thinking/deliberations into two discrete compartments. Thus, for example during the first trial, the Supreme Court ruled that what Amanda Knox said (or rather what the prosecutor claimed she had said) before she had been told she was an official suspect could *not* be used as evidence in the *criminal* trial, but *was* admissible in the *civil* one, being heard by the same people! The same applied even more starkly in the case of her former boss, Perugia bar owner Patrick Diya Lumumba. His lawyer, Carlo Pacelli, was particularly resolute in his descriptions of Amanda. In court and on the steps outside he painted her in an adverse light, something supported repeatedly by Lumumba himself after his release.

The year between my waking-up to this form of injustice and the start of the appeal allowed me to study the defence forensic file prepared in the USA. But it seemed that the message was not going to get to the right people unless it was translated into Italian, so I organized and paid for this to be done; then sent it to selected people in authority in Italy, including my ministerial neighbour, Renato Brunetta, Attorney-General Angelino Alfano and Prime Minister Silvio Berlusconi. Earlier I had sent them a translation of the Afterword on the case in Douglas Preston and Mario Spezi's book *The Monster of Florence*.

A hard time seeking to convince the press and media

The year before the start of the appeal also gave me the opportunity to hear and meet at a conference in Perugia two American journalists, Barbie Nadeau and Andrea Vogt. I was able to maintain contact with but not to change their minds about what was their pro-prosecution stance; and Barbie by this time had, in any event, committed herself in print in a book, *Angel Face: Sex, Murder and the Inside Story of Amanda Knox* (Beast Books, 2010) that according to its advertising spin claimed to tell the true story. It drew extensively on what I considered unsupportable arguments. I taped the proceedings of the conference, and afterwards joined a group talking to Andrea. Clearly critical of Douglas Preston, co-author of *The Monster of Florence* she said, 'Now this is off-the-record, no one is recording this are they?' I realised I had left my tape recorder running in my pocket, apologised, and switched it off. She changed tack imme-diately — 'Leave that on,' she said; 'I want this recorded … if you ever, ever use that tape I shall personally sue you!' Nine months on when the appeal opened she had still not forgotten, despite my sincere apology.

After the Nencini verdict (February 2014) declaring Amanda and Raffaele once again guilty (*Chapter 2*), within weeks there was a BBC3

TV programme directed by Andrea entitled 'Is Amanda Knox Guilty?' but largely implying she must have been.

I was more successful in persuading at least one British journalist that he might have backed the wrong horse. Nick Pisa has the dubious honour of having re-minted Amanda's personal, self-declared child-hood sporting moniker 'Foxy Knoxy' as a pejorative tabloid emblem. It became shorthand for the supposed 'evil' this young woman had come to symbolise; eventually the label itself justified the witch-hunt (see generally *Chapter 10*). But during the appeal, I always found Nick courteous and receptive to considerations of evidence. I had first sent him an email in September 2010 when I read an article of his in the British tabloid press that referred in its headline to Foxy Knoxy. I offered to show him the defence forensic file and take him through evidence that persuaded me Amanda and Raffaele were innocent. To my surprise five weeks later he replied and offered to meet up.

We met in a café in Perugia shortly before the appeal began. Over a coffee, I gave him a précis of my proof that the two had been victims of a gross injustice, involving distortion of the evidence. I argued with him that the moral ground was not lost. I suggested that the honourable thing to do would be to publish a *mea culpa*, and start fighting for justice. This course might also be prudent for his newspaper(s), if and when the truth was revealed and Amanda and Raffaele freed. At the end he said, 'You have persuaded me, David; I think you are right and they are innocent.' Thereafter and although the headlines didn't change at once, the slant of his articles did. The headlines, I guess, were not written by him, but those charged with circulation. But even Nick didn't change his mind completely until the final outcome.

Observations from court during the appeal

Finally, towards the end of November, I went to the first court session at the start of the appeal. I attended 19 of the 20 sessions as they dragged on for over a year. I soon realised that at the back of the courtroom there was a separate world that interacts with the official proceedings more than one might expect. I slowly inserted myself into this world. I was one of two doctors and the only British non-journalist who attended court regularly. Mostly, I studiously avoided talking to prosecutors, preferring to maintain a degree of anonymity.

I soon learned that in order to be sure of getting into the courtroom as a member of the public, I needed to arrive early; and made a point of catching the earliest local train and arriving around 8 am for proceedings which notionally started at 9 am, but more often around 9.30. I learnt that they only allowed in the first 20, and that Italians are not respecters of the British custom of queuing. So on the day when Amanda protested her innocence in person I stood to miss out by one place, and only heard her because one those before me left the courtroom unexpectedly.

Courtroom ritual

There were several other public regulars, mostly elderly residents of Perugia and I became quite friendly with them. The ritual was well-rehearsed. A swarm of cameramen rushed in and stood on seats or stepladders just behind the dividing barrier. As Amanda and Raffaele were ushered in between two bereted prison guards, cameras flashed, mainly trained on Amanda. Then after the entry of the judges and jury the cameramen departed and the visitors' area was left largely empty. Many of the journalists went off to their special room, to watch the proceedings on CCTV and chat among themselves. One of the seemingly more attentive ones, who has become a friend, was Frank Sfarzo, who had followed the case from the earliest, and like me soon became convinced of Amanda's and Raffaele's innocence. His ironic humour made his blog a 'must' until it was shut down by the authorities. He is still facing two long drawn out (and to my mind absurd) charges of *calunnia* against the police, at taxpayers' expense.

An invitation to meet the prosecutors

A daily ritual was played out between prosecutors and journalists. Quite naturally, the 'favoured' ones were those who wrote what the prosecution liked the world to hear. In January 2011, with the help of the journalist for *The Independent*, Peter Popham, whom I had met at the time of my first meeting with Mario Spezi, I had an article published in *The Independent on Sunday*. In it I drew parallels with the false conviction and imprisonment of Stefan Kiszko (see *Chapter 6*). My involvement in Kiszko's release may have lent some authority to what I, as a retired former professor, might have to say. And it was also good to demonstrate that the opinions on the Perugia case were not drawn along strictly national lines. At the next hearing in February it was clear that this article had come to the attention of prosecutor Mignini, as he asked Nick Pisa if he would act as my interpreter, and invited me to meet him and talk. During the next interval Nick told me of this request and that he had told Mignini my Italian was good enough. 'Nick,' I replied, 'I have never put my head in a crocodile's mouth. As far as he is concerned I don't even speak English.'

I did, however, decide to try to tilt courtroom opinion in favour of the accused. A naïve idea, I know. I would speak to any and every journalist I came across, and explain why I believed the pair were being railroaded. I even had coffee on a couple of occasions with Barbie Nadeau, and she did to her credit listen. At the end she said, 'I hear what you're saying David, but how can you *know* they are innocent? I replied, 'We don't have to *know* they are innocent, the prosecution has to *prove* they are guilty.' She asked if she could quote me, but as far as I know she never did.

I made a point of speaking to the family and friends of the defend-ants, who were sitting on the right hand side of the courtroom facing the judge. But I usually sat behind the prosecutors, on the left, to give the jury wind of at least one dissenter. As things began to heat up when the expert witnesses presented their assessment of the DNA evidence, I was alarmed to see prosecutor Manuela Comodi laughing and chatting to Maresca (the Kercher's lawyer) and apparently not paying complete attention to the slides being shown by the expert witnesses. At the end of this first session I fixed her in the eye from 20 metres and challenged her loudly and angrily in my best Italian: 'That was disgraceful—you were laughing!' She asked, 'Who was that?' whereupon I quickly vanished. An Italian journalist, Alessandro Penna from *Oggi* magazine (an Italian glossy weekly that has been consistently pro-innocence), said it was good but that my Italian was incorrect, or I might have been held in contempt of court. I had used the word *disgrazia* which means 'mistake', rather than *vergogna* for 'disgrace'. Nevertheless after the coffee break there were no more smiles or chit-chat that day.

John Follain: A critique

The journalist and author John Follain was throughout a supporter of the prosecution case. He alone had to suffer the flushed embarrassment of having his shoulder squeezed by Mignini as the latter left the courtroom after his final summing up in the appeal. Yet, earlier, Follain had been nominated in the Magazine Journalism Awards of 2008 for his interview with Amanda's parents for a *Sunday Times* article that led Mignini to sue them for *calunnia* (slander). While Mignini is still, in theory, prosecuting Amanda Knox's parents, Follain and Rupert Murdoch's *Sunday Times* avoided the fate of others less fortunate or wealthy.

Follain's book *Death in Perugia: The Definitive Account of the Meredith Kercher Case from Her Murder to the Acquittal of Raffaele Sollecito and Amanda Knox* (Hodder & Stoughton, 2011) (later re-issued as *A Death in Italy: The Definitive Account of the Amanda Knox Case* (a mass-market paperback)) was published shortly after the 2011 Hellmann acquittals, and seems to have been written with two possible endings in mind. It provides intriguing insights into the Perugian police and prosecutors. For example, Follain tells us that Detective Superintendent Monica Napoleoni 'liked to wear her silver shield-shaped badge as a pendant on a chain around her neck and occasionally tucked her semi-automatic ordnance pistol into a Louis Vuitton handbag.' Also that, 'For her turn as a witness, the detective swapped the jeans and casual clothes she always wore on duty for her navy-blue police uniform.' He tells us also that when Rudy Guede was caught in Germany, Napoleoni was '… delighted … but frustrated that she hadn't been the one who arrested him.' And he gives some idea of the prosecutorial grip on the Kerchers when he says, 'They sat next to the detective Napoleoni, who proudly wore her police badge on a chain around her neck.'

Follain's insight into Mignini is equally revealing. Thus we have: 'Autopsies didn't unsettle Mignini as they did several of his colleagues, and he didn't bother to wear a mask.' And '[H]e … wanted to be as closely involved as possible as if he was a detective himself.' Yet no journalistic curiosity as to why that might be! And of the murder scene we have, 'From the very time he'd looked into her bedroom his hunch had been that only a woman could have been so shaken by the sight of the victim as to seek to hide the body.' So the public prosecutor starts with a psychological hunch, coming in a flash to the seemingly improbable opinion of a woman perpetrating a crime of sex and violence on another woman. And, 'The DNA finding quickly became public'—one wonders why.

Follain says Mignini first interrogated Amanda in Capanne Prison (according to Amanda—in her book—he interrogated her from 1.30 am on the morning of November 6 in Perugia's Questura, when she was under the impression that he was the Mayor of Perugia and there to help her. Mignini has confirmed this in an interview). Anyway, 'Mignini had thought long and hard about the best way to tackle Amanda. 'Her greatest strength was her intelligence; her greatest weakness was her fragility.' But as to his perception of a woman's emotions: '"They were telling me I was guilty … After hours"—Amanda said and then broke off. She brought her hands up to her head and covered her ears … "[T]hat gesture again," Mignini thought to himself—and [she] started to cry. As Amanda wiped the tears away with her fingers, Mignini immediately made a point of requesting that the tears be noted for the record.' No inkling is given as to how tears were to be used against a young woman he criticised elsewhere for not showing enough emotion. We are then told that, 'Mignini was still seething as he strode out of prison. He had never carried out such a tense interrogation.' We are hearing here a seasoned public prosecutor talk about a 20-year-old American girl, hardly the head of the Gomorrah.

Follain goes on to describe how Mignini loved reading history books, especially tales of great battles, and that in some ways he saw 'what awaited him in court as a battle.' And how he rose and began his final request for the sentencing of the accused: Knox was a narcissist, he said, who nurtured anger and was unusually aggressive. She manipulated people, indulging in theatricals and transgressive behaviour. She had little empathy for others, suffered from 'emotional anaesthesia', and had a tendency to dominate relationships. It was in fact the contrast between this speech, and the pleas of an obviously innocent girl, that persuaded me to become informed and then involved in fighting for justice in this case.

During the appeal, says Follain, Mignini was 'pulling the strings', but for the most part did not speak. Manuela Comodi was his chief spokesperson. Of her in the first trial, Follain reveals that 'Comodi saw Amanda as the instigator. She was a charismatic figure, capable of influencing others, and she was the driving force who had drawn the group together setting in motion the spiral of events'. From which we can gather that there was allegedly substantial bias against Knox. One of the most objectionable ploys used in summing-up at the end of the first trial was to show an animated cartoon (production cost €180,000) of what the prosecutors imagined had happened (which Follain himself claims was Comodi's idea). 'For most people what you see on TV exists; what you don't see on TV doesn't.' But Follain does not want us to believe the second prosecutor is completely heartless, and tells us that she '... watched Amanda and Raffaele leave and suddenly thought to herself: "They're going to be convicted, I'm sure of it." She then thought "How absurd, how terrible for two such young kids to have so many years in jail ahead of them."'

The Kercher's lawyer, Francesco Maresca was a friend of Mignini, and so it is said had been suggested to the murdered girl's family by him. Follain writes that on Day 1 of the trial, 'Whatever the reason was, Amanda's smiles and laughs exasperated Maresca. "Let's see if either of them will be laughing when it's all over," he remarked.' And this is from the man who is supposed to wait until they have been found guilty before pushing for reparation. He is very sensitive to innocent behaviour from a young woman who on St Valentine's day wore a T-shirt with the Beatles message "All you need is love". Apparently, Maresca could hardly contain his anger. 'Amanda's gone too far. It's fine to declare yourself innocent all your life but there are limits. I can't stand this frivolous attitude. It's offensive to the court, and it's especially offensive to Meredith's family.'

While on the subject of insensitivity, at the end of the appeal this same Maresca actually put the photographs of Meredith's naked body on a loop for the whole court to see no less than three times. The previous evening Mignini had at least asked for the public area to be cleared, so he could show the same photographs; that degree of sensitivity was not shown by the Kerchers' own lawyer. But in the eyes of Follain, Maresca too clearly has a real heart as was evidenced after Amanda and

Raffaele's acquittal … 'Seeing her lawyer Maresca looking crestfallen, Arline (Kercher) asked him "Are you alright?" Maresca was amazed that she should be concerned about him at such a moment. "Yes, yes" he replied, "and you?"'

We repeatedly witness such seemingly misplaced deference to those connected to Meredith, as the prosecution confuses the tragic loss of a daughter or friend with solid evidence against those accused.

Press and media when the court was in session

One feature I noted was the extent of (arguably excessive) tolerance shown by the judges for the conduct of the prosecution, for example during the evidence of the expert witnesses. And how could the judges allow key participants to walk out of the courtroom when the accused was presenting her case? It was as if it was a game, in which they were both players and umpire. Yet one had the impression, which Frank Sfarzo says was not the case during the original trial, that at least the judges and jury were all attentive, and if they had prejudices they did not reveal them.

All but the journalists were excluded from court for the announcement of the court's decision, which came late in the evening of 3rd October 2011. A hostile crowd of hundreds gathered with the hordes of journalists and photographers outside the courtroom. I met up with Miriam Spezi, who had been refused entry to court along with her journalist husband. She spoke to some young people in the crowd, and said they were all *colpevolisti* (siding with the prosecution) and thirsting for blood. We placed ourselves behind a friendly CNN reporter for the announcement. Nick Pisa meanwhile seems to have confused the announcement of guilt on the charge of *calunnia* against Amanda (for having supposedly pointed the finger at Lumumba), with the couple being found guilty of murder. He declared on air, from inside the courtroom, that the main charges had been upheld, this at the very moment when Judge Hellmann was declaring the two to be innocent because they did not commit the crime. Our CNN reporter was not so hasty, and with his earpiece pressed tight told us, 'They're free!,' whereupon we whooped with joy, while many in the crowd bayed '*Vergogna! Vergogna!*' (Shame! Shame!). Miriam was frightened I might be lynched.

Two years later: The appeal against the appeal

Along with many others, including the families involved, I assumed that the appeal by the prosecutor to the Supreme Court would be notional, but it wasn't. John Follain, when he hailed me the morning after the appeal clearly thought otherwise. 'Time will tell, David, time will tell,' he said. Many of us, including Judges Hellmann and Zanetti were horrified to realise the extent of what seemed like power behind the scenes. If the defence had realised this, and had also worked as hard there, the outcome might have been different. But even they did not seem to appreciate how much the judicial playing field in Italy seems to be tilted in favour of upholding convictions. Would it be different, I wondered, when the case returned to the Supreme Court for the second and final time?

The court in Florence is a strikingly spiky and grand modern building, as imposing in its appearance as it is unimposing in its proceedings. The former Cross of Calvary has been replaced by a declaration in Italian that 'Everyone is equal before the law.' I attended most of these sessions. The president, Judge Nencini, looked a reasonable man, but disappointingly he followed the 'script' written from on high by the Supreme Court, first session. That frustration was certainly the view of Judge Hellmann, who I have met for discussions on a number of occasions after his retirement. This time there was minimal consideration of new evidence, and what was heard was ignored. It was, when I think about it, a complete waste of everybody's time.

'A nonsensical pile from Nencini (viz a *nonsencini*)'

Over five days I read the whole 337-page Nencini 'Motivation Report', translated many parts of it into English, made 47 pages of notes and wrote an article for *Ground Report* (a global citizen platform that enables anyone to publish news reports and videos). In it I raised a number of concerns. I wrote that I found it hard to conceive of a less impartial piece of judicial sophistry, revealing as it did the momentum behind confirming the guilt of Amanda and Raffaele. I asked if it was going too far to suggest that there may have been some kind of 'conspiracy' to save face by allowing the convictions of two innocent youngsters for murder to stand? Was it the case of a system supported by a compliant press, which chose this outcome rather than bringing into line one or more of its own? Commenting on the break-in, I wrote:

> '…which Nencini agrees was simulated. It is not as if in Florence they are not aware of Guede's propensity to break in, as they refer to it…and agree he was highly qualified to do so, but reverse the logic by saying he would not be that stupid. Why, I ask, should one be expected to believe that he would suddenly become sensible? In fact the document is riddled with examples of how Nencini uses Guede as a witness against Knox and Sollecito, even when he is blatantly lying (which is most of the time, and is doubtless the reason he was thrown out of the Caporali family). We are also supposed to believe Guede would have taken the sensible route into the flat that the ageing non-robber Nencini would have used. He says that to go in through Filomena's window *non avrebbe alcun senso* [i.e. would be daft]. And he would have no interest in simulating a theft in that way, knowing the police would have spotted it since breaking in was "an activity Rudy Guede did not entirely disdain"! So we now have the absolutely shocking news that burglars must…be sensible and break in using keys. That way, I suppose, no-one will ever suspect them.'

I continued, sometimes in irreverent fashion, by comparing some descriptions of what was supposed to have happened to 'Harry Potter magic' and pointing-out countless defects in the prosecution account most of which feature elsewhere in this book.[1]

Postscript: A week after the declaration of innocence
It is easy to be right with hindsight, and one thing I can honestly say is that I thought it was possible, if not probable, that the fifth session of the Supreme Court, at the eleventh hour, would realise that the evidence weighed more than saving face for the system. The reason for believing this is that this case was different; the eyes of the whole world were focused on the outcome, and I felt that its very international and highly polarised nature would at last mean that court would look at the evidence,

---

1. The whole article is reproduced at www.groundreport.
   com/a-nonsensical-pile-from-nencini-viz-a-nonsencini/

and once again, and this time finally, declare them innocent. And, miracle of miracles, five Supreme Court judges made a just and courageous decision and did so, doubtless in the face of much pressure to do otherwise.

Six months later — The 'motivation' report

Once again, the Supreme Court's decision was followed by the detailed (Marasca) 'motivation report,' setting out its reasoning. It was published on September 7th 2015, and makes for confused reading, as it treads a delicate path between procedure and accuracy. Marasca takes as its judicial function to consider the appeal against the Nencini Court judgment in its own right. In doing so it is not directly critical of the first session of Cassazione that rejected the Hellmann appeal and set up Nencini. Instead, it says that the Nencini Court was obliged to consider all aspects of the previous trials and most notably hard evidence, and that in this, it failed.

Thus, Nencini should have been critical of the role of the press and media, and the rush of Perugia's police to 'solve' this crime. It should have been critical of the early investigation, including the incredible and careless destruction of computers. It should have identified the contradictions between the different witnesses (without needing to state that their evidence was downright inadmissible). It should have acknowledged that any evidence provided in the Guede trials (*Chapter 2*) and appeal could not be transferred to this case. It should not have accepted the nonsense of a selective clean-up of evidence.

Above all it should have understood that scientific evidence is what matters, and that the DNA evidence against Amanda and Raffaele was not merely non-existent, but bogus, since there was contamination and the tests unrepeatable. DNA evidence that did not follow international guidelines or any recognisable scientific principles and should have been thrown out. In this and other respects, Marasca reiterates the rules of evidence, saying that it is not sufficient for a judge to convict on a firmly held belief of guilt, unsupported by facts.

There are also many other areas where Marasca appears to fall short. Once again he puts undue emphasis on the so-called *calunnia* of Amanda against Patrick Lumumba, without making reference to the absence of the interrogation recording, which the police were obliged to make and which could have revealed the circumstances in which the accusation arose and whether or not coercion occurred.

There is no mention anywhere of the possibility that someone in authority might have sought to conceal the truth. Marasca even theorises a possibility that Amanda and Raffaele could have been at *Via de la Pergola* on the fateful night, whilst simultaneously stating that it is impossible that they could have taken part in the murder without leaving evidence, such as that left by Guede. He states that the crime would have been very difficult for one person acting alone, without noting that since Amanda and Raffaele were absolved, this line of theorising requires one or more extra perpetrators, for whom there is no evidence either. Marasca also fails to acknowledge the internal contradictions pertaining to the break-in, such as glass shards on the outside of the shutters and the pattern of debris within the room, which should have led Nencini, as well as the police and earlier courts, to question the prosecution assertion that it was faked. And having cleared Amanda and Raffaele of involvement, the identity of the supposed perpetrator remains a chimera.

And, as with all previous judgements there is no suggestion that the semen stain should have been tested to further confirm Guede's complicity or identify an elusive co-perpetrator. Marasca firmly concludes that Nencini should have found Amanda and Raffaele not guilty, without acknowledging that there are any lessons to be learned from the errors in the process for the benefit of future defendants. The European Court of Human Rights has ruled on many similar cases from Italy and elsewhere but there is little evidence that any of its criticisms have percolated downwards and impacted on the workings of the Italian system of justice, where the same errors risk being repeated. Changes to police practice and judicial procedure are vital (See the closing chapter).

CHAPTER 4

The Psychopathology of the Press

'It's easier to fool people than to convince them that they have been fooled.'

Mark Twain

As noted in *Chapters 1* and *2*, corporations are psychopathic by nature and by law, having all of the rights of an individual, whilst being answerable only to their shareholders. It follows that they require outside control. One only has to consider the modern-day international finance and banking crisis to realise that unregulated corporate institutions are single-minded in the pursuit of profits and will seek to evade and ignore any regulation that interferes with this aim. Controllers of the media are no different, whether working through the printing press, the airwaves or the internet, although here the picture can be more subtle. News is seldom untainted by manipulation, whether at source or in the editorial process.

The nature of corporations and the press

Commercial publishers generally have two aims. The obvious one is to increase paid for circulation and therefore profit. Crime has always been part of this picture. Lurid tales of sex and violence have been staples of publishing since the press was invented. The prurient interest of the public is aroused, sales soar and the increased income goes straight to the bottom line. The murder of Meredith Kercher immediately stood out, even in an age when news could be sourced instantly from almost anywhere in the world. This story ticked all the money boxes of the gutter and not so gutter press. This was confirmed when one of us talked to a group of British journalists at the back of the court in Perugia and asked why they had bought and embellished such an obviously dubious story — 'We didn't dare *not* print it, and have a march stolen on us by the *Express*,' said one, 'We simply had to be there first with the sensational news.' With which the *Express* reporter agreed, 'Yes, we had no choice, we couldn't let the *Mail* be the one to break the story, even if we had some doubts. My editor would have fired me.'

Newspaper magnates also like to wield political influence and increase their wealth by indirect means even if this means tinkering with — some might say 'subverting' — democratic processes. Editorial coverage is slanted to favour one political party over another because the election of a government of a particular colour is believed to be more likely to assist an owner's business plan. But it is the first aim, the straightforward increase in sales driven by controversial crime stories, which concerns us here.

The transmission of news has been revolutionised in the past two decades as the internet has been added to the established delivery systems of print, radio and TV. In addition, self-publishing through blogs and comment sections on news sites has 'democratised' the expression of opinion, not always in furtherance of the truth. So now people access the news from three main sources; print, the broadcast media and the web.

The story of Meredith Kercher's murder spanned two continents and three countries: the victim was English; one of the alleged killers was American, one Italian; other protagonists were African and the location was Italy. So let us look at how the case was covered in Italy, the UK and the USA and how this differed. Was the news tailored to match the prejudices of mass audiences in the three countries where interest in the case was greatest?

Press coverage in Italy

Italy has a prurient tabloid culture, not unlike that of the UK, though in some ways more extreme, since the contrast between the way people actually live and the way they wish to be perceived is arguably greater. Sexism and double standards are part of everyday life and this is reflected in its media. The popularity of the former premier Silvio Berlusconi seemed to increase as news of his infamous 'bunga bunga' parties and allegations about his sexual activities with under-age girls gained more coverage. Meanwhile, Amanda Knox was vilified for owning a joke vibrator, and was tricked into admitting to having had more than one sexual partner, and two one night stands (*Chapter 2*). Amanda's Italian flatmate Filomena Romanelli spent the night of Meredith's murder at her boyfriend's house, just as Amanda did. However many young Italians still live with their parents until they are married, so their sex lives are often confined to their cars, and pretence of abstinence before marriage can be maintained. The firm hand of the Roman Catholic Church still holds sway, especially in the former papal states, including Umbria, although its teachings are increasingly ignored. Meanwhile a confused population has been raised on Berlusconi-owned trash TV replete with topless game shows.

Specialist magazines with large circulations ensure that a widespread interest in lurid crime is catered for, and these include coverage of investigations and prosecutions in progress as well as closed cases. There is no restriction (as there is in the UK) on pre-trial publicity, and this ensures that defendants become public property from the moment they are arrested. Prosecutors and the police leak and brief information to keep their versions of the truth in the news. As a by-product un-sequestered juries (not kept from outside influences, e.g. in a hotel, etc.) are free to arrive at unreasonable and unsupportable convictions based on supposition rather than evidence.

Coverage of the Kercher murder was unprecedented, even by Italian standards. Gabriella Carlizzi was already prominent for suggesting a devilish Masonic conspiracy theory for the Monster of Florence murders to prosecutor Mignini. She seems also to have ignited his interest in the notion of a satanic sex game gone wrong. Such was the saturation coverage in the Italian press, that by 2009 Amanda was voted the most prominent woman in Italy in a poll by one TV news programme, putting her ahead of then US vice-presidential hopeful Sarah Palin and then French first lady Carla Bruni Sarkozy. Her junior school nickname, 'Foxy Knoxy', the first choice phrase for UK newspaper headlines (see also *Chapter 3*), was rendered into Italian as 'Evil Fox', a sleight of hand that could not have helped her defence.

As described in *Chapter 2*, information about Amanda's sex life was cleverly extracted from her by the irresponsible and totally illegal ruse of having a 'doctor' tell her that she was HIV positive. No doubt this unethical ploy was intended to trick her into revealing details of a postu-lated sexual relationship with co-defendant Rudy Guede, a man she claimed to hardly know. This did not happen since she was telling the truth.

What the 'news' did induce was a diary entry in which she gave a lifetime list of men she had had sex with, mostly back home in Seattle, as she naïvely tried to identify the possible source of her supposed HIV infection. The lifetime total was seven including Sollecito (by current Western 20-year-old standards perhaps unremarkable). Her diary was promptly stolen and the contents given to the Italian press, where the number was spun as being that of sex partners in less than two months in Italy. Never mind that the use of this diary ran counter to Article 8 of the European Convention on Human Rights (Right to Respect for Private and Family Life). It was dynamite in Italy, Britain and elsewhere. Knox was painted as an amoral sex fiend and thus capable of anything. The subsequent news that the HIV 'test result' was a false positive was quietly passed over; as was the way it had been used.

Mignini's concern with the sexual aspects of the case was also used to publicise Knox's ownership of a toy vibrator, which had been given to her as a joke by a Seattle friend and which she had foolishly brought and kept in a toilet bag in her bathroom. Italy, like the UK, is apparently not yet ready for female masturbation or any reference to mechanical assistance. In the same way, Raffaele's interest in Japanese *Manga* comic books was implied to be the hobby of a degenerate.

So a careful programme of character assassination was pursued, accom-panied by misleading and inaccurate stories about the investigation itself. News coverage was complicated by the fact that the first language of Amanda and her family is English. Far from being a problem for the Italian Press, this was successfully turned into an advantage for the pros-ecution. Her statements could be badly translated and their meaning twisted. This process started on the night she was arrested when a simple text message '*Ciao*, see you later, good night' was interpreted as 'See you really soon so we can go to my place and kill my British roommate.'

Another notable mistranslation demonstrated that irony does not travel well. When Knox learned that the police had chosen a random knife from Sollecito's apartment as the murder weapon, she speculated in her diary as follows:

'Raffaele and I have used this knife to cook, and it's impossible that Meredith's DNA is on the knife because she's never been to Raffaele's apartment before. So unless Raffaele decided to get up after I fell asleep, grabbed said knife, went over to my house, used it to kill Meredith, came home, cleaned the blood off, rubbed my fingerprints all over it, put it away, then tucked himself back into bed, and then pretended really well the next couple of days, well, I just highly doubt all of that.'

This expression of confusion was then cleverly translated into Italian with the following spin (shown here translated back into English):

'That night I smoked a lot of marijuana and I fell asleep at my boyfriend's house. I don't remember anything. But I think it's possible that Raffaele went to Meredith's house, raped her and then killed her. And when he got home, while I was sleeping, he put my fingerprints on the knife. But I don't understand why Raffaele would do that.'

So by deft (and not so deft) sleight of hand, the prosecution, followed by the Italian media and then by the UK and USA media, turned Amanda's doubt into an accusation against Raffaele. The perverted version went around the world, boosted by journalist Barbie Nadeau's use of it in her 'Daily Beast' blog and her subsequent book *Angel Face.*

Throughout this process of obfuscation and character assassination no Italian newspaper or journalist, so far as we are aware, smelt a rat except for one man, a Perugian blogger Frank Sfarzo. At first he went along with the stories he was reading, but when he looked more closely he began to realise that the prosecution theory didn't add up. He also noticed that the crime theory had no basis in fact. The 'facts' were sourced later to make the theory work. Frank's blog was written in English and called 'Perugia Shock.' It was to continue for over five years as he became the source of many of the corrections and clarifications that would help torpedo Mignini's prosecution case. His outspoken 'no-bullshit' essays, written in a unique and sarcastic, almost pidgin English style, soon attracted a fierce following. As time went on, other Italian publications, notably news magazine *Oggi*, also became increasingly sceptical of Mignini's version, but not until after the first trial of Amanda and Raffaele ended with a 'guilty' verdict in December 2009.

The UK press

The UK enjoys what is probably the most diverse daily newspaper portfolio in the world. The compact size of the country means that all the main population centres can be served reliably from central print and distribution centres and in addition there are separate Scottish, Welsh, Northern Irish and regional dailies. Every point of view is catered for. 'Serious' (formerly broadsheet) papers like *The Times, Telegraph, Guardian, Independent* (now defunct in hard copy) and *Financial Times* cater for an educated market. The middle market is served by the *Daily Mail* and *Daily Express*. The 'red tops', *The Mirror, Sun* and *Daily Star* primarily serve the blue collar market.

Fierce competition for circulation, throughout the 20th-century, fostered price wars, giveaway promotions and special offers by market leaders. In addition, some editors and reporters eager to be first with the juiciest stories used morally dubious and sometimes illegal methods. At various times the challengers for the highest circulation were the *Daily Mail*, the *Daily Express*, the *Daily Mirror* (now *The Mirror*), the *Sun* and the *News of the World* (again defunct: see later), all of which had lengthy spells at the top of daily or weekly sales charts. These were the true mass-market stars and relied on a diet of crime and sleaze to stay at the top.

In 1896 Lord Northcliffe launched the *Daily Mail* using the motto 'get me a murder a day.' It was an instant success and by 1902 circulation had grown to over a million, the highest in the world. Other papers emulated and even improved on this formula, in particular the Sunday paper the *News of the World* which had peak sales in the 1950s of almost eight million. It was infamous for unmasking adulterous vicars and public figures who frequented prostitutes as well as serialising the adventures of fallen women and spendthrift football pool winners. Competition for market share and advertising increased further in the 21st-century as the internet lured readers away, intensifying a gradual decline in sales.

By now publishers and editors had become ruthless, and some of them employed freelance investigators to tap phones and trawl through dustbins in search of anything embarrassing that could be turned into a story. Even members of Britain's royal family were not immune to this treatment. In January 2007, News International, the owner of the *News of the World*, was implicated in a phone-hacking scandal and its royal editor Clive Goodman and private investigator Glenn Mulcaire convicted of the illegal interception of phone messages and sent to prison. The paper claimed that this was an isolated incident but in 2011 an out-of-court settlement with actress Sienna Miller prompted a fresh police investigation. This eventually uncovered illegal recordings of hundreds of celebrities and crime victims. The effect on the reputation of the *News of the World* was so great that in 2012 it was closed down. Although the *Daily Mail* was equally reliant on celebrity stories and was rumoured to deploy similar tactics, nothing was proved and it managed to escape much of the opprobrium heaped on its rivals.

Sub judice laws in the UK mean that crime coverage needs to be carefully managed, as information about people charged with criminal offences in Britain cannot be published until after the verdict or before someone pleads guilty voluntarily. Even during trials, coverage is supposed to be limited to reporting the bare unembellished facts of what occurs in court. Innuendo and misinformation about those who are merely suspects and have not yet been charged can also be costly as several newspapers discovered after printing exaggerated stories about a retired schoolmaster, Christopher Jefferies. He was interviewed in connection with the murder of Joanna Yeates in Bristol in December 2010. He was released without charge and a Dutch engineer, Vincent Tabak, was subsequently convicted. Jefferies pursued successful libel cases against eight newspapers and was reportedly paid over £500,000, and two were also found guilty of contempt of court for reporting information that could prejudice a trial.

Coverage of the Kercher murder, which was to be tried outside Britain's jurisdiction, was devoid of such restrictive niceties. There is no *sub judice* rule in Italy so anything and everything can be reported. The unlikely murder scenario, in which one young woman was supposed to have killed a female flat-mate with the assistance of two male friends, was outlandish and therefore immediately gripping. The UK press was well aware of its freedom to report every lurid and supposed detail. Accuracy was not a consideration for a case unfolding in another country.

The Rome correspondents and stringers for the British press made their way to Perugia immediately. As discussed in *Chapter 3*, John Follain of the *Sunday Times* was one of these and swiftly established a firm working relationship with prosecutor Mignini. Others like Nick Pisa, whose by line could be seen in several newspapers, also set up camp in town. Mignini was an experienced prosecutor. He had harnessed the Italian media in his pursuit of the Monster of Florence and his 'bizarre' theories about that case had earned him notoriety. Now he was (apparently fortuitously) placed in charge of what was the crime of the year.

Seemingly, Mignini started briefing immediately as his theories and comments began to appear in UK newspapers within 24 hours. Follain was able to report in the *Sunday Times* of November 4th 2007, i.e. 48 hours after Meredith's body was discovered, that the police were looking for a female suspect who was close to the victim; in other words the prosecutors must have already settled on Amanda Knox (since the English girls had left town, and her two Italian flatmates were both lawyers, and duly 'lawyered-up'). Mignini and his officers must have dismissed the break-in as faked from the moment they visited the scene, and had honed in on Knox because she and her boyfriend Raffaele had been first on the scene and had called the police.

Follain was to remain close to the case throughout and published *Death in Perugia* in 2012, already discussed in *Chapter 3*, which serves as a virtual primer for Mignini's take on the crime. Follain is also remembered for his interview with Amanda's parents, published in the *Sunday Times Magazine* on June 15th 2008: see later in this chapter. While Follain may have had a key role in the saga, another newspaper, the *Daily Mail*, swiftly took centre stage as the leading purveyor of Knox and Sollecito gossip. The newspaper occupies a unique place in the British psyche. It is loathed and loved in almost equal measure. It was Britain's first daily newspaper to be aimed at the lower-middle class market, newly literate through mass education, and it combined a low retail price with plenty of competitions, prizes and promotional gimmicks, as it fiercely fought for circulation in the inter-war years. Its owner Lord Rothermere was a friend of both Mussolini and Hitler and he directed the *Daily Mail's* editorial stance towards them in the 1930s.

In a 1933 leading article, 'Youth Triumphant', Rothermere praised the new Nazi regime's achievements, and this statement was adapted as Nazi propaganda. It stated, 'The minor misdeeds of individual Nazis' would be 'submerged by the immense benefits the new regime is already bestowing upon Germany.' It has been suggested that this was a reference to violence against Jews and Communists rather than detention of political prisoners. *The Mail* was also editorially sympathetic to Oswald Mosley and the British Union of Fascists. This editorial approach was enthusiastically received by a large section of the middle-class who instinctively supported rigour and discipline and feared that a Communist Germany might trigger another war.

The Mail was also the first British paper to sell a million copies a day and was, from the outset, primarily a newspaper for women, being the first to provide features especially for them. It remains the only British newspaper whose readership (at 53 per cent) is more than half female. Its extensive health and celebrity coverage enables it to follow a largely retrogressive and anti-feminist political line without apparently offending its women readers. It takes an anti-abortion stance and its skill at miscasting the views of those it disagrees with is illustrated by this headline from 2007, 'Meet Dr Death, the Lib Dem MP Evan Harris who backs embryo experiments, euthanasia and freer abortions.' Thus it cleverly capitalises on the guilt of many of its female readers who have had abortions themselves or who have friends who have done so. It also understands the *schadenfreude* felt by many who feel fortunate not to be in situations like that of Amanda. The Kercher murder story had everything its female readership finds fascinating—a grisly tale and a 'girl-next-door gone bad.' By April 2013, it was able to list 403 separate stories about the murder at its website.

The *Daily Mail* really comes into its own with its internet operation. In January 2013 a five year growth plan paid off when it overtook the *New York Times* to become the most viewed newspaper site in the world, with over 100 million monthly visits on some measures, thanks to the addition of many American readers. The secret of its success was to turn the website into a separate operation from its print sister, with a more focused approach on celebrity gossip. This cemented its female reader-ship and made it compulsory reading for everyone in show business.

The *Daily Mail* was ruthless in chasing down Amanda Knox, and its coverage of the Kercher murder showed it in the worst possible light for several years. As soon as Amanda was arrested, it (along with other British newspapers) sent reporters to Seattle to try to uncover her alleg-edly salacious and criminal past. Journalists arrived on the University of Washington campus and questioned anyone who had even a remote relationship to her. According to the *University of Washington Daily*, a British tabloid journalist from the *Daily Mail* contacted its writer Ben Schock, who had lived on campus in Terry Hall with Amanda during her freshers year, and the paper then reported that Schock had a 'serious romance' with Knox, although he told the *Daily Mail* he 'only went out casually [with Knox], and always in a group. It just really irritated me because I didn't say anything that would lead [the reporter] to suggest we were in a romantic relationship.' The *Daily Mail* also failed to report that Schock is openly homosexual. Author Candace Dempsey was particularly critical of the behaviour of British tabloids in her blog, 'Italian Woman at the Table' and singled out the *Daily Mail* in both its print and online editions for particular excoriation in an interview: 'It's there [and] it's permanent,' she said. 'If you don't really understand the Internet, you don't understand this case. A tabloid, such as the *Daily Mail*, will run a story on the case and fill it with dubious facts that outlive more balanced updates,' Dempsey said. Proof that coverage of the Kercher murder was generating sales was revealed by Andrew Seliber, another friend of Knox, who along with fellow student Ben Parker said it offered them as much as $40,000 if they would provide information related to Knox's personal life, an invitation they declined.

As far as the *Daily Mail* was concerned, Amanda and Raffaele were simply two more celebrities whose lives could be reduced to banalities and trivialities, leavened, and seemingly often driven, by leaks which may have come from the prosecution. The same pictures and much of the content would be lifted and repeated in further articles so that each one became little more than a thinly disguised repetition of what had gone before. The success of this approach was confirmed by monitoring web traffic, not only to the site as a whole, but to each individual page. Popular 'characters' would be featured more frequently as online visits continued to climb. Further feedback was solicited in the form of comment sections below many articles, where readers could engage in a virtual jousting match about the merits of the opinions in the pieces and these comments could themselves be 'arrowed' up or down in green or red by other website visitors. Most arrows angrily pointed towards a presumption of guilt. As a business model, this became the acme of online 'news' and features presentation.

The *Daily Mail* in print and increasingly online became the main source of information about the Perugia case. What it provided was partial, biased and omitted any criticism or questioning of the prosecution narrative. This continued for nearly eight years, with censorship of any comments that suggested possible criminality involving the police or prosecutors. The defence was scarcely mentioned and no attempt was ever made to cover the story in a balanced or accurate manner. This was helped by the fact that the prosecution arguments always came first in court, in the morning, after which the reporters would leave the courtroom empty for the defence to make their reply. Myth and spin became truth to most readers as its operation swept all before it. Meredith's nationality had ensured a pro-British, 'support the victim' approach, regardless of the facts of the case and Amanda's almost unique role as the supposed female organizer of a vicious murder, ensured the continuing fascination of prurient reader. The process was simple: talk to Mignini or another prosecution contact and project this into the latest 'smear', knock out an article and then swiftly move on to the next job. In fact, serious examination of the implausible and increasingly eccentric prosecution narrative was discouraged, lest scepticism should lead to the gravy train hitting the buffers.

Although the *Daily Mail* took the lead in covering the murder, *The Sunday Times* and its Italian correspondent John Follain were crucial in the development of one of the supplementary lawsuits that the case generated. Follain's early period of reporting on the case culminated in a 5,000 word colour magazine feature published on June 15th 2008. He set out the backdrop to the murder and quoted extensively from an interview he had conducted in Seattle with Knox's parents Edda Mellas and Curt Knox and Amanda's younger sister Deanna. It remains the longest and most sympathetic interview with members of Amanda's family to be published before her release. The family had decided, seven months after the murder, that they could no longer sit back and watch while Amanda's character was destroyed. Curt had been advised to use a PR consultant to field the media opportunities that were presenting themselves. He had chosen Seattle firm Gogerty Marriott and they had set up the interview with Follain.

As already described, by November 6, an exhausted and terrified Knox had been interrogated continuously by police for eight hours until she signed a statement at 5.54 am. Her family says that despite her good marks at university, Amanda was not fluent in Italian, but no professional interpreter was present, only a police officer who could speak English and who was not always there. Amanda was given no food and no water for all of that time. 'I've never been so scared in my life,' she told Deanna later. Father, Curt Knox says: 'Amanda was abused physically and verbally. She told us she was hit in the back of the head by a police officer with an open hand, at least twice. During the night, the interrogation was taken over by Mignini (who Knox believed to be the mayor of Perugia) who allegedly told her, 'If you ask for a lawyer, things will get worse for you' and 'If you don't give us some explanation for what happened, you're going to go to jail for a very long time.' Mother Edda Mellas adds tearfully: 'She was told she wouldn't ever see her family again, and her family is everything to her.'

Amanda gave them a description of the officer who allegedly struck her, but at that time it could not be published for legal reasons. In her book she identifies Rita Ficara, said to be a *poliziotta* with a past history of physical abuse of prisoners (though these are only allegations). The Perugia police have denied striking her and have said she understood what she was signing. This interview led to a charge by Mignini against Amanda's parents, of *calunnia*; but exempted John Follain and *The Sunday Times*. The case is due to be heard in the summer of 2016. The case against Amanda for saying she was struck was 'quietly' thrown out by a judge in Florence in January 2016!

The USA press

An early problem was that newspapers in the USA failed to send any reporters of their own, preferring the more economical option of using UK and Italian stringers. As noted in *Chapter 3*, two of these were Andrea Vogt and Barbie Nadeau, who are both married to Italians, and based in Rome. Both were wedded to the prosecution line. Nevertheless with the passage of time, coverage in the American media became progressively more sympathetic to Amanda and Raffaele, but by missing the crucial first ten days, any hope of influencing global perception of the pair was lost.

In contrast to the weakness of the American press, much of the best work revealing the innocence of Amanda and Raffaele, and the role of Rudy Guede, and the seeming corruption of the proceedings has come from the USA. Candace Dempsey, Bruce Fisher, Nina Burleigh and Mark Waterbury have all published excellent books on the case, with important contributions also by Douglas Preston, John Douglas and Ron Hendry. Amanda Knox and Raffaele Sollecito have published two personal accounts in the USA about their ordeal, while their publication and distribution has been blocked in the UK and Italy. Raffaele's book is currently a subject of yet another *calunnia* charge by Mignini, against him and his co-author Andrew Gumbel. The analysis of the forensic evidence carried out in the USA by the likes of Greg Hampikian and others working for the Innocence Project have been excellent. A major problem, however, has been that they had little impact in Italy where the case had to be fought.

In the USA, press coverage of the case was in the main superficial and cursory, at least up to the end of 2009. Even the leading newspaper from

Amandas home town, the *Seattle Times* paid scant attention to the story. Another newspaper, *Seattle Post Intelligence* published regular updates from both Candace Dempsey and Andrea Vogt and thus covered both innocence and pro-guilt angles. Dempsey would go on to write the leading unbiased (or pro-innocence) book on the case.[1]

The *West Seattle Herald*, whose reporter Steve Shea was an early advocate of Amanda's innocence, catered for her local neighbourhood of West Seattle. On Vashon Island, a short boat trip from the city and home to Curt Knox's family, an enterprising resident, Karen Pruett, covered the case and eventually became a key figure in the Knox-Sollecito innocence campaign. But it was US television that led the way in campaigning for innocence, with journalists like Doug Longhini, Peter Van Sant and Paul Ciolino using phrases like, 'railroad job from hell' on CBS *24 Hours* specials. They opened the door to balanced coverage nationwide. Their work was augmented by Seattle's own King 5 Television with Lynda Byron who travelled to Perugia at key times.

America is a big country where murders are commonplace, so serious coverage built slowly as more and more people gradually became aware of the curiosities of Italian justice. After the Judge Hellmann acquittal of 2011, the whole world watched as Amanda Knox, after a BA flight from London to Seattle, made her first public statement on American soil before a forest of microphones. Foolishly we all thought that her release would be the end of the matter, but Giuliano Mignini knew better.

---

1.   Berkley, *Murder in Italy*, 2010.

CHAPTER FIVE

Internet Trolls

One of the most bizarre aspects of the prosecution of Amanda Knox and Raffaele Sollecito has been the existence of a sophisticated online pro-guilt publicity campaign. It began before they had even been charged, well before their first trial began, at a time when Knox in particular was being portrayed in the media as an 'evil murderess.' The evidence against the pair was alleged to be convincing and as described in the previous chapter much of it had been leaked to an eager press.

Despite efforts by their families, conviction appeared to be a formality. A small group of Amanda's friends in Seattle fought a brave but largely ignored campaign for her innocence. Against this background, surely there was no need for an online pro-guilt campaign? Yet this is exactly what occurred. Amanda has been subjected to one of the most vicious trolling campaigns in online history. It goes well beyond simplistic name-calling and death threats. Two websites were set up to turn up the heat. One claimed to be interested in 'True Justice for Meredith Kercher,' but has directed most of its energy against Amanda and her supporters; the other was a chatroom, 'Perugia Murder File' (PMF) that in time split into two chatrooms seemingly after a falling out amongst members.

Attacks on Knox are 'all for Meredith'

Misplaced sympathy for the victim is an inadequate explanation for the depth and intensity of the response, which includes Twitter, online comment sections and whole websites dedicated to attacking Amanda and Raffaele. On Twitter and on two dedicated forums, a band of trolls uses multiple identities to target news organizations and journalists. This is the phenomenon known as 'organized trolling.' Izabella Kaminska of the *Financial Times* of London has studied organized trolling:

'There have always been trolls, of course, but that's not what we're addressing here. What we're talking about is the overt corruption of the system due to increasingly organized interests understanding that if they shout loudly and prolifically enough, and in unison, they may be able to push their particular agenda to the top of the public's attention, usually by crowding out the last remaining objective faculty on the network. Logically speaking, this inevitably leads to a point where the reader—no longer capable of differentiating trustworthy messages from corrupted ones, but burned many times by falling into the enemy's trap—gives up entirely, and ends up trusting nobody at all.'

The Kercher murder arguably attracted more attention than any other crime this century. It is open and shut. No intelligent, objective observer can truly support the guilt of Amanda and Raffaele. So why do superficial contributors continue to write, 'We will probably never know the truth?'

The impact has been immense. Trolls have succeeded in persuading many in the media and elsewhere that there is a credible case against the pair. On Facebook and on Twitter in particular, 'armies' of trolls with multiple identities engaged in a 24/7 campaign to libel them, by repeating disproved myths, inventing new ones and indulging in character assassination. The Twitter war is vicious and unending. It is difficult to judge what affect it had outside the closed world of Perugia murder obsessives, but given the modern media's love affair with instant messaging it may be assumed that it had some impact on journalists. Understandably, activity quietened a little after the final March 2015 Supreme Court ruling. But even then only a little.

There are two kinds of trolls, leaders and followers. Followers (some might say 'sheep') are those who hide behind anonymity and wallow in *schadenfreude*. They have been around forever but the internet has given them a new platform and increased, if dubious, power. More interesting, particularly in this case, are the leaders, the early adopters, the pioneers. They are more dangerous. They set the agenda for the followers and they were determined to bring down Amanda and Raffaele from day one, almost as if they had some special stake in the outcome.

Why do trolls matter?

Trolls matter because they can pervert justice. Justice depends on honest police and prosecutors, competent defence lawyers and impartial judges and juries. Too often all these pieces are not in place. Meredith Kercher's death was a tragedy, and one man — Rudy Guede — was responsible. Seven years later, a second tragedy was that two innocent people were still living under a cloud of suspicion. This is the case over which internet trolling came of age and it has not been a pretty sight.

The followers — and what drives the trolls

Two factors — *schadenfreude* and confirmation bias have combined to enable and to sustain online vilification. The World Wide Web is a powerful democratising force but it has also given a louder voice to the ignorant, the bigoted and the dangerous. *Schadenfreude,* or delighting in the misfortune of others, is said to appeal to people with low self-esteem who feel better when those around them have bad luck. Brain-scanning studies have shown that it is correlated with envy.[1] The magnitude of the brain's *schadenfreude* response could even be predicted from the strength of a previous envy response.

As described in *Chapter 10,* the mob has always loved a murder or a hanging and today's media has an unparalleled ability to broadcast a story. *Schadenfreude* has featured throughout history. After 1783, in the UK, hangings were moved indoors and spectators had to be content with baying from outside the prison. Deprived of a ringside execution seat, the public's fascination with murder shows no signs of waning, as the continuing popularity of the 'true crime' genre attests. One crucial element is missing from books and movies — audience participation.

Confirmation bias (*Chapter 1*), has shaped the cases described in this book. Once a narrative has crystalised in the mind it is almost impossible to shift it. Facts that undermine the original message will be ignored. Nobel prize winner, Daniel Kahneman points out in his book, *Thinking, Fast and Slow*[2] that the halo effect, where we tend either to like or dislike

---

1. See http://www.nytimes.com/2009/02/17/science/17angi.html?_r=0 and the journal *Science* — http://science.sciencemag.org/content/323/5916/937.abstract
2. Penguin, 2012.

everything about a person, is a petrifyingly powerful factor in our lives. It means that first impressions not only count, but that almost nothing else counts at all. Terry Pratchett through his character Lord Vetinari sums this up:

> 'Be careful. People like to be told what they already know. Remember that. They get uncomfortable when you tell them new things. New things…well, new things aren't what they expect. They like to know that, say, a dog will bite a man. That is what dogs do. They don't want to know that man bites a dog, because the world is not supposed to happen like that. In short, what people think they want is news, but what they really crave is olds…Not news but olds, telling people that what they think they already know is true.'

(Through the character Lord Vetinari from, *The Truth: A Novel of Discworld*)

Biased interpretation explains how people, seeing the initial evidence, form a working hypothesis that affects how they interpret the rest of the information. So Amanda and Raffaele were up against confirmation bias in their first trial—big time. The prosecution and the media saw to that. And their prior history as well-behaved students from middle-class homes fostered *schadenfreude* for those who enjoyed seeing them brought down a peg.

Trolls harass and threaten offline as well

For some trolls, campaigning for guilt online was not enough. They took the fight to the employers of prominent innocence campaigners in attempts to get them fired from their jobs. This tactic succeeded in the case of former FBI agent Steve Moore, who was sacked in 2010 from a top security job at Pepperdine University. Many others suffered similar attention, up to and including death threats, including against one of this book's authors. The effectiveness of these campaigns was sometimes blunted because the writers hid behind fake cartoon character identities although in some cases they were revealed. In Washington State, a Superior Court judge Michael Heavey whose daughter had attended school with Amanda also spoke out. Trolls complained to the Executive Director of the Commission of Judicial Conduct in Seattle.

Hijacking of the Wikipedia page

The relevant Wikipedia page for the case, styled 'Murder of Meredith Kercher,' was controlled, from its earliest days, by editors who argued that Amanda and Raffaele were guilty. They correctly recognised that for journalists new to the case, Wikipedia would be an early port of call, so control of this page would shape the narrative. All attempts by incoming contributors to create a balanced article were expertly repulsed. Editors fought over changes in 'discussion' or 'talk' at mind-numbing length. Even the decision to define the case as 'controversial' was debated for several pages as filibustering attained art form status. Eventually, innocence campaigners organized a petition to Jimmy Wales, Wikipedia's founder. Once alerted, he took a personal interest in the case and arranged for new contributors to assist in editing it. He commented, 'I just read the entire article from top to bottom, and I have concerns that most serious criticism of the trial from reliable sources has been excluded or presented in a negative fashion.' A few days later he followed up, 'I am concerned that since I raised the issue, even I have been attacked as being something like a "conspiracy theorist".'

The page slowly began to improve but a wholesale revision was delayed until after the Hellmann acquittal of 2011. Even now a rearguard action against reason persists. Three weeks after their acquittal, incoming editor, 'SlimVirgin' admonished one of the hard-line editors,

> 'I think you have a conflict of interest editing here, because it's clear from your many off-wiki posts that you're an anti-Knox activist, and some of the posts have amounted to personal attacks on her, rather than simply discussing the case. You should not be editing a Wikipedia article about a living person when you've crossed the line into activism against that person...I therefore think you should consider not editing this article again or any of the others about Knox.'

The impact of the trolls, combined with superficial newspaper, radio and TV coverage was to mislead some legal commentators who should have known better. US TV presenter and former lawyer Nancy Grace spoke out against the 2011 acquittal, 'I was very disturbed because I think it is a huge miscarriage of justice,' Grace said. 'I believe that while Amanda Knox did not wield the knife herself, I think that she was there, with her boyfriend, and that he did the deed, and that she egged him on. That's what I think happened.'

Amanda Knox, Raffaele Sollecito and their families are victims who will have to bear the burden of accusation and expense for the rest of their lives for doing nothing more than defending their innocence. Trolls still attempt to taint them forever as killers and they continually claim that their supporters have 'sprung' a murderess with a 'PR campaign.' Even after the final decision and declaration of innocence by Italy's Supreme Court, which is under Italian law absolutely the last word on the case, the problems Amanda, Raffaele and their families face in trying to regain their reputations and secure their rehabilitation remain immense.

Online purveyors of defamation and hate will do well to remember that they can run but can't hide. Sooner or later, the worst of such trolls may find themselves in the dock.

The curious case of Harry Rag

One driving force behind this pro-guilt campaign, one of the first of the internet age, is the self-styled, 'Harry Rag', who may have taken his name from a song by the 1960s British rock band The Kinks. Rag has commented on other cases, but nothing compares to his (or maybe her?) obsession with this one, where he is treated with a respect bordering on adulation by other pro-guilt trolls. This has led to speculation that he may be in receipt of privileged information or even in direct contact with prosecution sources. There is little doubt that discovering the identity of Harry Rag would be a key to understanding the organized trolling PR campaign against two innocent people.

When he was banned from one site in mid-2008, Harry Rag adopted another strange pseudonym, 'The Machine', and he uses both. His first post was as early as November 18th 2007, 12 days after Meredith's murder.

A year later, and before the trial started, he was writing as follows (we have asterisked* anything manifestly and demonstrably wrong).

'There are two excellent pro-evidence,* pro-victim websites about the Meredith Kercher case. True Justice For Meredith Kercher: http://truejustice.org/ee/index.php. And Perugia Murder File; http://perugiamurderfile. freeforums.org/index.php. ALL the judges who have been involved in the case: Claudia Matteini, the judges at the Italian Supreme Court, Massimo Riccarelli, and Paolo Micheli thought there were serious indications of Amanda Knox's and Raffaele Sollecito's guilt and refused to grant them bail on the grounds that they are mentally unstable, dangerous and could reoffend. The case against Amanda Knox and Raffaele Sollecito is formidable.* There are 13 pieces of forensic evidence that link Amanda and Raffaele to the crime,* including Amanda's DNA on the handle of the knife found at Raffaele's apartment* and Meredith's DNA on the blade,* and Amanda's bare footprints set in Meredith's blood* and Raffaele's DNA on Meredith's bloodied and cut bra.* Amanda and Raffaele knew precise details about Meredith's body* which they could only have known if they had been present when Meredith was murdered. Amanda herself admitted she was present when Meredith was murdered in her handwritten note to the police on 6 November.* Amanda and Raffaele not only gave conflicting witness statements, but also gave completely different accounts of where they were,* who they were with and what they were doing on the night of the murder.* In the light of the judges decisions so far and the forensic evidence which was independently confirmed as accurate and reliable, it looks extremely unlikely that Amanda and Raffaele will be found not guilty.'

The catalogue of disinformation is much greater than this. The following was collected and passed to the authors by pro-innocence activist Karen Pruett in 2010 (again using asterisks to emphasise blatant errors):

- On 5 November 2007, Knox and Sollecito were confronted with proof they had lied and were given another opportunity to tell the truth.* However, they both chose to tell the police even more lies.*

- Sollecito's new alibi was shattered by computer forensic evidence and his mobile phone records.*
- Knox accused an innocent man, Diya Lumumba, of murdering Meredith despite knowing full well that he was completely innocent.* She didn't recant her false and malicious allegation against Lumumba the whole time he was in prison.*
- Knox's account of what happened on 2 November 2007 is contradicted by her mobile phone records.*
- Amanda Knox and Raffaele Sollecito both gave multiple conflicting alibis.*
- Neither Knox nor Sollecito have credible alibis for the night of the murder despite three attempts each.*
- At the trial, Sollecito refused to corroborate Knox's alibi that she was at his apartment.*
- Rudy Guede's bloody footprints led straight out of Meredith's room and out of the house.* He didn't lock Meredith's door,* remove his trainers,* go into Filomena's room or the bathroom that Meredith and Knox shared.* He didn't scale the vertical wall outside Filomena's room or gain access through the window.* The break-in was clearly staged.* This indicates that somebody who lived at the cottage was trying to deflect attention away from themselves and give the impression that a stranger had broken in and killed Meredith.*
- Guede had no reason to stage the break-in and there was no physical evidence that he went into Filomena's room.*
- The scientific police found a mixture of Amanda Knox's DNA and Meredith's blood on the floor.*
- There was no physical evidence that Rudy Guede went into the blood-spattered bathroom.* However, the scientific police found irrefutable proof that Knox and Sollecito tracked Meredith's blood into this bathroom.*
- Amanda Knox's DNA was found mingled with Meredith's blood in three different places in the bathroom: on the ledge of the basin, on the bidet, and on a box of Q Tips cotton swabs.
- Sollecito left a visible bloody footprint on the blue bath mat.*

- Amanda Knox left a bloody shoeprint on the pillow under Meredith's body.*
- Knox's and Sollecito's bare bloody footprints were revealed by luminol in the hallway.* Knox's DNA and Meredith's DNA was found mixed together in one of the bloody footprints.*
- An abundant amount of Raffaele Sollecito's DNA was found on Meredith's bra clasp.* Sollecito must have applied considerable pressure to the clasp in order to have left so much DNA.* The hooks on the clasp were damaged which confirms that Sollecito had gripped them tightly.*
- Amanda Knox's DNA was found on the handle of the double DNA knife and a number of independent* forensic experts — Dr. Patrizia Stefanoni, Dr. Renato Biondo and Professor Francesca Torricelli — categorically stated Meredith's DNA was on the blade.
- Sollecito knew that Meredith's DNA was on the blade which is why he twice lied about accidentally pricking her hand whilst cooking.*
- The defence experts were unable to prove that there had been any contamination.* Alberto Intini, head of the Italian police forensic science unit, pointed out that unless contamination has been proved, it does not exist.*
- Amanda Knox voluntarily admitted that she was involved in Meredith's murder in her handwritten note to the police on 6 November 2007.* She stated on at least four separate occasions that she was at the cottage when Meredith was killed.* She also claimed that Sollecito was at the cottage. *'

It is not necessary to go through the above postings sentence-by-sentence, but simply to say that virtually everything is wrong, and virtually all of it lines up perfectly with the prosecution theory.

Anonymous blogging

One of this book's authors (David Anderson) believes that he has established the likely identity of 'Harry Rag' but not with the degree of certainty that allows for its publication here. We are however able to provide some of the background to this below.

A brush with Harry

In September 2013, as the retrial of Amanda and Raffaele was about to start in Florence, a consultant for the BBC, Ross Fitzpatrick, organized an interview between Raffaele Sollecito and Stephen Sackur for the BBC's no holds barred programme *Hardtalk*. Meeting and talking to Raffaele, it seems, persuaded Fitzpatrick of the accused couple's innocence, and Raffaele came over well. This seems to have infuriated Harry Rag. Then early that December, Fitzpatrick was engaged in a Twitter conversation with Rag, and for some reason became convinced of his identity, addressing him on Twitter as 'Bill' (name changed). Michelle Moore, a staunch defender of innocence, spotted this on Twitter and contacted Fitzpatrick. So I (David Anderson) later also contacted him, whereupon he clearly came under some pressure to back down. However in doing so he wrote the following; 'My suspicion [of his identity] is just that, but one that I am sure is correct.'

So in December 2013 I wrote to the complaints department of the organization I believed to be his employer. I presented my evidence in person and in writing, saying that it strongly suggested to me that their employee might be trying to influence the outcome of a criminal prosecution. I suggested that they had a moral duty to investigate the allegations. I had analysed the entries over five years by 'The Machine' (Rag's alter ego) on the TJMK website, and his responses to comments, and found strong evidence that he was attending to this in working hours. The response to all of this was to dismiss my concerns as irrelevant. I referred the matter higher and received the same response.

Harry Rag's exultation at the Nencini verdict

Rag's activities heightened as the result of the Florence retrial approached. By February 3rd 2014, the Nencini verdict had been declared, reconfirming guilt, and in Amanda's case increasing the sentence. Rag was exultant on Twitter. His 840 Tweets and re-tweets from the period 27th January to 4th February that year included 26 cold approaches to journalists saying, 'Find out why #amandaknox was found guilty of murder by reading the official court documents: http://themurderofmeredithkercher.com/'.

I provided this to the suspected employer as a clear example of how Harry Rag was trying to influence the press. In my response to the rejection and in my reply of February 7th 2014, I gave my reasons for the matter to be pursued. Hearing nothing, after further contact on 2nd April I eventually received by email a confidential copy of the report outlining the nature of my complaint, and the reasons it was being archived. Half an hour before the report was to be published I was informed by email that it was embargoed indefinitely.

The baiting of Harry Rag

The next event of relevance occurred following the publication in April of an article by Rag on a blog called 'justice4ever', in which he repeated his standard pro-guilt assertions. I decided to use this as an opportunity to try and make him angry, and in the process perhaps to expose his identity. I wrote…

> 'You know who I am, but who are you, Harry Rag, that you lie so much over such blatant and corrupt injustice? Is it pure emotion, or does the clink of money enter as a supplementary motive as well? And is it true that you are also 'The Machine', who posts so prolifically if mechanically (though for some reason rather less of late) on the TJMK…website? You have said so in the past, so you can hardly deny that. And is it an unfortunate coincidence, or just a rather revealing slip of the nom de plume that TMJK is an anagram of TJMK? At all events it only seems fair for you to reveal who you really are, and as you admit to being a machine, just who or what is driving you.'

After a response from another poster I continued:

> 'Who do you see in the mirror when you shave badly of a morning? Not Harry Rag, surely. What do your friends call you? The Machine? Or "Bill"? And is it truth or lies that many of your colleagues are whispering (sotto voce out of misdirected sympathy) behind the closed doors of [your] employer…Make the others proud instead, by finally coming out…After

all, that is surely what [your day job] should be about — transparency and truth, not rags and machines.'

Then on the blog I got a revealing reply, which contained the following:

'I politely recommend seeking professional psychological help with your unhealthy obsession with discovering my identity. You've already lodged a complaint about [Harry Rag] which led to an investigation. Your wife and full-time carer should keep you away from the Internet before you hurt Meredith's devastated family any more…'

And in response to a reply from a fellow pro-guilter he wrote:

'Yes, it's true. The fact he unquestioningly believed [who I was] without any proof whatsoever speaks volumes about his gullibility and naïvety'.

I was immediately blocked on justice4ever. I made a copy of the exchange, and shortly afterwards found that the whole section after my first challenge above had been deleted from the website. In his anger Harry Rag had revealed information he could only have got directly or indirectly from the complaints department I had written to in December 2013. He had forgotten for a few crucial moments that the employer had contacted him and not Harry Rag.

The pernicious effect of anonymous pseudonyms

So are we being over-sensitive or paranoid? In this case the victim's family members have always said all they are interested in is finding the truth about who killed Meredith, but this is hardly aided by misleading pro-prosecution websites. Meredith's father John Kercher Snr writes in his book, *Meredith*:

'Throughout all of this the True Justice for Meredith Kercher website has been a vital resource, without which it would have been difficult for us to appreciate fully the case that unfolded around Meredith's murder.'

This is the website to which, under the pseudonym 'The Machine' Harry Rag contributed 41 articles over a six-and-a-half year period from August 2008. The simplest way to discover whether there has been a prejudicial effect is to ask what would have happened had the author acted without the cover of these pseudonyms. It was bad enough to have lawyers representing the family in the civil case say such things inside and outside court under the imbalanced pro-prosecution laws of Italy. But the same comments from a named individual, whoever he or she is, repeated *ad nauseum* on the internet, should surely be censored as a prejudicial attempt to influence the outcome of a trial. One lesson of this case, therefore, is that bloggers should be constrained under international law to blog using a registered and true identity. That way there can be no such abuse, such as we have seen here—promoting the conviction of two innocent young people, contributing to future unjust prosecutions.

The interests of justice cannot be served by anonymous trolling about a live case but there seems to be little appetite by the world's legislatures to tackle this problem. The most useful solution to this problem would be the removal of anonymity.

CHAPTER SIX

The Murder in England of Lesley Molseed

We have seen from earlier chapters that there are problems with police and justice systems in Italy. However, our purpose is not to pick on one country, but to examine these in the context of injustice in general; and we are interested here in systems that at least claim to seek justice.

It is instructive to take one case from each of the other countries indirectly involved in the case brought against Amanda Knox and Raffaele Sollecito, namely England and the USA. Such case histories should highlight differences, and help suggest what changes might need to be made to prevent such personally and financially costly disasters in the future. In medicine, illustrative case histories help to personalise otherwise sterile afflictions, and the same should apply equally to the law. This chapter looks at a notorious miscarriage of justice from England.

The Kiszko Case

Stefan Ivan Kiszko was convicted and spent 16 years in prison for the murder in 1975 of a young and particularly small girl, Lesley Susan Molseed. Like Amanda Knox and Raffaele Sollecito, he too should never even have been considered a suspect. In the 40 years since Lesley Molseed was murdered and Stefan Kiszko falsely convicted there have indeed been substantial changes, especially in the light of even higher profile injustices including those concerning the Guildford Four and the Birmingham Six.

We have selected the *Kiszko case* for three main reasons.

- *First*, because as a young consultant physician I (David Anderson) was personally involved in Stefan's medical management and 16 years later his exoneration and release. It was a rude awakening to injustice. I want to share some of the lessons I learnt from the case, and what I might have done differently with the benefit of hindsight.

- *Second*, better than any other case, it illustrates the advances in identification of murderers from DNA evidence, specifically small amounts of semen, and many years after the crime. It is therefore powerful testimony to conserving evidence. With the Kercher and Kiszko cases we have clear examples of what might be labelled 'seminal cases of 'The Law' breaking the law. In the Kiszko case, as we shall see, techniques caught up with the passage of time, and proper DNA-analysis ultimately and miraculously identified the true perpetrator: 30 years too late for Kiszko, and 12 years after his death.
- *Third*, in examining what went wrong in 1975/6 we might be forgiven for thinking that we are looking at Italy today.

It is not that the *polizio-judicial* powers in Britain don't also sometimes make appalling and sometimes unjust or even malicious mistakes; but there are at least some mechanisms for learning when things go wrong, and then putting them right for the future. Italy, however, seems to be stuck in a time warp. There are, however, pressures underway to change this, as well as an increasing realisation, illustrated well by the Kercher case, that injustice is everyone's business. In England there is slightly less pretence that papering over cracks to save face is more important than repairing the underlying structure. And there is also a better separation of powers, so that errors have a greater chance of being exposed.

A friend of mine once said, talking of the famous Chinese 'face'; 'The British care just as much about face as the Chinese; they just don't make so much fuss about it'. The same applies to the powers that be in all walks of life in Italy as in China. From a psychopathology viewpoint, there is in Great Britain therefore more unspoken recognition of the need to confront CNE in professionals and their professions. And there are marginally more effective detection mechanisms and safeguards.

Existing works on the Kiszko case

An excellent book on the Kiszko case, *Innocents: How Justice Failed Stefan Kiszko and Lesley Molseed* by Jonathan Rose, Steve Panter and Trevor Wilkinson was published in 1997 (Sage). A second, by barrister Michael O'Connell, to be entitled *Delusions of Innocence*, is not yet published at the time of writing; he has generously let me review a draft. According to O'Connell this case illustrates at least five causes of miscarriage of justice in the UK. These are: police misconduct; false or fabricated confessions; perjury by witnesses; wrongful visual identification; and bad trial tactics and defence conduct. With the possible exception of the last of these, all five, as we have seen, appeared to surface in the case of Amanda Knox and Raffaele Sollecito. Once we have looked at the case, it will be worth examining how changes put in place since 1975 in Britain have, if at all, improved the situation.

My first contact with Stefan Kiszko

In August 1975. I took up my first senior medical post as Senior Lecturer in Medicine and Consultant Physician at Manchester Royal Infirmary. Within a few days of arriving I was asked to see a sick patient of Ukrainian extraction, Stefan Ivan Kiszko, on the Haematology Ward. He worked as a clerical officer for the Inland Revenue in the neighbouring town of Rochdale, and lived with his mother. His father had died five years earlier in his early fifties from a heart attack. Stefan presented as an abnormally developed and extremely sick 24-year-old with severe malnutrition and anaemia, primary testicular failure, and atrophic pea-sized testicles. His anaemia was caused by a severe dietary deficiency of the B vitamin folic acid, caused by a grossly imbalanced diet, and a lack of fresh vegetables enhanced by a high intake of cider. His blood haemoglobin concentration was 3 g/dl (20 per cent of normal) and his anaemia the most severe the consultant haematologist had seen in 25 years of practice. It actually necessitated blood transfusions, something extremely unusual for anaemia in a young man.

Hypogonadism and its laboratory diagnosis and treatment had formed a part of my MD thesis three years previously. As the probable cause of his eunuchoidism I made the provisional diagnosis of Klinefelter's syndrome, in which the testicular failure results from an extra X chromosome. This causes a failure of the sperm-producing seminiferous tubules, and the condition of azoospermia (inability to produce sperm). It also causes secondary partial failure of production, by the interstitial (Leydig) cells, of the male hormone testosterone. The diagnosis of classical XXY

Klinefelter's syndrome was not in fact confirmed by blood chromosome analysis, leaving the possibility of XY/XXY mosaicism. At all events, this did not affect his management. I explained to him that based on his gross testicular atrophy he could not produce sperm, and that the same defect also meant he produced much less of the male hormone testosterone than normal. I reassured him that replacement with injections of testosterone was straightforward, and would greatly improve his wellbeing.

Stefan lived quietly at home with his mother Charlotte in Rochdale. There was nothing in his past history to suggest any propensity to violent or disturbed behaviour. He was devoted to his mother, an immigrant from Slovenia, who had worked for many years in a cotton mill, and as a result suffered from the severe industrial lung disease byssinosis. Stefan's employer found him reliable and diligent. His pride and joy was his car, a bronze Hillman Avenger. He was tall (six foot two inches); this is because in eunuchs the long bones continue to grow for far longer than in normal males, since the growth plates close late. He was also overweight, and had difficulty walking, being flat-footed and having suffered from a fractured ankle that had needed plating some 18 months previously. Osteoporosis is unusual in normal young men but is a typical feature of those with longstanding testosterone deficiency.

I took a careful history, and told Stefan what my diagnosis was. We had a conference with the other doctors involved, at which Stefan was present. He would not, I explained, be able to father children, but with hormone treatment should be able to have a normal sex life and marriage. As is to be expected in such a condition, he had only been through a partial and delayed puberty. Nevertheless Kiszko expressed a normal interest in girls, and was keen to start male hormone injections. He had masturbated as a late teenager but not recently. I explained that there would be an increase in sex drive, and he would experience the normal level of increased aggression and drive seen as boys go through puberty. He would start to get erections and to masturbate again.

Kiszko was delighted at the prospect of developing more normally. Unusually for endocrinologists, but because of experience with one other patient who had been slow to adapt, I started him on an injection every three weeks at half the normal dose of testosterone, so that he could come to terms with his adult male sex urge gradually. On December 9th 1975, I saw Stefan for the second time in the endocrine clinic, and he appeared to be in much better health and was effusive in his gratitude; he told me he had started to develop normal male sexual urges. He had had his second injection of 125 mg Primoteston given by the district nurse on October 3rd 1975, with later injections at the same interval being given by his GP. December 9th was the last time I saw Stefan because of extraordinary events that, unknown to both of us, were starting to unfold in his home town of Rochdale, and would soon envelop and destroy him.

Lesley Susan Molseed

Lesley Molseed (formerly Anderson) was a frail but bouncy eleven-year-old, the youngest of four children, who had been born with congenital heart disease, which had been finally operated on successfully; she was the size of an eight-year old. She lived with her mother, stepfather Danny and her sister and brother. At lunchtime on Sunday October 5th 1975 her mother sent her on an errand to the local baker. It was actually her brother Freddie's turn, but he was playing football. He never forgave himself for this and it may have contributed to his eventual suicide; but Lesley was an irrepressible young girl, who loved going on errands, and she negotiated with her mother a three pence bonus. She never returned, and there was a massive police hunt for her and her presumed abductor.

Early in the morning three days later David Greenwell, a joiner from Nottingham who was working in Rochdale, had passed the night asleep in his van in a lay-by on the A672 road at Ripponden about ten miles from Rochdale, rather than face a long journey home. Getting up that morning he scrambled up a steep slope to a flat area of ground above the road to relieve himself, and his eye was caught by a piece of blue cloth. On closer inspection it was the body of a small girl lying face down. She had been stabbed 12 times. After killing her, the perpetrator had masturbated on her body. Greenwell immediately contacted the police. Obviously a paedophilic, psychopathic sexual predator had violated and killed her.

If we pause now to consider the logical way to find Lesley's killer, we would concentrate on the crime scene, in order to come up with clues, and also to help form a profile of the killer. The forensic team found various items there, which included a felt tip marker pen, to which they later attached much importance in targeting Kiszko. And of course they performed a thorough examination on site, and later at a *post mortem* examination. A paedophilic killer had stabbed her viciously and repeatedly from behind and had then masturbated on her body. They would have known the perpetrator would have been covered in blood, the knife having pierced the girl's heart. Obviously it was a sexually active adult male, capable of persuading or forcing the diminutive Lesley to get into his car; he was possibly therefore known to and trusted by her. Away from the crime scene the highest priority would be given to descriptions of a small girl in a blue coat in a car with a man; and then climbing or being dragged 30 feet up a steep slope on this remote country road.

We would be looking for a man in reasonable physical condition. That information alone should have excluded Stefan Kiszko, who was still lame from his fractured ankle, and recovering from an exceptionally serious anaemia and gross hormone deficiency. At the time of Lesley's abduction and murder Stefan had been out of hospital for less than three weeks, after a stay of six weeks for a severe illness. Despite this, once they found he had a sex hormone deficiency the police became fixated with the three-letter word 'sex'. If they did any sort of simple criminal profiling, those charged with the investigation lost sight very early on of the most basic elements of this crime, and how it pointed to a man in normal physical health. Furthermore the police clearly did not give enough weight to the right kind of witness in trying to piece together the events surrounding the innocent Lesley's abduction.

Overwhelmed by spurious raw data

After this horrific crime the police were overwhelmed with mainly well-intentioned reports from members of the public coming forward with all sorts of information, that they seemed to have no sensible way of sifting and categorising. This was before the police had computers, and West Yorkshire Police were using a punched card system, which through the prism of 40 years now looks ridiculously cumbersome and archaic. The officers in charge quickly formed an image of a man, who they believed would have revealed himself as an obvious child molester, who they reasoned would probably have exposed himself. With little lay understanding of how psychopaths stalk their prey, they followed their own naïve instincts, pursuing lines for which they had no evidence. In particular they attached great importance to descriptions by young children of men near to Lesley's house who 24 and 48 hours before her abduction had or may not have exposed themselves.

Important witnesses ignored

Meanwhile, the police seem to have glossed over what we now know to have been, and they should have recognised as, the highly relevant observations of a local resident, Mrs Emma Tong. At 1.30 pm on the day of Lesley's disappearance Mrs Tong saw a little girl wearing a blue gabardine hooded coat sitting in the front passenger seat of a cream coloured car that needed respraying, outside her house in a street in Rochdale quaintly named Well I'th Lane. The little girl seemed to be handling a present of some sort which, smiling, she held up to show Emma Tong. Shortly afterwards Mrs Tong saw a man in a brown tweedy jacket get into the driver's seat and drive off with the little girl. On seeing a photograph of Lesley in the newspaper on October 11th, six days later, she was immediately convinced it had been Lesley and she reported this to the police, but the information was not given adequate weight. She gave a perfect description of Lesley, and had remembered the gap in her front teeth. Her evidence clearly pointed to a cream coloured car. This sighting should have been given the highest priority.

Even more extraordinary was the lack of attention given to evidence from lorry driver Christopher Coverdale. Between 3.45 pm and 4 pm on October 5th, the day of Lesley's murder, he was driving on the A672 Oldham to Halifax road in the direction of Ripponden, by Rishworth Moor, when he saw a little girl wearing a blue gabardine jacket with a hood being helped up a steep embankment or hill overlooking the carriageway, by a man in a brown coat. He remembered thinking this was foolhardy in the light of the bad weather. He reported this sighting to the police on October 24th, when he first became aware of Lesley's murder, and later led them to the area that was only yards from where her body had been found on October 8th. Evidently he was the last person to see Lesley alive, probably a few minutes before her assailant stabbed her to death. So why was this not put together with Mrs Tong's observations? They now had a good description of a reasonably fit man, who had persuaded Lesley to climb with him up a steep embankment. Overlooking two such powerful accounts speaks at the very least of questionable investigative competence, arguably something more worrying.

Police pressurised to solve the crime

The massive number of punched data storage cards were useless for retrieving data. The West Yorkshire and Greater Manchester Police were swamped, and rapidly became unable to see the wood for the trees. There was no way they could even keep up with, let alone analyse reports. There was, naturally, a great deal of pressure to solve the crime, but appeals to the public led to much irrelevant data, but which although spurious, helped when it came to Kiszko's prosecution and conviction.

Because Lesley was a young girl, the police concentrated on reports by local young girls of men who had supposedly exposed themselves around the time of her abduction. There is in fact absolutely no logic to this line of argument, but it was turned into a main arm of the prosecution case. Children are notoriously susceptible to suggestion (and some tell outright lies) and evidence from them has therefore to be treated with great care. And one 13-year-old and two of the older girls admitted years later that they had made up the stories 'for a lark'. One of the principal episodes, on October 3rd, in fact, turned out to be milkman Maurice Helm who had been seen emptying his bladder by the roadside near the youth club; he went to the police later and explained the confusion. One young girl, Debra, told how on October 4th in broad daylight when she was with her friends Maxine and ten-year-old Ann Marie, a man had exposed himself to them with an erect penis; he was said to have a long scar on his left leg (Kiszko was never examined for such a scar). One month later Maxine thought she saw him again and identified the man as Kiszko; this claim, which she clearly believed, led directly to the police's first interview of Kiszko. Maxine made another statement on 30th December, one week after Kiszko had been charged, stating that the man was clean-shaven, about five feet ten inches, and 'sort of shuffled'. Although Kiszko was six feet two in height, he did have an odd gait, and this was taken as corroborative evidence. These girls were never cross-examined in court. The importance given to their testimony was underlined when the judge in sentencing Kiszko commended Maxine for her sharp eyes that had led the police to Kiszko.

As already described, in early-September Stefan had been extremely ill, with such severe dietary anaemia that he had needed a blood transfusion. He was grossly malnourished and had also been grossly sex hormone deficient, and was still recovering from the effects of his ankle fracture 18 months before, and subsequent operations. But police were looking for an outsider, and he looked odd and acted oddly, and that was enough for them to pursue him to the point of arrest. Remember, they desperately needed to solve this crime, and to do so quickly. As we have argued regarding the Perugia murder, that can be a recipe for disaster and possibly 'sloppy' work.

The sequence of events that led Kiszko first to be suspected, then targeted, and finally coerced into making a false confession are well described in Rose's and McConnell's accounts. Reading these I wonder whether there was more to Stefan's mental health at that time than just the behaviour of a physically immature 'Mummy's boy'. He was both careless and inconsistent in the stories he gave as he was questioned at home on four different occasions. Certainly there is much to indicate that his brain function in August would have been damaged by his malnutrition and a folate deficiency so severe it had led to gross anaemia. With a heavy intake of cider, it is highly probable he was also suffering from deficiencies of other B vitamins, notably thiamine, whose deficiency is well recognised as a cause of recent memory loss, confusion and confabulation. Many of the problems and initial suspicions with the police centred on his changing story about where he was on dates around Lesley's murder, and when he first drove his car after leaving hospital. An additional problem was that he and his mother were at that time in the process of moving house in Rochdale from 31 Crawford Lane to 25 King's Road, which put him under considerable additional physical and mental stress at a time when he most needed to rest.

A disjointed sequence of police interviews

Over the six weeks starting on November 5th a month after Lesley's abduction and murder, Stefan was interviewed in his home on four occasions, by three sets police officers totalling seven in number. He made the fatal mistake of talking to the police, not once but several times, each time digging himself deeper into trouble with conflicting accounts over dates and details, and signing statements on the spot that were based on immediate memory.

He was visited first at 10.20 pm on November 5th, by WPC Shaw and PC Oliver. This was after he had been identified by Maxine and a young boy as the man who had indecently exposed himself at 12.45 pm, the day before Lesley's murder, and again that night. Kiszko said correctly that he was out of hospital on October 4th, but had been at home with his mother; he told the officers also that on that day he had been in a friend's car taking things round to Kings Road. He showed them his own car, the bronze coloured Hillman Avenger, which he claimed he had not driven for several weeks, on account of his bad leg. He had in fact visited Manchester Royal Infirmary on October 3rd, where he had been given his second injection of 125 mg of slow-release testosterone. Later evidence presented in court revealed that on the afternoon of October 5th, the day of Lesley's abduction, he had driven with his mother and his aunt to visit his father's grave. This was not discussed with officers Shaw and Oliver, who seemed only to be interested in the accusation by Maxine that he was the man who had exposed himself on October 4th, one month previously and whom she had just identified outside his house. In retrospect, however, it is obvious that the police had decided that the murderer had probably been revealing his deviant tendencies by exposing himself to young girls. As time went on it became progressively more apparent that pursuit of this link was taking centre stage in police strategy, and to the exclusion of other lines of enquiry and evidence.

The second police visit to Stefan was in the afternoon of November 7th, two days later, this time by two plainclothes detectives, Detective Sergeant John Mawson of the Bradford Drug Squad, and Detective Constable Colin Russell of Greater Manchester Police. They informed Kiszko that they were making enquiries into the murder of Lesley Molseed. He was not cautioned. There is no indication that they were aware of the above visit made by officers two days previously, but Stefan quickly told them, and asked what he was being accused of doing on October 4th. On this second occasion he incorrectly stated that he had been in hospital that day, and tried to find the discharge letter, but couldn't in the chaos of moving house. He was then asked if he had access to a vehicle and what it was. He was then set a trap, by being asked to make a statement concerning his whereabouts on October 4th, without being cautioned that it might be used in evidence against him, and of his right to remain silent. He signed a written statement on that date to the effect that as far as he could remember he was still a patient in Ward 4M of Manchester Royal Infirmary, that he couldn't remember the date of his discharge, but if he had been discharged he would certainly have spent all day at home as he was unable to walk. So we have the extraordinary situation that two days earlier he had given two officers information which was factually correct, and which he now contradicted with wrong information. But perhaps his memory was on this day particularly bad.

Then three days later on November 10th the same two police officers returned, having checked the dates with Manchester Royal Infirmary, and Kiszko agreed he had been mistaken. They made no attempt to try to identify or trace the friend he had said on November 5th had helped him move belongings on October 4th. Mawson then said that his information was that Kiszko had access to a white saloon car, probably a Vauxhall Viva. This is interesting since this was the colour of the car Mrs Tong had seen outside her house. Kiszko again emphasised that the only car he had access to was his bronze ('spice coloured') Hillman Avenger, referred to in his statement of three days earlier. And at this point he caused himself further problems by referring to the first visit to his father's grave having been on Sunday 12th October (i.e. one week after Lesley had been abducted and murdered).

The fourth visit concerning Lesley's murder, this time by Detective Sergeant John Akeroyd, accompanied by Detective Constables McFadzean and Whittle, all members of the West Yorkshire Police task force, took place six weeks later, on Sunday December 21st 1975. Clearly in the intervening six weeks the police investigation had made no progress, until a link was made by the police between the supposed acts of indecent exposure on October 3rd and 4th and the murder of Lesley Molseed on October 5th. They had three days earlier, on December 18th, gone to the Turf Hill Estate to make more enquiries.

The purpose of the visit on the 21st was to remove Stefan from his house and his protective mother to the more coercive and intimidating atmosphere of the police station. They did this by inviting him, rather than arresting him, thereby paradoxically depriving him of rights he would have had as a suspect. They did not inform him that they wanted to interrogate him about the murder of Lesley Molseed. Kiszko, knowing he had nothing to do with it made the fatal mistake of believing that his innocence would save him. When Sergeant Akeroyd went into the house the other two police officers went into the garage, and started to examine the outside of the Hillman car, which Michael O'Connell argues, must have been to look for signs that it had been resprayed. Of course it had not been. In the event Kiszko agreed to drive his car to the police station for a chat. This, fatefully, separated him from his protective mother, as well as providing the police with the car for closer inspection.

Final interrogation

It is unclear where Stefan was eventually interrogated, although in law he was technically free to leave at any time. The only record of what happened to Stefan over the next 36 hours is what was recorded by the police officers, clearly under the direction of their boss, Superintendent Dick Holland. What they wrote is obviously not to be taken at face value as they were setting traps for a man they already felt certain was guilty of something. Between mid-morning on Sunday 21st December when he drove to Rochdale Police Station and 3.30 pm the following day, Stefan Kiszko signed a written confession to the murder of Lesley Molseed which included details of the crime that only the murderer or the senior police officers involved in the investigation knew.

Remember, we now know with absolute certainty that he was innocent of this heinous crime. It therefore follows that, wholesale and inexplicable coincidences apart, this information can only have been fed to him by one or other of the police officers. McConnell in his account tries to reconstruct the sequence and timing, which is difficult because none of the three officers were keeping contemporaneous notes, and times were not noted, as was required by the then Judges' Rules. But it is clear they tied Stefan in knots over the dates in early-October; the indecency episodes were supposed to have taken place on October 4th, a Saturday, and Kiszko refers to this linking it to the 'day when the little girl went missing'. He said the first time he went out in his car was the following Sunday, which was the 5th. But they got him to commit to the 12th.

He then attributed his confusion to his illness, and the injections he was getting, which led to his revealing that the latter had been given to him to stimulate his sex drive and he had started to be interested in girls and to masturbate again. They repeatedly changed their questioning between events on October 4th to those on November 5th, bonfire night. Signs of his later paranoia emerge when he suggests someone may have been trying to get him into trouble as he worked for the Inland Revenue.

It is evident that up to this time the police were unaware that Kiszko was being treated for hypogonadism (which in any case they confused with impotence). However, the transcripts show that the fact that he previously had no interest in girls and that the injections were to try to help him was pivotal. In the first afternoon session, Detective Constable Whittle asked Kiszko for his car keys, went and examined the car and found several sex magazines with nude girls under the carpet in the boot. This again was seen as inconsistent with his assurance about lack of interest in girls. He was asked to empty his pockets, which revealed two knives — one for cleaning the battery of his car and one for cutting string. His late father had given him a number of knives when they went on holiday in Austria.

He was then asked where he had been on the night of October 3rd. Remember, it was now four days before Christmas. At 6 pm on December 21st, his interrogation restarted for the third time, and this time Superintendent Holland, the officer in charge of the murder investigation, accompanied Akeroyd. They had with them various items taken from his car including more knives, sweets and balloons (later used as evidence that he was enticing children), and some felt tipped pens. They also found pieces of paper with car numbers on them, one of which was seen as highly incriminating. While he was detained, Holland, Akeroyd and two others went to his house and searched it illegally and without a warrant. They seized a knife, some scissors, and ampoules of testosterone he had been prescribed in hospital for the GP to inject.

'Arrangements were made for Kiszko to be accommodated in the police station overnight,' the records state. Of course he was put in a cell. He was therefore all but unlawfully arrested. It is extraordinary that his defence team never raised any objections to his questionable detention either before or during his trial. In the middle of the night, at 1.45 am on December 22nd 1975, after he had been there for 15 hours, Kiszko was interviewed again. Superintendent Holland asked about his treatment, and again about a specific car, number ADK 539L, he had recorded in red; he could not say when he had recorded this. It was seen as highly incriminating, because this car had passed the murder scene one hour after Lesley's disappearance. There are no records of where or when he slept, or what food and drink he was given, while detained, but he felt nauseated, quite probably from the ketosis that goes with fasting.

Holland and Akeroyd interviewed Stefan again at 11.30 am on the morning of Monday December 22nd, starting again with the car registration number claiming, 'I now know that car was at the scene of a murder at Ripponden at 2.30 pm on October 5th.' Although this car was traced to someone now living in Manchester, it had in fact been sold the previous year. Kiszko was in the habit of recording car numbers of people he thought were harassing him in some way, or who had infringed the law. On a previous occasion when he had gone to the police, a PC Bell had actually told him to record the car number of any such person! There was no evidence that Kiszko had noted the number on October 5th, indeed this would have been an extraordinary thing for him to have done if he had just murdered or was about to murder a little girl.

Kiszko's false confession and retraction

Then Detective Superintendent Holland did a strange thing, and left his junior colleague alone with Kiszko, and according to the agreed account Stefan almost immediately confessed to killing Lesley, saying,

'Oh this is terrible. It's those damn injections. All this would never have happened…you see I can't help myself when I've had my injection…(I picked her up) on that Sunday the day that I killed her.'

Akeroyd then cautioned him, reminding him that he had the right to remain silent.

'Are you telling me…?'
'Yes, I killed that little girl.'

The sergeant opened the door, called out, and almost immediately Superintendent Holland and Chief Inspector Steel were there. Then over the next three hours they worked on Kiszko and got a perfect fake confession (which had been written by Holland), which included several crucial unpublished details known only to the murderer and to the police.

Only then was he allowed access to a solicitor, whereupon he promptly and fully retracted his confession, claiming that he had only signed it because he had been told 'Then we can all go home for Christmas'.

You and I might think that this was extremely naïve, but then being naïve is not a crime; and very scant details are provided of the conditions under which Stefan was interrogated. We also know little of his mental state. In his retraction he went over every item of the confession indicating which was true and which false. What we can say with some certainty is that an officer or officers must have fed the incriminating details to Kiszko into his signed confession, and these later helped persuade the jury at his trial that he was the murderer. The fact that as soon as he was charged with murder and given a solicitor he retracted made no difference. Normal people (and juries) have extraordinary faith both in the honesty of police officers, and in the validity of confessions.

Understanding the mind-set of the police

It is worth pausing to try and look into the thinking of the police. The driving force here was Superintendent Holland, regardless of who else went along with him. And of course he was the man responsible for the investigation, with the most to gain from wrapping it up quickly, just before Christmas. First, it is clear that they were not specifically trying to cover for the real murderer (they didn't know who it was).

Second, Kiszko was abnormal emotionally and developmentally. He had gone through a partial puberty as a late-teenager, had started to masturbate then, and stopped when he became ill. According to the Kinsey Report of 1948 on male sexual activity,[1] 92 per cent of adult males masturbate. This activity as well as his testosterone production will have regressed under the influence of his heavy cider drinking, and his severe folate deficiency anaemia.

Third, there was the clear suspicion in the minds of the police after Kiszko kept changing his story over the exposure. They were sure he was lying, whereas in fact he may simply have had some persistent nutritional short-term memory loss. At all events, once they had reached a certain point of no return, they honed in on the next 'trick', which was both useful and necessary in order to persuade a jury to pronounce him guilty. They were probably tired of the case, and *in order to wrap it up before Christmas they needed a confession.* We noted the so-called Reid technique in *Chapter 1*; but in this case it may well be that all they needed was for him to believe that the truth would be revealed because he was innocent and that would shine through. In the first 325 Innocence Project exonerations on irrevocable DNA evidence, no less than 27 per cent had confessed to a crime they had nothing to do with.[2] As we will see in the next chapter, in cases where people were released in the USA on irrefutable DNA-evidence, at least 25 per cent were convicted because they confessed to a crime they had nothing to do with.

The author's memories of the case

Now nearly 40 years later I no longer have my notes, but my memory of this case is good, probably because of the lessons I mistakenly thought I had learnt. I cited Stefan's case for many years whenever I lectured to medical students and doctors on hypogonadism. I am also indebted to Campbell Malone, Kiszko's tireless solicitor, who has let me have copies

---

1. Kinsey A, C., Pomeroy W. B. and Martin C. E. (1948), *Sexual Behaviour in the Human Male*, Indiana University Press.
2. http://www.innocenceproject.org/causes-wrongful-conviction/

of files with newspaper descriptions of the trial, as well as my own New Year 1976 statement to the police.

Late on the last full working day before the Christmas Holiday (December 23rd) a Detective Inspector Cooper and a fellow detective from West Yorkshire Police visited me in my hospital office. They said that they had strong evidence that Kiszko had sexually assaulted and murdered Lesley Molseed. They had learned that he had been started recently on male hormone injections, and believed that these had tipped him over the edge. They said they had an overwhelming amount of circumstantial 'evidence' to support their case, including finding girly magazines, and sweets and five knives in the back of his car, and four girls who said he had exposed himself a few days before Lesley disappeared. They had taken him in for questioning on December 21st, and by December 22nd he had confessed to murdering the little girl. The officers were definite, and revealed in their conversation their conviction that he was guilty. I for my part said he definitely would not produce sperm, and that in a psychologically normal man the replacement male hormone would only stimulate sexual activity in the normal way. I told them he had seemed very happy with the treatment when I had seen him in the clinic on December 8th.

The officers returned in the early New Year with a written statement they had put together from notes they had made. I found this to be a quite inaccurate reflection of what I had said, and what I believed, and I therefore refused to sign it and indeed completely rewrote it. Specifically, I said that in my opinion Kiszko would be unable to produce sperm, and that the injection of testosterone would increase his sex drive as it does during normal puberty, but it would not turn a normal man into a killer. In order to introduce him to normal male hormone levels gradually, and because he had been so ill and malnourished, I had started him on half the normal dose. For many years after his conviction I used this case to argue that men who have not undergone normal puberty, and were therefore not used to normal adult levels of testosterone, should be started at half dose. Many endocrinologists were approached to criticise my treatment of Kiszko, and most said they would have given testosterone at twice the dose I had used. In fact, the police had charged an innocent Kiszko, so the dose was completely irrelevant.

Trial, conviction and eventual release

I was called to Leeds Crown Court to give evidence at Kiszko's trial in July 1976. Earlier in the trial there was intensive questioning of Dr Michael Tarsh, a psychiatrist, which by inference probably undercut the idea that Kiszko was innocent. Out of court I spoke to the defence barrister, David Waddington, who was also a Member of Parliament and went on to become Home Secretary in Margaret Thatcher's government and later Lord Waddington. I told him that testosterone replacement would not have induced violence in a previously psychologically normal individual against anyone, let alone a child. Puzzlingly, however, I was never called by the defence to the witness stand. The prosecuting barrister was Peter Taylor, who later became Lord Chief Justice, so this was a courtroom loaded with would-be high-fliers.

Waddington, who was defending Kiszko, whether he believed him guilty or not, tried hard to get him to plead diminished responsibility (thus in effect accepting that he had killed Lesley but in a reduced mental state and by implication transferring some of the blame onto his endocrinologist), in exchange for a lesser sentence: the effect being that he would avoid a mandatory life sentence. I presume it was feared that my testimony would have weakened this defence, which it seems was being toyed with without Kiszko's knowledge or agreement. But Stefan obstinately refused to admit to the crime, saying, correctly as it transpired, that his first confession was false (and arguably coerced).

Then one of the jurors overheard a conversation by the defence team suggesting that the defence thought Kiszko was guilty, whereupon she said she was a juror. This prejudicial fact was never taken up by the judge; the juror should have been dismissed, and if she had told other members it should have led to a re-trial before a different jury.[3] Neither happened; and after a trial lasting two weeks, Kiszko was found guilty of murder by a majority of ten to two. In his concluding remarks the judge, Mr

---

3. Statement by Philip Clegg, junior defence counsel — see Rose, Panter and Wilkinson, *Innocents*, 1997, pp. 254-5.

Justice Hugh Park, commended the police as well as the four girls who had identified Kiszko for their bravery and honesty.

Sentenced to life imprisonment, Kiszko, not surprisingly, went through a living hell, now confirmed as a 'nonce', being repeatedly assaulted by fellow prisoners, and eventually developing full-blown paranoid schizophrenia. He always protested his innocence, and his mother fought tirelessly on his behalf. Superintendent Holland, who had led the investigation, went on to investigate the Yorkshire Ripper case: see 'Postscript: the quest for the Yorkshire Ripper' later in this chapter.

Finally, Kiszko's mother Chatlotte, who used all the money she was awarded as compensation for her industrial lung disease (byssinosis) in defence of her son, called on the help of a new solicitor, Campbell Malone, who was impressed with her grit and determination. He found that the junior defence barrister under Waddington (Philip Clegg) had had serious doubts as to Kiszko's guilt. As a result of his efforts the case was finally reopened in the slow lane of justice, in 1989. David Waddington was by now Margaret Thatcher's Home Secretary, and by a curious coincidence, the Kiszko papers landed on his desk the very day he took up the post; to his credit he initiated a review.

In mid-1991, now a Professor of Endocrinology in Hope Hospital, Salford, I was approached by Superintendent Trevor Wilkinson, the police officer who had been put in charge of the review. He had found crucial evidence that was withheld at the trial, the most important of which was a report that there were sperm heads on scotch tape prints of dried semen on Lesley's clothing (the actual clothes had been destroyed in 1985). I was able to tell him that this meant Kiszko was innocent. The appeal was re-opened and Stefan was eventually released; he died six months later of a heart attack at the age of 41; probably he had inherited his father's familial hypercholesterolaemia, but undoubtedly the horror and stress of his imprisonment will have been a major additional factor. His mother, who had fought so hard for him, and who had used up all the money she was awarded for her lung disease, died six months later. The thing she was most proud of was being awarded the Freedom of Rochdale, in recognition of her courage. Lesley's mother April had the good grace to apologise to Charlotte Kiszko; she had been one of those vocal in calling for the restoration of the death penalty for paedophile killers.

DNA and the real killer

When Stefan was released the police, led by Trevor Wilkinson, reopened the hunt for Lesley's killer. Wilkinson shows how he became convinced that the real killer was a paedophile called Raymond Hewlett;[4] no charges were brought against him by the Director of Public Prosecutions, and the case was dismissed for lack of firm evidence.[5] This was fortunate, since eventually and almost by chance, 13 years after Kiszko's death, Lesley's true killer was found. The police had organized a DNA-profile to be made from the Scotch tapes taken from Lesley's clothing, and the result was put on the UK national database established from 1999. There were no matches. However, in 2005, in a suspected rape case, a man was submitted to a routine buccal scrape for his DNA-profile. The result did not match a sample from the rape victim, but was nevertheless put on the complementary section of the national DNA database where it perfectly matched that taken from the sellotape imprint from Lesley's clothes.

The man was Ronald Castree, a divorced part-time taxi driver, a father of four, who had been brought up on the Turf Hill Estate where the Molseeds had lived. As an adult he seems to have prowled that area. Indeed a lay magistrates' court had tried and convicted Castree of sexually molesting another little girl nearby in July 1976, during the very time of Kiszko's trial. The nine-year-old had managed to pull herself free and escape, and had been able to identify him. Castree was fined £25 and given a suspended sentence for this offence! Then three years later he abducted and assaulted a small boy, who also managed to escape. He was once again identified and convicted by the same bench, and on this occasion was fined £50.[6]

As indicated, Castree was convicted of Lesley's murder a third of a century later, in 2007, based on DNA evidence. It is interesting to compare its strength with that used in Italy by the first court in the case

---

4. Rose, Panter and Wilkinson, 'Who Killed Lesley Molseed?', in *Innocents*, 1997.
5. See *Chapter 22*.
6. ITV documentary *Real Crime: The Thirty Year Old Secret*, and see http://www.express.co.uk/expressyourself/205720/Married-to-a-murderer

against Amanda Knox and Raffaele Sollecito (ultimately rejected in the definitive Supreme Court ruling in 2015 (*Chapter 3*)). First, the source of the DNA was an imprint containing sperm heads, taken from clothing Lesley was wearing when she was stabbed to death. The body fluid (semen with attendant sperm) from which the DNA-profile was made pointed without any doubt to the perpetrator, linking him physically to the crime scene, and to the death of the murdered girl, and to attendant ejaculation. The evidence is as strong as the DNA-profile would be from the semen stain on the pillow on which Meredith Kercher's body lay (were the latter to have been examined). Since the sole function of sperm is to transmit the male portion of the genome to the egg, we are talking of concentrated DNA. In making the match, the possibility of confirmation bias does not enter into the equation, and there was no *a priori* reason for the laboratory to have suspected Castree. The tests were done at different times and in different laboratories, and matching was done by computer, and not with the eyeball of a human being who knows what answer is expected. Then, once the match was made, Castree had precisely the sort of criminal history including two convictions, to fit the profile of Lesley's killer. He was also a local man with a car, and finally he (and his car) matched the description of the man abducting a girl seen by Mrs Emma Tong and later Christopher Coverdale (see earlier in this chapter).

Analysis of the elements that led to false conviction

Enormous publicity surrounded the hunt for Lesley Molseed's killer, and Detective Superintendent Holland and his team were undoubtedly under great pressure. Yet it is hard to see any rational explanation as to why the investigation followed the course it did. Undoubtedly, however, at a certain point it started to undergo a sort of snowball effect, and as it did so other lines of investigation were shut down. The investigators became trapped by tunnel vision and extreme confirmation bias set in.

Some of the more extraordinary elements in this case are worth reiterating, and of course they point to intrinsic weaknesses in the English system of justice. We are now in the privileged position of knowing who the killer was. We do not know whether Castree knew Lesley, nor whether he had in fact exposed himself to girls on October 3rd and 4th, but this seems unlikely. The evidence of Emma Tong strongly suggests that the real killer enticed the little girl into his car with the offer of a gift, which Lesley had held up to show her. Since we know she died three hours later and was clearly cooperating with the murderer to the point of being assisted up the slope where she was killed, it is possible that a further enticement was the offer to help her look for her missing cat.

The new investigation

Once Kiszko was released, the murder enquiry was reopened. As a result of my being informed that the police had suppressed evidence that there were sperm heads, I recall telling Superintendant Wilkinson that the slides should still exist, and by that time the polymerase chain reaction DNA technology and forensic profiling meant that a few dried sperm would be enough. In fact what still existed was a scotch tape imprint of semen taken from the dead girl's clothes. It is to the credit of the forensic scientists that they were able to put a unique and probatory genetic profile from this still unsolved crime on the UK database. It was a further five years before Castree's profile was fortuitously also put onto the other half of that database, in connection with an offence of which he was not convicted.

This unfortunate story is explained in part by the public pressure on the police that always accompanies high profile murders. After two-and-a-half-months, and just before Christmas, the lines they were pursuing were drying up. We now know that this was in large part due to police shortcomings. Kiszko's conviction and then commendation of the police by Mr Justice Park must have helped Holland's promotion and in turn helped secure him an important role two years later when a spate of murders of prostitutes and other women began, by the so-called Yorkshire Ripper. This investigation was also mishandled, whether due to Holland's involvement or not, and when the killer Peter Sutcliffe was identified and convicted it transpired that the police had in fact interviewed and then released him no less than nine times.[7]

---

7. See Michael Bilton, *Wicked Beyond Belief.*

Confirmation bias and the false 'confession'

Arguably, the Lesley Molseed investigation was incompetent throughout. This is evidenced not so much by the fact that the police took special note of accounts of exposure related by children, as by the neglect of at least two major witnesses (Tong and Coverdale: above) who had seen Lesley with the real killer. Not only was the car quite different in colour and make from Stefan's, but they suppressed the account by Coverdale. Yet this was obviously of high credibility because he had taken the police to the exact place where he had seen the man pulling the small girl up a slope, moments before she was brutally stabbed to death. To bury such an important lead defies explanation.

Meanwhile under pressure, the thing that led them to Kiszko was the evidence of children one of whom later admitted they had made it up 'for a lark'. Stefan for his part was mostly interrogated about the exposures reported by the children. He was tricked into driving his car to the police station, and believed it was to talk about these incidents, not about Lesley's murder. The police were convinced they had the killer, and they applied the notorious Reid technique and then used every possible tactic to extract what turned out to be a false confession that Kiszko then signed.

It is pointless to allocate blame on one or more police officers, but this case provides strong argument for the video-recording of all interrogation sessions from beginning to end. We have seen the same thing in the so-called 'confession' of Amanda Knox, and her supposed incrimination of Patrick Lumumba. As soon as he had a solicitor, Kiszko retracted his confession, saying he had signed it because he was induced to do so by being told, 'Then we can all go home for Christmas.' Six months later, however, ten out of 12 of the jurors believed that confession was real. Interestingly, the real killer, Ronald Castree, has never confessed.

It is certain that the police and forensic team knew that the murderer had masturbated on Lesley's body after he had stabbed her multiple times. And they had found sperm heads on scotch tape impressions of the girl's clothing. Kiszko admitted that once he had started on testosterone he had started to masturbate into a handkerchief (behaviour that is perfectly normal), and the forensic officers both examined this and got him to produce a fresh semen specimen. None of these showed sperm heads, so at this point there was clearly the active suppression of vital evidence. The logic runs, 'We've got our man, because of this … and a confession; we can't back down, so we'll suppress the exculpatory evidence.'

Sucked into a judicial black hole

Once someone is sent for trial by jury, although the notional presumption is of innocence, it changes to a contest between two opposing truths. The stories are heard and decided by amateurs (the jury) selected at random from all walks of life, each and every one of whom who would probably prefer to be somewhere else. It is a black hole of unknown and uncontrolled force, whose power becomes for all practical purposes insuperable once the jury has decided to convict.

In Britain, jury members are assumed both individually and collectively to be fair-minded, to give equal weight to prosecution and defence, and to consider only evidence presented in court. They are guided in their decision-making by a supposedly impartial judge who sits *super partes* and rules on admissibility of evidence, offers information on the law and, at the end, sums up and gives guidance on what they have heard. He does not himself make the verdict, but he substantially influences it, intentionally or otherwise. Throughout much can go wrong, even if and when no-one has been dishonest; and the outcome depends to a great extent on chance. The trial is still essentially medieval in structure, being originally derived from the belief that the jury receives the truth from God (who of course does not make mistakes). But the jury are human beings, who live in the community and are inevitably influenced by the opinions they have heard. They are instructed to pay no attention to anything other than what they hear in court, but they too are subject to prejudices and confirmation bias.

Within a jury there are individuals of differing personalities, intelligence and prejudices. And since the prosecution presents its arguments first, the jury starts with the strongest possible case against the accused, and many will decide on guilt at that point; once they become hard-wired the defence will have great difficulty in shifting them. Furthermore, in 1976 there was no Crown Prosecution Service to stand as a buffer between the police and the decision on who to prosecute in the first place and disclosure of prosecution evidence was not required as it is now.

Looking at the trial accounts and from the evidence that emerged 16 years later and finally led to Kiszko's absolution, the police clearly withheld crucial evidence. The prosecution was forceful, the judge seems to have been biased and the defence fatally weak. Thus Kiszko denied absolutely that he had abducted and murdered Lesley and said he had never met her. But his barrister David Waddington wanted him to restate his original confession so he could face a more sympathetic court by accepting the lesser charge of manslaughter on the basis of supposed diminished responsibility induced by male hormone injections.

Waddington seemed to want to argue that those injections, Jekyll and Hyde-style, had turned him into a 'monster', although I explained to him this was not the case. He was heavily criticised by the prosecution and later by his fellow junior barrister for trying to 'ride two horses.' At all events the double-edged argument can only have undermined Kiszko's claim that he was innocent.

Misconception about hormones and aggression

I found it astonishing that, as the endocrinologist who had prescribed the drug and having been called to attend as a defence witness, I was not asked to testify and stand up to cross-examination in court. This in a sense also denied real medical science and expertise a proper defence before a lay jury. I would have argued that there is no way this treatment would have turned a normal man into a monster. This is not how testosterone works; it will simply have stimulated that individual's normal direction of sex drive. If an individual was predisposed towards violent behaviour, this would have been evident in some way already. Testosterone is not a drug; it is a natural hormone, produced by every normal adult male at an amount of around 2.5 g per year. This is a relatively massive quantity in hormone terms. And I had started him on half the normal replacement dose, so he was at that stage merely at a transition on the way to achieving the normal adult male testosterone level.

Weaknesses in Kiszko's defence

I believe that Waddington 'bought into' the police story of the first confession and did not believe Kiszko, although the latter performed solidly in the witness box, and had the confidence that his innocence would somehow speak for itself. He did not understand the magnetic force of the judicial black hole. There are to my mind several crucial mistakes the defence made; the first was to fail to argue, based on irrelevance, against admission of testimony by the children, whose accounts of exposure related to two days and one day before Lesley's abduction. These accounts, which turned out much later to be false, conformed to the lay and police view of paedophiles; bore no clear connection with the crime; and were at best highly prejudicial to Kiszko. The proceedings followed the pattern that had been used by the police in their interrogations of Kiszko, where they had started on the subject of the exposures, and then having trapped him in the police station and put him under great stress, switched to accusations about Lesley Molseed.

The judge bears some responsibility for allowing this testimony. The girls, who had changed their story, were not cross-examined and as already explained on their own admission many years later some of them had made-up the story 'for a lark'. 'We were very young at the time,' one said later. It is highly probable that the testimony would have broken down under cross-examination in court of any or all of these girls. The importance given to their irrelevant and misleading written testimony is revealed by the judge at the end of the trial having commended them, showing that he too had 'swallowed' the police story and their part in it.

A further gross weakness is that Waddington, presumably persuaded by the first confession which contained facts ostensibly only the killer would know (seemingly fed to him by the investigators), was convinced that his client had in fact killed Lesley Molseed. His junior deputy was much less sure and many years later he expressed his concerns to Campbell Malone (above). It was Waddington who decided not to call me to give evidence as an expert witness, perhaps because I would have weakened the power of his second horse (diminished responsibility). And as already mentioned there were other defects which can be laid at the feet of the defence, one of which was that a jury member was told on good authority that the defence team were discussing a guilty plea based on diminished responsibility (above). The judge was told and should have dismissed the jury and restarted the trial with another one. It should have been pushed for by the defence, but perhaps they were embarrassed by their own lapse.

And what about the witness Emma Tong? She was called to testify at Kiszko's trial, but her evidence was discounted, presumably because it conflicted with the police's preferred hypothesis, and of course if accepted would have embarrassed both police and prosecution. But at least her testimony was heard in court, while even more incriminating information from lorry driver Christopher Coverdale was completely ignored. It is not even clear that the defence were aware of the Coverdale testimony. In this case, the Coverdale cover-up becomes central, because it suggests the police were turning a blind-eye to the true killer and his *modus operandi*.

The role of press sensationalism

In contrast to what happens in Italy, in the UK there are at least notional controls on what the press can publish before a criminal trial that might prejudice the case for the defendant and there are stiff penalties for those who flout them. Before trial and after charge, the press are not allowed to publish anything but the bare facts of arrest, charge, etc. and certainly not anything prejudicial to the accused. Then during the trial they can only state what has happened in court, which begins with the prosecution and its opening statement: it always makes out its case first. It is hard to imagine that in such a controversial case as child's abduction, and sexual killing, there is not some inherent prejudice in the minds of jurors. After all, what possible reasons could there be for the police and prosecution to get this wrong, let alone to deliberately frame an innocent person? Campbell Malone was able to show me copies of the newspaper clippings, including an interview with an anonymous specialist (myself (David Anderson)) after Kiszko's conviction, saying he wished he had not given him the drug. This was true, I felt in some way to blame. But now, nearly 40 years later, what I feel I was really guilty of was being too trustful of those whose job was to secure that the killer was behind bars; for them and their jobs it seems to have been better to have anyone behind bars than no man at all. If so, what then became important was the so-called eleventh commandment; 'Thou shalt not be found out'!

The horror for Stefan

Before the trial, while Stefan was being detained in Armley Detention Centre but had not been declared guilty, his life in custody was not too bad. But once a man is convicted for a horrendous sexual crime, he becomes a 'nonce' and is fair game for all the other prisoners to attack. This was to be Kiszko's fate in prison, where he was riled and repeatedly assaulted by fellow prisoners, and as I have already indicated he eventually developed overt paranoid schizophrenia, coming finally to see even his beloved mother as part of a grand conspiracy. He believed they were out to get him because he worked in the tax department. There were already suggestions of mild elements of paranoia in his behaviour before, notably the noting of car registration numbers. And undoubtedly he did not behave completely normally, probably because after his hospital admission he was far from fully recovered, not least from his severe folic acid deficiency anaemia.

I had only met Stefan twice—once in hospital, and once at outpatient follow-up. For my own part, I believe that if I had known him for longer as a patient I would have realised with more certainty that he could not have been responsible for this horrific murder, and I might have acted more decisively with the police. Then when approached several years later by a phone call from a solicitor, I might have felt more of an obligation to help him too. But I had been forced by events into a position where I felt in some way responsible for unleashing a hidden killer.

The long road to innocence and freedom

Stefan's mother never doubted his innocence, and was a fearsome fighter on his behalf. She was fortunate to come in contact with a caring solicitor, Campbell Malone, who took on her case *pro bono*; she also threw in the sizeable award for compensation for her industrial lung disease that she received from the government, to her son's defence. In England (in contrast to Italy), there is no automatic right of appeal. The initial trial may be a little fairer, in that to my mind the dice are not so heavily loaded in favour of the prosecution, but this case shows that, especially when there is a great deal of pressure on the police, it can still become a contest. It is a contest that can be rendered grossly biased if, as in this case, evidence is distorted or suppressed by those whose job is to carry out the investigation. If a confession can be elicited, prejudice can then be further reinforced. Normal people, and this applies to members of the jury, refuse to face the fact that almost anyone, when put under sufficient pressure and compounded by sleep deprivation, can be made to confess to more or less anything. Their priority at all costs becomes just to get some psychological peace and sleep.

Paradoxically, the one factor that led David Waddington to take his eye off the ball, and that may well have contributed to his weak defence of Kiszko, was the very factor that may also quite by chance have led to Kiszko's ultimate release. That was the suppression of the medical profile of both Stefan (he was sick and could produce no sperm) and the guilty man (he was healthy and could). This in turn opened the way many years later and long after Stefan's untimely death, for the conviction of the real murderer, Ronald Castree. Maybe Waddington's real ambition and interest lay in politics. To his eternal credit, when in a position of power as Home Secretary, he distanced himself from any errors he may have made at the trial and immediately put the matter under an independent review.

Finally a sound police investigation

Far from engaging in a whitewash, Superintendent Trevor Wilkinson proceeded to carry out a thorough investigation. Crucially, he uncovered evidence that had been withheld from the defence, concerning the presence of sperm heads on adhesive tape imprints taken from Lesley's clothing. In the Autumn of 1991, he and another officer visited me in my office at Hope Hospital and presented me with this evidence.

I knew from the miniscule size of his testes that Kiszko would not have produced sperm, and had already told the police this back in 1975. What I was unaware of is that the police knew that the perpetrator had produced sperm, but had chosen to ignore or suppress this because they felt the numbers were small! I was immediately able to tell Wilkinson that this one piece of evidence meant that he had been falsely convicted. Superintendent Holland's role and that of the prosecution's Home Office forensic scientist, Ronald Outteridge, have been questioned, including as to whether either of them ignored or failed to recognise that Kiszko was azoospermic; having examined the handkerchief under Kiszko's pillow into which he masturbated and a fresh specimen produced to order on the evening of his detention.[8]

Almost immediately, things were set in motion for Stefan's release, but he had developed paranoid schizophrenia so this had to be to a mental hospital. When he eventually left there he was never able to return to a normal life. The importance of my 'seminal' testimony was such that early in 1992, when I had moved to become Professor of Medicine at the Chinese University of Hong Kong, I was visited in person by two police officers from West Yorkshire Police to take a formal written statement.

One final twist to this story resulted from the extremely rapid development of methods for connecting DNA to particular individuals, by exploiting a series of unique inherited differences in the structure of the parts of DNA that are not concerned with coding for genes. I remember discussing with Wilkinson and Campbell Malone, Stefan's solicitor, the possibility that even though Lesley's clothes had been destroyed, the pathology laboratory slides should surely still exist, and that using the technique of polymerase chain reaction (PCR), as little as a few sperm might be sufficient. Fortunately they were able to recover the adhesive imprints from the pathology laboratory files, so the profile was put on the national database, which finally led to the conviction of Ronald Castree. It is worth noting that this aspect of the investigation stands in stark contrast to the abuse of DNA-analysis as applied in the framing of Amanda Knox and Raffaele Sollecito for the murder of Meredith Kercher, as I have already described has been severely criticized in print by one of the pioneers of DNA forensics, Professor Peter Gill.

---

8. The situation remains open. After Kiszko's acquittal, both were issued with summonses claiming that they suppressed evidence, but the case was stayed by a JP on the grounds those more senior might have been responsible, and too much time had passed for a fair trial. 'The decision not to prosecute the pair, initially private but revealed after pressure from MPs, has left the wrongdoing unresolved, even though the scale of the miscarriage has been detailed in several books': see, e.g. https://www.theguardian.com/uk/2007/nov/12/ukcrime.martinwainwright

What is the current relevance of the Kiszko case?

The fact that the confession contained information only the perpetrator and the police knew is surely we would suggest evidence he was framed by being fed such incriminating information. He was convicted only ten years after Britain had abolished the death penalty for murder. After Kiszko's conviction there were strident cries for its restoration in the special case of paedophile sex murders. At the forefront of this campaign were Lesley's mother April and her family members. To their credit, however, they retracted and apologised to Stefan and his mother Charlotte, once he was cleared.

An important lesson is that families of murder victims tend to side with the prosecution; and since the priority is to establish guilt beyond reasonable doubt I believe that they need to be excluded from the proceedings. Vengeance is the enemy of reason and a fair trial. The Kiszko case is also of great relevance when we consider the use and abuse of DNA evidence, a technology that has been spearheaded in the UK and the USA. When Kiszko was tried and convicted, DNA profiling had not been developed and no one realised just how hardy DNA was against degradation. Who knows for how many thousands of years DNA, that personal blueprint for life, can remain unchanged and intact in a dried state?

In this case, the police and forensic teams saw no reason to keep Lesley's clothes, so one lesson in this fast changing world is that no one has a crystal ball to see into the future. Crucial evidence should not be destroyed just because a conviction has been achieved and 'legal truth' determined. Semen stain traces should not be discarded. Fortunately a tiny trace had quite by chance been conserved, and it was this that finally 30 years later led to the capture of Ronald Castree.

DNA is everywhere, and the fact that Castree's was on an adhesive tape imprint from the Lesley Molseed's clothes where it had no reason to be was highly incriminating. Sperm are virtually pure male DNA-transmitting machines. So we would do well to contrast this with the decisions of not one but four courts in Perugia and Florence to *refuse* to do a DNA-profile on putative semen stains on the cushion on which Meredith Kercher's lifeless body was found. Perhaps this should also suggest that lawyers and judges need something of a scientific education.

Instead, what we see all too frequently in courts is scientifically ignorant lawyers and prosecutors, supported by amoral 'experts' trying to push the limits of extreme DNA-profiling to where simple environmental contamination comes into play. Now that Knox and Sollecito have been finally declared innocent, attention is being directed back to Rudy Guede and a possible accomplice. It will be interesting to see whether semen traces on the cushion on which Meredith's body was found will finally be subjected to DNA-profiling; if indeed the cushion still exists. If it does, and the DNA belongs to Guede, then he acted alone. Since in January 2016 Rudy Guede has called for a re-opening of his case, this would be a good place to start!

Weaknesses in investigation, the false confession, and confirmation bias

All this talk of DNA analysis, and demonstrating innocence is important, but maybe it misses the main point. That concerns the structure and procedures of our police and judicial systems, and how adapted or otherwise they are to solving crimes of violence. What the Kiszko case illustrates is that after a horrific murder the investigations pass into the hands of people who may not be best suited to solving them; they have responsibility, but no real power, and that puts them under great pressure to come up with a solution—any solution that will stick. It would be interesting to know whether in such cases there is any serious attempt at psychological profiling. I have found no suggestion that there was any criminal psychologist involved at an early stage in the Molseed enquiry. Instead and arguably the police fell back on the time-honoured medieval technique of inquisition and witch-burning (considered in *Chapter 10*).

First, you find someone outside the group who might have done it. Outsiders don't defend themselves well. Then you concentrate on obtaining evidence that they committed the crime, including by excluding exculpatory evidence. This is what Peter Gill calls the prosecutor's fallacy. And one important instrument is the forced (and therefore false) confession. Most normal people just won't believe an innocent person will confess to something they did not do, even under conditions of sleep deprivation and extreme pressure. They *know* they would never do that themselves; and so they don't give any credence to a retraction. *One confession under unrecorded conditions is worth a lifetime of subsequent denials.*

So the Kiszko case is potent evidence of the need for all police officers to video-record the whole of every interrogation session, and then to make this over to the defence. The man who did kill Lesley Molseed has *never* confessed; yet the evidence against him is overwhelming. Just as a forced confession is not evidence of guilt, so the lack of a confession is not evidence of innocence.

Once she was dead, nothing was going to bring Lesley Molseed to life again. So what was all the hurry about? Yes, there was pressure to prevent the murderer from striking again, but this is different from the pressure to save face. In this case, in large part because the wrong person had been accused and was then convicted, the perpetrator was able to abduct at least two other children in three years, and when caught the courts used derisory penalties.[9] A part-time taxi driver who abducts and tries to assault eight or nine-year-old children, and is reprimanded not once but twice with £25 to £50 pound fines is evidence of a dysfunctional justice system. Nowadays, any incident where children report sexual assault is taken very seriously and anyone found guilty would hardly be sent home after paying a paltry fine. The (late) *News of the World* campaigned on this. There is now the Sex Offenders Register. Post a series of high profile cases (including that of the entertainer Jimmy Savile), an assault and court appearance that was followed by another would almost certainly attract a prison sentence even if the first such offence did not.

To the credit of England's legal system, once Kiszko's innocence was exposed, the police redoubled their efforts to find the true killer. Amazingly, Wilkinson's team then once again went after another wrong man, but the independent Director of Public Prosecutions refused to bring a case against him, believing there was a strong probability he would not be convicted. In the end DNA was the only method. There were also later half-hearted efforts to bring criminal negligence charges. Unfortunately the law as it stands is too often concerned with punishment, rather than learning the lessons from one's mistakes. Much more

---

9. The first such episode was actually before the trial of Kiszko, but clearly the police had already closed the Molseed murder enquiry in anticipation of a conviction.

effective would have been a without-penalty audit meeting directed at the professionals involved to help prevent similar errors in the future. Furthermore there seems to be nothing in the law akin to the investigation of the airline disaster 'near miss', which is taken just as seriously as the recovery and examination of the black box after a fatal air crash.

Postscript: The quest for the Yorkshire Ripper

When police have to investigate complex and horrific murders, they are invariably put under great pressure from the press and public for a quick resolution. It is easy for them to be enticed or forced up a blind alley, then to over-commit, and then fiercely to defend their position. As we saw with Kiszko, public reputations and obstinacy on the part of investigators then reinforce confirmation bias, with potentially disastrous results. This may be especially so in high profile and horrific multiple murders by a ruthless but intelligent psychopathic killer. Probably the most extreme example of this in British criminal history is the notorious series of brutal murders of young women, perpetrated over a wide swathe of the North-West of England between 1975 and 1981, by the Yorkshire Ripper, until almost by chance he was finally caught red-handed. This man, Peter Sutcliffe, was a married, long distance lorry driver who lived in Bradford. Since one of the main ripper investigators from 1976 onwards was Detective Superintendent Dick Holland, a small diversion into this case seems relevant. The story is extensively documented by the journalist Michael Bilton in his book *Wicked Beyond Belief.*

In those punch card pre-computer days, Holland and his boss, Chief Constable George Oldfield, became immersed 'hands on' in the details of the investigations, instead of taking a more reflective and analytical role. In the process, several investigations that would with hindsight have led to Sutcliffe being identified as the killer were aborted: as it was, police interviewed Sutcliffe no less than nine times. Investigative omissions involved a failure to match tyre marks left at the scene of the crime to cars picked-up on CCTV in red light districts; failure to compare multiple and remarkably accurate Identikit pictures of the killer by eight survivors of his attacks; and to fully pursue the trail of a new five pound note found in the bag of one of the murdered women, a prostitute. Instead, disastrously, investigators became convinced of the authenticity of taunting letters and tapes sent to them, from a man calling himself The Ripper. This man came from Sunderland, well away from the Leeds-Bradford area; as a result of this embedded belief, police for several years excluded any man without a Geordie accent.

Bilton documents how the hoaxer was identified 25 years later as John Samuel Humble, by salivary DNA from an envelope. Realising the sick joke had gone too far, Humble had at one point even telephoned the police to say it was a hoax! But so great was the police commitment to the Geordie killer theory that Humble was ignored. This hoax, and the weight given to it (despite gross inconsistencies) was a major factor in leaving Sutcliffe free to kill at least three more times in a spree that finally saw 19 women from all walks of life dead, eight severely injured, and the whole of England terrorised. Humble was eventually convicted, in 2006, and sentenced to eight years in prison for perverting the course of justice. One the face of it, Sutcliffe seems to be an obvious psychopath, but his mental state has been categorised differently over time and there has even been talk of him being returned to a normal prison location.

CHAPTER SEVEN

Injustice in Texas: The Case of Darlie Routier

From the USA we might have chosen any one of literally hundreds of cases of unjust prosecutions. Debra Milke, Kirstin 'Blaise' Lobato, Damien Echols and the West Memphis Three, David Camm, or the Central Park Five, to mention a few. Scarcely a day goes by when there is not another case of a falsely imprisoned individual being revealed in that country.

One case that stands out to us is that of Darlie Lynn Routier, a young wife and mother at the time of her conviction, and now (2016) aged 45. It is arguably a stark illustration of the worst and of the most Kafkaesque depths to which a justice system can sink. Texas-based crime writer and journalist, Kathy Cruz has written a book *Dateline Purgatory* that deals with many aspects of this harrowing case, and includes much new insight into the character of Darlie, and the frightening events that led to her being targeted and sentenced to death for the murder of one of her sons on June 6th 1996.

We will return later to the more general problems of 'The Law' breaking the law in the USA, where the number of people in prison has tripled since 1980, and now stands at 2.3 million, where prison conditions are generally appalling, and sentences exceedingly harsh. There have been 1,283 executions since 1976 when the Supreme Court suspended its earlier moratorium on the death penalty, and over that time there have been a massive 134 Death Row exonerations. Four private prison companies are listed on the Wall Street Stock Exchange, and they all generously support the two main political parties. Every political candidate wants to be seen as tough on crime, something encouraged by the fact that public prosecutors and district judges are elected to office. And there is the disgrace of Guantanamo Bay, where not even lip-service has been paid to justice.

Fairytale turned nightmare

Darlie Lynn Peck was 19-years-old when she got married to her teenage sweetheart Darin Routier (everyone in the family seems to have had a first-name beginning with D). On the surface Darin and Darlie's was a fairytale relationship. They had three boys, of whom the youngest at the time of the murders was six-month-old baby Drake. When her life fell apart on June 6th 1996 they were living at 5801, Eagle Drive, a large suburban house in a rich suburb of Rowlett, close to Dallas. Six months after Drake's birth, Darlie, as happens with many mothers, was slowly recovering from post-natal depression. At its worst she had expressed in writing to her husband thoughts of suicide; but seemed to be comforted by a heart-to-heart chat with him. She made it clear that one thing she held onto was the love of her boys. By all accounts Darlie was an extremely popular, generous and loving mother, who adored her sons, and was generous to their friends. No one in the family says anything bad about Darlie, who lies at the extreme positive end of the empathy scale. This picture of a lovely person extends to her relationship with fellow prisoners and staff as she sits on Death Row.

That fateful night, Darlie was asleep downstairs on a couch in front of the TV (still switched on) with her two oldest sons, Damon aged five and Devon aged almost seven, who had fallen asleep on the floor. An intruder broke in at dead of night, cutting the screen of an unsecured window downstairs; and repeatedly stabbed the two boys in the chest. They died within minutes. He sexually assaulted the sleeping mother. Kathy Cruz suggests that one (or possibly two) intruders first anaesthe-tised her with an ether/toluene mixture. Darlie awoke and tried to fight him off and was stabbed in the right arm and right side of her neck.

After a seemingly inadequate police crime scene investigation, Darlie was finally placed in the frame, derided by some as a heinous witch, and condemned to death for carrying out a crime that was pathologically, psychologically, physiologically and physically impossible. A system designed to protect the innocent got it so wrong.

Darlie's husband Darin was sleeping with the baby upstairs. It is not clear what happened first, but at around two am she felt groggy when she was awakened by Devon crying, 'Mummy, Mummy' and she saw a man wearing a baseball cap standing over her. She and the two boys were viciously stabbed by the intruder. Husband Darin was wakened by her screams. Damon died immediately and Devon on the way to hospital. She had tried to fight off the intruder and the stab wound in her neck extended to within two millimetres of the right carotid artery. The chain she was wearing was impaled in the wound, forced there by the knife. She had a defensive stab wound on her right arm, and multiple bruises to her arms that were extensively and well-documented and photographed in hospital. Darlie rang the emergency line 911, while Darin tried hopelessly to resuscitate Damon. Devon was already dead.

Tape-recordings of her desperate emergency call are available on the internet, and show a shocked and extremely distressed woman, who cannot understand what happened, horrified that her sons ('My babies') were brutally stabbed and are dying: http://www.fordarlieroutier. org/911Call/ ... Here is how it starts ...

00:00:00 911 Operator #1 ... Rowlett 911 ... what is your emergency..

00:01:19 Darlie Routier ... somebody came here ... they broke in ...

00:03:27 911 Operator #1 ... ma'am ...

00:05:11 Darlie Routier ... they just stabbed me and my children ...

00:07:16 911 Operator #1 ... what ...

00:08:05 Darlie Routier ... they just stabbed me and my kids ... my little boys ...

00:09:24 911 Operator #1 ... who ... who did ...

00:11:12 Darlie Routier ... my little boy is dying ...

00:11:25 RADIO ... (unintelligible) clear ...

00:13:07 911 Operator #1 ... hang on ... hang on ... hang on

00:15:03 Darlie Routier ... hurry ... (unintelligible) ...

00:16:01 911 Operator #1 ... stand by for medical emergency

00:18:11 Darlie Routier ... ma'am ...

00:18:19 911 Operator #1 ... hang on ma'am ...

00:21:26 Darlie Routier ... ma'am ...

00:23:00 911 Operator #1 ... unknown medical emergency ... 5801 Eagle Drive ...

00:24:00 RADIO ... (unintelligible) ...

00:26:24 Darlie Routier … ma'am …

00:27:12 911 Operator #1 … ma'am … I'm trying to get an ambulance to
   you … hang on a minute …

00:28:20 RADIO … (siren) …

00:29:13 Darlie Routier … oh my God … my babies are dying …

The crime scene was soon completely trashed by the various invasions of the emergency services, and police and crime scene investigators. There were obvious signs that an intruder had entered through an open downstairs window. But the official version of this double killing was apparently being scripted as the work of someone in the house. From 30 minutes after his arriving at the crime scene retired crime scene investigator James Cron declared that there was 'something fishy'.[1] The bad on-site forensics were amplified by poor records, which conflict with crime scene photographs, and the seemingly less than efficient collection of evidence. And this was supported in court by other questionable prosecution witnesses and also by the blood spatter analysis of Tom Bevel whose expert evidence has also been queried in other cases, including of David Camm, who was wrongly convicted of murdering his wife and young daughter;[2] and Warren Horinek whose shirt was spattered with his wife Bonnie's blood as he undertook CPR following her gunshot suicide.[3] Blood spatter is one of many forensic techniques called into question by a prestigious US Committee's report on Strengthening Forensic Science.[4]

Darlie was given first aid, and eventually taken to hospital where she received emergency surgery, and she was discharged home three days later. The stab wound on the right side of her neck extended to within two millimetres of the carotid artery, and was stopped by her necklace which had to be dug out of the wound. She also had a defensive knife

---

1. Kathy Cruz, *Dateline Purgatory*, p. 4. 'Despite the bloody chaos that spanned several rooms, Cron later told the jury he had determined within minutes that the crime was an inside job.'
2. Camm case — http://www.wcojp.org/bevel-credibility.html
3. Horinek case — https://www.texasobserver.org/a-bloody-injustice/ and Cruz, Kathy, *Dateline: Purgatory: Examining the Case that Sentenced Darlie Routier to Death*, Texas Christian University Press, Fort Worth Texas, 2015.
4. 'Strengthening Forensic Science in the United States: A Step Forward,' Committee on Identifying the Needs of the Forensic Sciences Community, National, Research Council (2009). See National Academies Press at: http://www.nap.edu/catalog/12589.html

wound on the right arm that needed five stitches, two stab wounds on her left shoulder, and numerous bruises. Case notes document a mother in shock and grieving for her children, and needing heavy doses of tranquillisers, something that was misinterpreted as indicating a heartless and callous woman. Almost immediately her questions and reactions were being amplified by the police as inappropriate. They later claimed that her neck wound was self-inflicted, despite the fact she is right-handed, her necklace was impaled in the wound, and as Cruz points out, is a highly improbable injury a woman conscious of her looks would use.

Darlie's distress is repeatedly noted by nurses in the hospital records, but when it came to her trial a different picture emerged, following what seems to have been tutoring of the nurses and doctors, and exclusion of the evidence of those who stuck with their original contemporaneous hospital records. Photographs as she lay recovering in hospital, suppressed by the court and never shown to the jury, show Darlie had extensive defensive cuts and bruises. At least one juror, who was interviewed by Cruz, says the jury were never shown these, and he would not have been persuaded of her guilt had he seen them. Darlie, whose panties had been removed during the attack, recalled having a rape test, and the cost of a rape kit put on her hospital bill, but the result mysteriously disappeared. She was in hospital for three days after undergoing emergency surgery. For much of this time she was heavily sedated and tranquillised with Xanax. When she left hospital they kept her and Darin waiting for three-quarters of an hour before they could view the bodies of the children in the morgue.

It is clear from subsequent events that almost immediately she was targeted as principal suspect, with police work that strongly suggests tampering with and ignoring evidence that would have backed-up Darlie's story of an outside intruder.

The boys were buried holding hands, side-by-side in a single coffin, on June 14th, the day that would have been Devon's seventh birthday.

Conviction: Justice or 'just is'?

We have already alluded in earlier chapters to Franz Kafka's caricature of legal systems in *The Trial*. Darlie's tragic case focuses a singularly strong light on many aspects of the psychopathology of 'The Law' breaking the law and to our minds the crass stupidity of many supposedly normal people, in a supposedly civilised society.

Different states in the USA very enormously, and many guard their judicial rights aggressively against federal interference, but all too often unprincipled police and public prosecutors can target innocent individuals, and destroy their lives. On that fateful night, 26-year-old Darlie's life was doubly destroyed, first by the brutal murder of her two oldest and dearest sons, and then by a court order for her own judicial killing. This set out to pin this brutal killing on the person who most loved her children, by damaging, distorting and destroying evidence, and painting her in the eyes of the public and the jury as a 'monster'. And yet for the time being it seems nothing can be done to bring common sense and compassion into play to have this gross injustice reversed. For reasons that are far from clear, and without challenge from the defence team, the trial was switched from liberal Dallas (population two million) to the tiny and ultra-conservative Republican town of Kerrville; (population 20,000). Arguably this produced a jury that was more likely to convict.

The trial was held in the middle of winter, and the courthouse was freezing cold. Seven months after the attacks, Darlie was convicted and condemned and viewed by many as a modern-day witch, and an unimaginably evil mother, to stand as a symbol of universal hatred.

There are many things that ran against Darlie, one of which was that Judge Tolle was about to retire, and wanted to fix the date for the trial to start before the end of the year. Then the prosecutor in charge of the case, Greg Davis, following in the tradition of former Dallas prosecutor Henry Wade appears to be proud that he has sent more people to death row than any other.[5] In our opinion, this case stands as a living monument to collective human gullibility, as it faces a system strongly favouring

---

5. See http://www.wacotrib.com/news/courts_and_trials/mclennan-county-prosecutor-likely-holds-active-death-row-record/article_548a4b86-4742-5f0a-aa35-bce4a41ad89a.html. By Tommy Witherspoon. Davis had prosecuted 22 death penalty cases, and failed to obtain a death sentence in only one. Kathy Cruz (see earlier footnote) page 42, quotes attorney Skip Reeves 'He's a very effective and competent prosecutor, there's no doubt about that', Reaves says of Davis. 'I think he does anything and everything he can to get not only a conviction, but a death sentence. I think he feels absolutely no guilt. I think he's convinced he's doing the right thing'…Reeves says (20 death sentences) is a number that many people may find admirable…'.

the prosecution. We believe there are few cases that can compare in their improbability with that brought against and, so we would argue, 'pinned on' Darlie Routier. And this, as with the Knox/Sollecito case, raises the uncomfortable possibility that the primary crime (the break-in and murders) and the secondary 'crime' (shortcomings in the investigation and evidence gathering) might conceivably in some way be linked (see later in the chapter). Another interesting similarity is that both crimes had been defined as an inside job, with a faked break-in; with Darlie this was within 30 minutes of the police arriving on the scene.

Weaknesses in confrontational judicial systems

Darlie's case also points to most if not all of the weaknesses in confrontational trial systems. It illustrates how the media can be abused both outside and inside the courtroom; how a determined prosecution can be strengthened in the eyes of a jury by a less than effective, some would say poorly constructed, and ultimately ineffective defence. And how, once a person has been convicted, the case passes from a presumption of innocence to a presumption of guilt, as the obviously innocent but now convicted-as-guilty person is sucked through a judicial black hole. It shows how, in the USA, once a wrong decision has been made, the gates of justice are padlocked shut, in a way that, theoretically at least, does not apply in Italy, where everyone has the right to what is at least intended to be a fair appeal.

Darlie's case also illustrates just how big the gulf can be between the common sense of obvious innocence, and the common and monstrous nonsense of 'established judicial guilt'. In our view it shows how people with CNE and so without conscience can hide openly within supposed justice systems. If allowed free rein, they can then easily use technical and legalistic trickery to transform the victim of a heinous crime into its official perpetrator. And be allowed to get away with it. We see in this case, courtesy of all the worst faults of supposed justice systems, how a victim can be morphed into the supposed perpetrator that a judge and jury will actually choose to condemn to death. It shows how there may be two ways to spell justice. And the second is 'just is', and once the jury has washed its hands of a case and its members have long since gone home to the comfort of their beds, their collective decision in effect lasts forever. The 'just is' system is not measured in the days or weeks of a complex trial, but years or decades, through a simple failure of the system to admit, 'We may have been mistaken', and to re-examine what by any standards is an exceedingly improbable prosecution hypothesis. It illustrates that after conviction, a justice system with all the human frailties that that entails, may suddenly become impossible to question.

Crime author Barbara Davis: A shaft of light

There are many hidden twists to this tale, but one of the most moving concerns crime author Barbara Davis who initially wrote *Precious Angels*,[6] a book that related to her belief that Darlie Routier was guilty. After publication, Christopher Brown, author of another book on the case, *Media Tried, Justice Denied*,[7] approached Davis. Reluctantly the latter agreed to meet him and he presented evidence to her of what he argued were 'official lies and distortions' that Barbara Davis had initially swallowed. To her credit, rather than resorting to the easy exit of confirmation bias, she listened to the evidence, examined it and was quickly persuaded by it. She changed her mind, and ultimately became a prison friend of Darlie and a staunch advocate of her innocence. It shows real courage for a journalist and writer to admit that she was wrong, and then to try to help remedy matters. She asked for Darlie's forgiveness, and true to character Darlie forgave her. It may be wholly unrelated, but it is a disturbing fact that two years later police gunned to death Barbara Davis' own son at the door of his home and with his mother there, following an anonymous tip-off. Barbara is a brave woman with the guts to denounce her own formerly misguided self. We do not encounter many stories of courageous writers who have switched from the role of witch-hunter to champion of innocence.

Another interesting feature of this case is that both sides of the Routier family have stood solidly behind Darlie throughout, and to this day protest her innocence and are fighting for her release. This applies equally to her in-laws as to her mother and her husband who in 2011 divorced

---

6. Dutton/Signet, 1999.
7. Ad Vice Marketing Inc., 1999.

her, although he has not remarried. All of them speak consistently of the absolute impossibility that she would have turned on her two boys. Furthermore, the case is now so notorious that, at the time of writing, the recently released and exonerated David Camm, a man who tragically has been deserted by the family of his murdered wife, has taken up Darlie's case as his first task on behalf of the Innocence Project. As already discussed, David Camm is one of a number of innocent people originally convicted in part by questionable evidence of 'blood spatter analysis' given by expert Tom Bevel.

Tampering with witnesses

We have already seen the prosecution was highly selective in the witnesses it used, excluding any who would attest to Darlie's distress in hospital, and arguably tutoring (or 'coaching' as it is sometimes known) others. They also greatly weakened her defence by naming many of her family members as prosecution witnesses, and then not calling them. This meant they were excluded from the trial, and rendered unable to speak out in her defence: not the only indication of police targeting her. It was also highly disadvantageous to the defence that the judge allowed two police to plead the Fifth amendment (above).

Failure, omission, negligence or incompetence?

There are serious omissions in the investigation of the crime scene, and in the basic forensics. By their own accounts, the police within 30 minutes had decided to concentrate their attention on the mother. There was a bloody fingerprint that does not belong to anyone in the household, which has not been examined, despite containing enough characteristics to be useful. They initially claimed it was a child's, but failed to take fingerprints from the two murdered children, whose bodies had to be exhumed two years later for this purpose. It does not belong to Darin Routier, Darlie or either of their murdered sons.

Several witnesses stated that they had seen a dark-coloured car outside the Routier's house the day before, and that this same car was seen there on the night of the murders, with two men apparently acting suspiciously. The driver had been seen by Darlie's neighbour Karen Neal acting suspiciously in the week before and others had seen it parked outside on the night of the crime. So far as anyone can tell, the police made no attempt to identify the car or men.

Outside the house there was a sock belonging to Darin, which was bloodstained. This has never been examined forensically or for the DNA-profile of the blood. There was a pubic hair found at the crime scene, which has not been profiled for DNA. Much of the so-called expert testimony on behalf of the prosecution was suspect. Accounts of Darlie's injuries as being consistent with self-inflicted wounds are simply nonsense, and denied by the photographs taken in the days after the murders.

Might the investigation be compromised?

One important question is why the police decided almost immediately that the murders were the work of the mother. It may or may not be relevant that a dark car was seen hovering outside 5801 Eagle Drive on the night in question. So far as we can establish, the investigating team steadfastly ignored this potential lead. The mystery car becomes of particular relevance when we come to examine whether the murders were the work of America's most prolific, but little known, serial killer, Edward Wayne Edwards (see later in this chapter), whose *modus operandi* regularly involved compromising investigations.[8]

Convicted because of silly string?

One of the most damaging pieces of evidence that was used at the trial was a film clip taken clandestinely a week after the murders, at the boys' graveside. At the end of a service in which Darlie is clearly grief-stricken, her 16-year-old sister persuaded the family to celebrate Devon's seventh birthday, by firing silly string on the graves. The jury saw the clip of Darlie firing silly string in a loop eight times, and one juror said this was the item of 'evidence' that persuaded him of her guilt. Taken out of context they saw a heartless woman, not a loving and grieving mother.

---

8. For allegations in the public domain over this and other failures concerning the lead detective's son, who at the time was awaiting trial for a drive by shooting, see http://whatliesbeyond.boards. net/thread/1814/june-6-1996-guilty-railroaded (As to which we cannot comment one way or the other and do no more than draw attention to this for the purposes of completeness).

When questioned about the covert filming at the funeral, Inspector James Patterson and his assistant Chris Frosch pleaded the Fifth Amendment and the judge allowed this. The jury was never informed and the judge ruled against any revelation as to the circumstances of the 'silly string' video or whether the filming was lawful.

Why, and how, could a mother do this?

Darlie's supposed motive was to make their life simpler. All the evidence indicates that she was a loving and devoted wife and mother with absolutely no past history of violence, that the boys were 'jewels in her eye'. Court testimony by her mother-in-law indicates her being a perfect daughter-in-law, who loved and was loved by the whole family. It seems clear that the family had some financial problems, and that her husband Darin was not above contemplating a shady business deal, about which more below. But all the evidence suggests that Darlie herself, when she heard of this, was appalled and made Darin drop any such plan. Much was made of her vanity, and the fact that she had had breast implants, but this is of absolutely no relevance to the crime.

It was, one would think, never remotely plausible that she could have murdered her two beloved children and then stabbed herself in the right side of her neck and arm to cover up. Instead, her conviction appears to have been the direct result of suppression of evidence, combined with rubbishing of the crime scene, character assassination, a less than solid defence and to our mind an over-zealous district prosecutor, Greg Davis, intent on securing a conviction and death sentence.

The most pertinent question to ask is, 'Why do this to an innocent woman, with absolutely no previous history of violence?' There may be no rational answer if, as described at the start of this book, there are CNEs in positions of power working within a system created in their own image. But the authors strongly suspect that there must be even more to the case than that.

Death Row

Killing a five-year old in Texas is a capital offence, and hence Darlie was sentenced to death by lethal injection. She is currently one of seven women in Texas on Death Row for murder. She was never tried for the murder of the older boy, Devon, for reasons that are obscure; there are elements of evidence that might have persuaded the jury that she had nothing to do with his death (such as the use of another knife, which was never found) and which thus could have affected the case against her in relation to the murder she was charged with.

At the time of writing, she has been on Death Row for 19 years, and all appeals for a retrial have so far been unsuccessful. Appeals for DNA-analysis have been vigorously resisted. She was accused, tried and convicted of murdering one of her two young sons on the most contrived and improbable evidence.

Alteration of transcripts

One extraordinary element in this case is that the trial transcripts were unreliable; these are what jury members have to refer to in coming to a verdict. There were no less than 33,000 errors.[9] This in effect led to them being given the wrong information that Darin Routier had said the utility room door had been locked, lending support to the theory of a staging of the crime scene. The errors, which were later painfully unscrambled, significantly interfered with Darlie Routier's 1998 appeal, and some have argued that this should have led to a retrial. But, alas, once you have been convicted in the USA, it is extremely difficult to get a judgment overturned whatever the errors in this regard.

What was the role, if any, of Darin Routier?

Looking at the records and at his testimony in court, there seems with hindsight to be no reason to suspect that Darin Routier had any direct hand in his son's murders. He was sleeping upstairs with six-month-old baby Drake, and was awakened by his wife's screams. He slipped on his shorts, ran downstairs and did his best in an impossible situation to try to resuscitate first Devon then Damon. But each had been viciously

---

9.   Kathy Cruz, *Dateline Purgatory,* page 147 (in November 1998, at the time of Darlie's appeal). 'Expert Susan Simmons was appointed to reconstruct the trial record. It was Simmons who ultimately revealed that there were 33,000 errors in the transcript.'

stabbed through the lungs, so Devon died immediately and Damon on his way to hospital.

However, it is known that Darin had a history of minor illegal activities. He had been involved in insurance scams; the first, three years before, had involved his car, and when Darlie found out she was furious. Then, shortly before the murders, Darin had approached the same contact, Barry Fife, who had been involved in the car insurance scam, to discuss having his house burgled, probably by a man called Ben Claybour, who immediately disappeared to another state.

Darin seems to have supported his wife and still says she is innocent, but admitted that if she had died he would have been convicted of the murders, as the police would have gone after him. It is, on the face of it, surprising that they didn't do so anyway. One wonders whether, as with the prosecution of Amanda Knox, there is more than an element of misogyny, and going after the least likely perpetrator.

Ten years after the murders, Darin asked for and obtained a divorce. He has not remarried. Drake, who was brought up by Darin's parents, has recently developed leukaemia. It is hard to imagine what further disasters might be piled on Darlie Routier.

Main lessons from the case

The same elements that we have seen in our other two cases appear to have operated here, and it is hard to pinpoint their relative importance. How is it possible that a judge and jury were persuaded of the guilt, against all the odds, of a mother with an unimpeachable past suddenly turning on her own progeny, and then stabbing herself? This is so totally contrary to the biology of our species, in which the mother invests everything to bring up the next generation. A defining feature of humanity is our incredibly long childhood, in which we are almost entirely dependent on the nurture of our mothers.

These two boys were the light of Darlie's life. Even when five weeks before their murders she had, in a fit of severe post-natal depression, expressed suicidal thoughts and then phoned Darin in a call for help, it was clear that the boys were what she most lived for. The same is apparent in the five minutes of heart-rending recorded telephone call to 911 (partly set out earlier in the chapter) — 'Who would do this to my babies? Who would kill my babies?' From the written hospital records she was repeatedly in tears and devastated; what is also clear is that the police worked hard on the nurses and doctors in the days afterwards, and coming up to the trial, seemingly in the hope of getting them to say that her reaction was not appropriate. They only called staff to give evidence that helped their argument that she did not react as a normal mother would. And since in each case the prosecution proceeds first, in the absence of a very strong defence, confirmation bias will have operated.

Prosecutor Greg Davis has sent 20 people to Death Row in Texas. Some people might therefore describe him as ruthless, an 'accolade' applied to many prosecutors and investigators. Certainly, in Darlie's case he pushed for the death penalty and got it. It may be that lawyers (a breed not in any case much noted for their empathy) are placed, whether they like it or not, in a system in which their job can so easily be to target those who could well be innocent (the corollary being that the guilty go free).

Darlie's role in her own conviction

The case illustrates we believe that people pay more attention to confirmatory than to exculpatory evidence. Darlie has always seemed to be a woman who delighted in her own good looks, but that after all is a common aspect of femininity. It is unusual perhaps that she had bilateral breast implants, since she was apparently already well-endowed. When she appeared in court and spoke in her own defence she was easily wrapped in knots by the prosecutor pointing out inconsistencies in her different depositions to the police (most of which were not written down, and had been given when she was interrogated under the influence of the tranquilliser Xanax). But then, of course, prosecutors are professionals, who are trained and paid to undermine witnesses' evidence including through cross-examination. This is the nature of the adversarial system of criminal justice.

While Darlie was trying to come to terms with the slaying by a stranger of her two innocent boys, she and her family had absolutely no inkling that the police were collecting a distorted dossier against her. How was she, believing the police were looking for a tall intruder and violator dressed in black and with a baseball cap, to realise that the police had decided that she was the likely killer and that her behaviour would be held up to the scrutiny of the press, the public and by a jury.

All the time the police, it can be assumed, were working with prosecutors over how to use such material to construct a convincing picture of guilt six months down the line to 12 lay people, the jury, who knew nothing of the psychology of trauma and grief, or of the potential for miscarriages of justice, or for CNEs to be working within the police, courts or justice system. And is it conceivable as we explain below that somewhere in this mix one or more of them was being compromised by a psychopathic established serial killer?

This is just one case that shows it is high time for things to change in justice Texas-style, and to alter for future generations the cruel suffering of Darlie Routier. How many more years, and how much hard work by people who, like us, can see what to us are the obvious flaws in this case, will it take to have her released from her state-sponsored nightmare?

Even if Darlie, against all the odds, had been guilty of killing her own children out of the blue this would surely speak of some form of insanity such as schizophrenia that would require treatment and study, not extermination. The death penalty makes no sense anyway, but surely makes even less when the rules of a macabre and surreal bureaucracy dictates that it applies for the murder of one's own five-year-old child but not for that of his simultaneously killed seven-year old brother.

The USA's most prolific killer

It may be relevant to consider briefly a previously largely hidden USA serial killer, Edward Wayne Edwards, who died in 2011. He is an object lesson in how an intelligent psychopathic killer systematically exploited weaknesses in the US police and justice system. This has been chillingly analysed by retired detective John A Cameron in *It's Me, Edward Wayne Edwards, the Serial Killer you Never Heard Of* (Golden Door Press, 2016).[10] Cameron has painstakingly pieced together the horrifying truth that Edwards, who died of old age on Death Row in Ohio aged 78, waged

---

10. This can be downloaded free from John A Cameron's website. It makes for chilling reading. See www.coldcasecameron.com

a life-time of terror over large parts of the USA. The story is instructive for students of confirmation bias, which can leave investigators vulnerable to false or distorted evidence or to tempt them with the prospect of over-quick or 'fast track' convictions.

Born to a single mother, Christine Myers, in 1933, Edwards had a disturbed childhood. His mother died of gunshot wounds when he was aged five, and her father, suspecting the boy had shot her, had his name changed. He was handed over to a guardian, then a Catholic home run by nuns for disturbed and orphaned children. This experience, and the concept of Satan as the anti-Christ, undoubtedly influenced his *modus operandi*. Edwards escaped the home at age eleven and committed his first murder at the age of 12 under the noses of the authorities. Throughout his life he was imprisoned on many occasions for theft, robbery and arson. In prison in 1956 he was diagnosed as a sado-masochistic psychopath. He married three times and had six children, and used his image as a family man as effective cover. He wrote a book at age 36, *Metamorphosis of a Criminal*,[11] claiming he was a reformed, in which he documented, as a puzzle, many of his early murders.

Using evidence from Edwards' writings, and interviews, Cameron documents at least 168 murders by him over a 66 year period. In 1996 on his blog, Edwards, using a pseudonym, claimed 500 murders. Cameron lists many of the most horrific killings ever committed, including the Black Dahlia murder, Zodiac killings, the West Memphis Three, and the so-called Lipstick Killer. Edwards is known to have murdered three six-year-old children, including the child star Jon-Benét Ramsay.

He delighted in manipulating evidence to convict the innocent. At least 24 people were convicted for murders he had committed: several of these were executed. Advocates of the death penalty might want to ponder that. A minimum of 12 men convicted of Edwards' crimes are still serving life sentences, but the state, police or judiciary have found no incentive to release them and may have a vested interest in the opposite. Edwards was at one time on America's Ten Most Wanted list (but not for murder). He committed so many killings across swathes of the

---

11. Hart Publications, 1972.

USA that there was a perceptible fall in USA murders whenever he was imprisoned, rising again on his release. The perfect prison snitch (see *Chapter 8*), Edwards in many cases plea bargained for his early release in return for turning in fellow prisoners. And when out of prison, the first people he visited when he took his family to a new town were the local police, befriending them with his slick charm. He committed at least one of his murders while in a police uniform borrowed from his wife's brother.

In his most brazen murder, Edwards, who with his (innocent) wife had adopted a young man, got him to change his name, murdered him and successfully claimed $250,000 life insurance. In exposing the extent of Edwards' activities, Cameron has done a great public service. Unfortunately at the time of writing the authorities in the states where Edwards carried out many of his killings have shown a singular lack of interest, even for the innocent still serving life sentences. Once again, it seems the judicial black hole is being defended.

The continuing cover-up of Edwards' crimes and *modus operandi* is most strongly suggested by the fact that at the time of writing notwithstanding numerous requests by John A Cameron, the FBI have still not released the late Edward Edwards' DNA CODIS profile. This despite suspicion of his involvement in many other murders, in some at least where the perpetrator left his DNA. The most obvious of these is the murder one week after the Routier killings, of 18-year-old Angie Dodge in Idaho Falls, a favourite haunt of Edwards and a murder in which the killer ejaculated on the victim's body. The profile of the killer is known, but so far seems not to have been compared with that of Edwards. Meanwhile Chris Tapp is serving life imprisonment for involvement in this murder, based on a coerced and false confession.

So might there just be a connection?

This psychopathic 'monster' who would have been 63 in 1996 was still then highly active. The murders of two sons and subsequent framing of their mother would fit his *modus operandi* to perfection. The number 666, mentioned in the *New Testament's* Book of Revelations, has special significance for Satanists, for whom it represents the 'mark of the beast'.

Edwards might have chosen the 6ᵗʰ of June 1996 to carry out a murder anywhere. Devil worshipers hold 666 to symbolise the perfection of man's overall system separated from God and under the constant influence of Satan. So a *first* question is, 'Was *this* exceptionally horrific murder one that the psychopathic Satanist Edwards committed on that day?' *Second,* the two child victims were respectively aged five and six—perfect targets for Edwards, who killed several six-year-olds (including, on Christmas day 1996, Jon-Benét Ramsay). *Third,* throughout his life Edwards often manipulated the police and judicial system to nail his crimes on a further victim, using weaknesses in the system to do his dirty work. So maybe it would work rather well if the individual whose car was used at Eagle Drive, who had perhaps expected to take part in a routine break-in, just happened to be someone connected to the justice system targeted by Edwards, as was his usual style, for its vulnerabilities.

CHAPTER EIGHT

The Psychopathology of Victims and Victimisation

Trust and its exploitation by others

Most normal people are trusting by nature and make the assumption that trained professionals will do honestly and without any sign of malice what they are trained and paid to do. This does not include incarcerating innocent people. However we see from the three cases in this book that, on occasion, the professionals we trust to sustain justice may falter. And their 'victims' often inadvertently help.

After a murder the primary victim has ceased to exist, and from then on is replaced by one or more secondary or surrogate victims, often in the form of family members. We have seen how their need for resolution, plus confirmation bias, can be powerful forces to supplement the case against those who have been formally accused. Once a crime ending in murder has been committed the police assume the role of criminal investigators, with the declared aim of bringing those responsible before the courts for judgment. In pursuing this superficially laudable aim it is important to realise that *they are being paid to be successful, that is to obtain convictions*. It is only an assumption that because normal people want only the guilty to be convicted, all those in power will do likewise.

We have seen through the prism of three infamous and high profile cases that this may not always be case. People with constitutional negative empathy (CNE), even if not obviously psychopathic, have an innate tendency to engage in targeted aggression, and they are least likely to be found out when it is within their own special area of expertise.

The court is charged with the responsibility of weighing the evidence and convicting those they judge to be guilty beyond reasonable doubt.

However, once that hurdle has been passed, in the eyes of the law it ceases to matter whether or not the individual is *really* guilty. In fact, since the innocent person has now been judicially *defined* as guilty, the process then swings from its initial declared position of a presumption of innocence, through 180 degrees to a presumption of guilt. It is often perversely argued by judges and lawyers that the integrity of the justice system depends on this.

We have referred to this as a judicial black hole. Meanwhile all players in this game of 'catch the criminal' are human beings with their own fair share of faults, and their own separate though overlapping agendas. All players will have their own particular mix of intelligence, empathy, rationality and confirmation bias; these are largely if not entirely, separate from their particular roles in the drama that is being played for real.

The hypothetical psychopathic policeman or prosecutor

Let us now briefly consider the case of a hypothetical public prosecutor, or other person in a position of official or legal power, who happens to fulfil the criteria of constitutional negative empath Type p (psychopath) as described in *Chapter 1* of this book. That is, he or she has an inherent and lifelong defect of amygdala function whereby they fail to see in the distress of others a mirror of their own distress, and consequently lack the normal aversion to harming them, and so have failed to socialise normally. Such people must be assumed to exist within any profession. Indeed they might even be concentrated, by virtue of inherent properties of the system, within the general class of people attracted to become, for example, policemen or public prosecutors.

By her own admission in her revealingly honest book *Confessions of a Sociopath*, author M E Thomas admits to being just such a lawyer and successful public prosecutor. We have seen that life for the psychopath/sociopath/CNE, who through no fault of his or her own has grown up to be devoid of empathy, can be rather boring. With no true friends and therefore no real social life, he or she often tells lies when cornered and functions solely through control. As a child he or she has been a bully, and bullies have a tendency to work with other bullies to target weaker or more empathetic people.

As an adult such a person, lacking the normal aggression inhibition mechanism, gets spurious pleasure from engaging in *targeted aggression,* generally in their specialist area of expertise, where they are least likely to be caught. In a child murder case, for instance, a CNE policeman may focus on the most emotionally committed individual, such as the mother or father. They are the most vulnerable, and all that may be needed is a process that runs on apparent intuition, combined with shoddy police work. For the un-empathic individual, who sees and treats others as mere objects, there may be particular satisfaction from trapping and then exposing good people. And if the system allows it, such an individual will have developed a network of like-minded or at least compliant subordinates. For example there are perennial 'expert' witnesses, such as a psychiatrist I once knew, who boasted he would testify to anything for the appropriate fee; or the perennial 'experts' on blood spatter analysis, or arson. And obviously, hidden behind the anonymity of a pseudonym, there is a special place for such people to thrive as internet trolls, as we have seen with the notorious and enigmatic Harry Rag (*Chapter 5*).

In this chapter we look specifically at the way in which victims of injustice can contribute inadvertently to their own downfall or the downfall of others.

Supposed lack of emotion: A standard prosecution trick

There is great expectation by the public that, especially on the part of a friend or close family member of a victim, there will be openly displayed emotion and that its presence is a strong pointer to innocence. The flip side, or what can be painted as such, is seen and used by public prosecutors as a pointer towards guilt. In the case of Amanda Knox, it was the alleged cartwheel, or the purchase of supposedly sexy lingerie, or the comforting kiss filmed and recycled as 'making out' with her boyfriend. In the case of Darlie Routier it was firing 'silly string' on the boys' graves. Once such an accusation is made, it is easy to make it stick, and prosecutors know this.

First of all, there really are no rules on how we are supposed to deal with grief and shock; we each deal with them differently. Shock is the natural first response to the loss of a loved one, and is not necessarily accompanied by tears. The emotion displayed immediately is most likely to be panic, anger and horror. It is only later, and often much later, that grief and mourning set in. Furthermore, a strong character may well do most of their grieving away from the public eye, maintaining a stiff upper lip in public.

Amanda Knox was severely criticised by Meredith Kercher's friends for not displaying an appropriate emotional response; this was in stark contrast to the hysterical reaction of one of her Italian flat-mates, which matched much more closely the more demonstrative expectations of Italian women. *La bella figura* demands of Italians the open display of all emotion, the flip-side of grieving being the routine kiss on both cheeks when you meet a vague acquaintance of either gender, which is anathema to most Anglo-Saxons! Somehow a 20-year-old American girl confronted with the horror of her flatmate's death by stabbing was expected to conform to an Italian (possibly TV) norm, ignoring that she was in shock and overwhelmed by both the fact of her friend's death and terror at her own vulnerability. The victim could so easily have been her. Far from home, with only a lover whom she barely knew to protect and comfort her, she was sentenced in the public eye for a simple and completely impassionate kiss. People do not understand that often the first reaction to a severe threat is to freeze.

Viewed from the perspective of malicious or unjust prosecutions, generated by a CNE process well-attuned to expectations of empathy in others, we can see how readily such failure to conform in public can be exploited. Remember, one of the features of CNEs is that they lack emotional empathy, while being in full possession of cognitive empathy. They know what is expected of public displays, and may become expert at imitating the actions of others. Such individuals, and the systems in which they operate, become past masters at creating and then exploiting perceived appropriate displays of emotion.

Thus people asked how, only eight days after the sudden non-accidental violent stabbing of her two young children, could a mother fire silly string over their still warm graves? This is surely such an obvious aberration it must point to her guilt? As part of the targeted aggression against Darlie, for the prosecution to persuade a jury of this, at least four elements were brought into play. First, the fact that the filming was clandestine (and therefore arguably illegal) was concealed from the jury. Second, the judge, unknown to the jury, allowed two police officers to plead the US Constitution's Fifth Amendment (the right not to incriminate oneself). In a trial for murder, which in the end carried the death penalty for the accused, the professionals making the accusation were allowed to conceal the arguably illegal nature of the filming because it might incriminate them! Just how unethical does that sound? Third, the jury was not informed that the whole two hour funeral service and burial was recorded on film and this film shows plenty of grieving and displayed emotion by a devastated mother. Fourth, the idea of the 'silly string' had been suggested to Darlie by her 16-year-old sister Dana, as an aid to comfort her; and as described in *Chapter 7* at that point Darlie saw her children as looking down from heaven and sharing in the fun. It was her way of coping with her loss. And finally, the jury was shown just the silly string clip eight or nine times in a loop, reinforcing the opinion that it was inappropriate. This was much as the world was shown on TV *ad nauseam* an innocent kiss between Amanda and Raffaele, also effectively in a continuous loop. And outrageously in the Perugia appeal the 'murdered girl's lawyer', Francesco Maresca (acting for the prosecution), even showed photographs of Meredith Kercher's naked body in a loop, presumably in an attempt to shock the press and the jury. And he seemed to show no remorse at just how outrageous this was.

Manipulation of witnesses

Another element in these arrangements to demonstrate that the accused was lacking in appropriate emotion involves the manipulation of witnesses. Here again, the Darlie Routier case is illustrative. In a case as improbable as this, with little concrete evidence, and unconvincing forensics, it was necessary to create an emotional smokescreen. Therefore the prosecution called only those witnesses who were prepared after the event to make statements that complied with what was expected.

The hospital records, kept by many nurses and doctors, showed that Darlie was weepy and tearful in hospital; but under intense targeted questioning, false memories appear to have been implanted in certain witnesses, and these were the ones who were called to the witness stand. Contemporaneous records were ignored in favour of a prosecution approach of asking leading questions coupled with a failure of the defence to question this. Witnesses who would have testified differently were excluded. Thus were the defendant's personality and actions misrepresented and her credibility destroyed in the eyes of the jury.

Such elements are amplified in Italy where the investigation and trial processes are long drawn out, potentially providing multiple opportunities for the accused to slip-up in the eyes of the court and the public. One example from the trial of Amanda Knox will suffice, and again it stemmed from a well-meaning relative who had given Amanda a T-shirt with the Beatles message 'All you need is love' printed on it; thinking like an American she chose to wear this in a court appearance on Saint Valentine's Day. This was seized upon and amplified as being disrespectful of the memory of the deceased, by the lawyer representing the Kercher family, Francesco Maresca already mentioned above.

In the Stefan Kiszko's case, there were two important witnesses—Emma Tong and Christopher Coverdale—whose evidence clearly pointed to another culprit, and away from the frail Kiszko, who were essentially ignored. Coverdale's evidence seems even to have been concealed from the defence. Meanwhile the police and prosecution depended on the extensive evidence of children who had testified to Kiszko exposing himself—three of these (a girl Debra aged 13 at the time, and two older girls) admitted many years later that they made up the stories 'for a lark'. The defence did not see fit to cross-examine these girls in court. The stories of exposure on October 3rd were admitted to have been due to a milkman; so as part of his confession Kiszko even admitted to an offence that the police were not claiming had occurred.

The false confession

Of the three cases considered in detail in this book, only Stefan Kiszko actually ever confessed to the crime. Amanda Knox, we are told, closed her eyes and 'imagined' what might have happened, and this was then twisted and represented as a confession of sorts, then used to condemn her for slander against Patrick Lumumba. Both Kiszko and Knox immediately retracted, but the false confession holds a strong grip on a jury, and in the eyes of the public. Darlie Routier has never shifted from her story that a hooded or masked man stabbed her boys and assaulted her.

Few people can imagine the circumstance under which they would confess to a crime they did not do, and yet it happens to normal people all the time. Under pressurised conditions used in the Reid technique, and seemingly applied to both Amanda Knox and Stefan Kiszko, almost any normal person will eventually confess to or imagine something they did not do.

Professor James Duane of Regent University School of Law explains in painful detail why nobody should ever talk to the police unless their lawyer is present on a popular YouTube video.[1] This is why it is absolutely crucial that interrogations are filmed, so that the precise circumstances are recorded and can be seen later. The problem here, of course, is that there may be gaps in the recording or other influences at work. In the case of Kiszko, the reader will recall, his confession included facts that only the perpetrator and the police were aware of; this clearly shows that he was somehow fed this information (unless he was a remarkably coincidental maker-up of details).

There is an extraordinary example of a series of recorded interrogations on YouTube, posted with a commentary by Judge Michael Heavey, which led to the conviction of Chris Tapp for the brutal murder of 18-year-old Angie Dodge in her flat in Idaho Falls one week after the Routier murders. This shows interrogations which lasted a total of 24 hours over a week, using a gamut of techniques, including a police officer who knew Tapp from his schooldays, appearing to 'butter him up,' offering immunity if he implicated his friend, and planting him with false memories.[2]

The plea bargain
A plea bargain, as offered to Chris Tapp (above), comes into play when an accused person is offered a reduced sentence if they admit to something, or sometimes if they turn on a fellow-accused. It is common in USA, and elements of the plea bargain exist in Britain. In none of these

1. See https://www.youtube.com/watch?v=6wXkI4t7nuc
2. See www.judgesforjustice.org

three cases did the possibility of the plea bargain arise directly, although it was made clear to Raffaele Sollecito that he would get off lightly if he incriminated his fellow accused Amanda Knox. Fortunately for her, as indicated in Raffaele's book, *Honor Bound*, he resisted this pressure.

The true plea bargain is a weapon frequently used, especially in the USA, to convict others in the absence of compelling evidence. Thus, an offer may be made to the accused that will lead to a conviction, but with a much-reduced sentence. The flip-side of this is that the individual who doesn't confess and continues to protest his or her innocence, if and when found guilty, receives a harsher sentence. In the USA in states such as Texas where the death penalty still operates, the bargain may be that the prosecution will not press for this (but with no guarantee).

We saw in the case of Stefan Kiszko just how unfair it is to the innocent to insist on a full admission of guilt as a pre-condition to their early release during questioning. This unfairness is one further consequence of the unwritten but implicit belief in the absolute sanctity and veracity of the jury's decision, as it becomes the 'judicial truth'. Time and again it trumps the real thing. We have also seen in *Chapter 7* how serial mega-murderer Edward Wayne Edwards found time-and-again that he was used as a 'prison snitch' in return for early release, to make up confessions and other stories that got his fellow inmates convicted of crimes, allowing him out of prison early to kill again.

Fast track trials

Something underhand seems to have happened relating to the apparently sacrosanct nature of 'judicial truth' in the case against Amanda Knox and Raffaele Sollecito. Their co-accused, Rudy Guede, who was almost certainly the solo killer, was allowed a so-called 'fast-track trial.' The advantages to the guilty of taking this shortcut to justice in whatever country are enormous. It obviously also greatly simplifies things for systems that are hopelessly overloaded, giving reason to reward it. In Italy, the fast track automatically qualifies the person who has taken it to a reduction in sentence amounting to nearly 50 percent. And in Rudy's case, his sentence of 30 years was reduced on appeal to 16 years, and it did not even involve him making an unqualified admission of his own guilt. What it did was neatly sidestep the need to be cross-examined in court by the legal representatives of his co-accused, who throughout maintained their total innocence and were eventually exonerated.

The fast track procedure avoided the need for Guede to explain to the court why he had changed his statements first made to his friend Benedetti on a Skype call, in which he said that Amanda had nothing to do with it. Furthermore, it meant that all steps in Guede's case were a year or more ahead of those for Knox and Sollecito; and since Italy still maintains the absolute sanctity of the Supreme Court's ruling, and since the Supreme Court ruled that Guede had acted 'with others', then that conclusion was deftly used downstream by the prosecution in a full trial against Knox and Sollecito. Now that the Supreme Court has finally ruled that Amanda Knox and Raffaele Sollecito are innocent, the need to sustain the Supreme Court decision over Rudy Guede (despite his never having had a real trial) still maintains the same conclusion. This is that though the other two had not actually participated in the murder they *might* have been present when Meredith was murdered! Judicial truth, however ridiculous, always trumps real truth and common sense.

Interestingly in the so-called Colne case against Annamaria Franzone, where she was accused of battering her three-year-old Samuele to death on her bed her lawyers advised her to take the fast track, even though she has vigorously maintained that she is innocent, and that Samuele was killed by an intruder. As a result, she too benefited from an automatically reduced sentence. The fast track allows a conviction to be made by one judge acting alone, and often being vague or obtuse in his or her judgment. Arguably, Italian justice is full of such anomalies.

False and contrived witnesses

Witness testimony can be notoriously unreliable, and such evidence was involved in convicting 25 per cent of the first 250 USA cases later overturned by the Innocence Project on the basis of incontrovertible DNA evidence.[3] Most of these were rape cases, in which the supposed perpetrator had been identified in a prisoner parade. One would intuitively

---

3. http://www.innocenceproject.org/causes-wrongful-conviction/

think that a rape victim would be able to identify with some degree of reliability her assailant. Often initial uncertainty is later replaced in court by absolute certainty, with the implantation of false memories and confirmation bias, and it is well-established that if the officer running the parade knows who the suspect is this will substantially increase the chance of that person being pointed-out.

In Italian justice, the exceptionally slow pace of standard proceedings facilitates the elaborate construction of willing, but extremely unreliable witnesses. It seems there has been little advance here since the medieval methods of trial by fire or drowning. According to modern judicial procedure, even in Italy witnesses are supposed to lead to the truth, not the obverse. However the public prosecutor there, if extremely devout as well as unrestrained by mere facts, may decide on the basis of a revelation who is guilty of the murder, and then construct judicial truth by creating placebo witnesses from nothing. It is refreshing to see this and other abuse of evidence is strongly criticised in the final 'motivation report' released in the case of Knox and Sollecito (*Chapter 3*).

To see related examples of this type of event, the reader can refer to Preston and Spezi's book *The Monster of Florence*, which is replete with people accused on the basis of completely non-credible witnesses, such as the famous alphabetical ones, used to convict Pacciani and his 'picnicking friends.' It is hard to imagine a court anywhere in the world would accept, as did Judge Massei in the trial of Amanda Knox and Raffaele Sollecito, the testimony of bench-sleeping heroin-addicted born-again anarchic Christian such as Antonio ('Toto') Curatolo (*Chapter 2*). I (David Anderson) was present at Knox and Sollecito's first appeal, when he gave evidence, and his testimony was rejected by Judges Zanetti and Hellmann. Yet two years later, and after his death, it was reinstated by Judge Nencini, on instructions from the first Supreme Court hearing, as part of the 'osmotic analysis' of the case that they had been asked to undertake. The final hearing by the Supreme Court (the Marasca hearing), seems to have taken a contrary view.

The so-called 'prison snitch'

Then there is the use of the so-called 'prison snitch' who may be offered a reduced sentence or an early discharge, in return for something that will help incriminate a fellow inmate. Of course, there is always the possibility that someone in prison might befriend someone who has some conscience and therefore wants to confide in a sort of safe priest-substitute. For this reason, it is possible that when the convicted child-murderer Mario Alessi, who shared a room with Rudy Guede in Viterbo Prison, claimed he confided certain details to him, he might have been telling the truth. He was after all prepared to repeat it under oath. Specifically and importantly, without any way of knowing that there were putative semen stains on the cushion on which the murdered girl's body lay, Alessi testified first on a sworn affidavit, and then in court that Guede told him that he (or someone) had masturbated over the dying girl's body. Reason enough, you would think, to do a microscopic examination for sperm heads on those stains that were revealed by the defence forensic experts using the fluorescence crimescope, and then if confirmed, by further DNA-analysis. Isn't it important, even in Perugia, to know who the killer was? For certainly that is his seminal calling card. Parenthetically, if it belonged to Rudy Guede it surely confirms the defence theory that he acted alone. Or would a burglar actually masturbate over a dying girl's body in the presence of another burglar who had dealt the fatal blow?

Confirmation bias and the exploitation of family anguish

One feature that many convictions of the innocent have in common is that close relatives of the victim, who in their anguish are desperate to know who the killer was, are persuaded at an early stage that the prosecution case is sound. Once convinced, they submit to confirmation bias, something to which we are all susceptible. For them, this can be enhanced by an innate trust of authority and the fact that they are unwillingly thrust into the spotlight.

Most of us, once committed to a particular story, especially one that is being constantly repeated, become increasingly reluctant to back down as we ourselves repeatedly retell it to others. And the more emotionally connected we are to a particular outcome, the more hard-wired our beliefs become. The more a particular story is retold, the more embedded it becomes. Natural sympathy for the victim from ordinary members of the public (from whom the jury will be drawn) can soon lend a specious authority to the official story, thereby reducing the likelihood that the accused can receive a fair trial. People with no direct connection with the deceased, but who are shocked by the prosecution story, then naturally reflect this bias. This is one reason why, in the UK, victims' families are largely excluded until after the trial (unless they happen to be legitimate witnesses), and there are strict reporting restrictions, once someone has been charged and up until sentence. The more horrific and unusual the crime, the greater is the pressure for it to be solved, and the greater the risk of convicting an innocent person or persons, to fulfil this perceived need. We saw this well illustrated in the improbable and contrived conviction of Stefan Kiszko.

Exploitation of sympathy for the family

From an early stage after Meredith's murder, the Kercher family was told that Amanda Knox and Raffaele Sollecito had taken part in a 'sex game gone wrong' which led to the murder of Meredith. As Amanda recently pointed out in a poignant TV interview, '[T]hey never had a chance even to think that I was innocent.' Initially, this bizarre accusation of a sex game included a third man, Amanda's employer Patrick Lumumba. Yet a Swiss professor had been with him in his bar all evening. But the police, under pressure from the prosecutor, rushed in to arrest him in the middle of the night. When Lumumba's alibi was seen to be water-tight and evidence of Rudy Guede was found all over the crime scene, the prosecution simply swopped one man for another.

After his release, while he initially accused the police of abuse, in time Lumumba neatly switched to the role of 'supplementary victim' of Amanda, who, under conditions of sleep deprivation and great psychological pressure had apparently 'imagined' Lumumba killing Meredith. And the sex game theory was dropped altogether by Prosecutor Crini in the Nencini appeal, and replaced with a hygiene motive!

This swopping of roles, and much else, was helped by the incredibly drawn out preliminary investigations and then trial, so typical of Italy's 'justice' system. The unwavering acceptance by the family of the prosecution story, already referred to, was enhanced by a number of things. First by the fact that the family's lawyer, Francesco Maresca, was introduced to them by the public prosecutor, Giuliano Mignini, a colleague, only four days after Meredith's body was found; and then that same day the police announced with a flourish it was '*caso chiuso*' (case closed).

Naturally the family believed that the lawyer representing them would be keen to uncover the truth. The sequence by which his assurances to them concerning the 'truth' will have affected their views towards Amanda and Raffaele have been described in earlier chapters. At the end of the first trial the Kerchers were awarded damages against Amanda and Raffaele. These amounted to a staggeringly large sum (around €10 million) to be paid to the Kerchers by the families of the supposed perpetrators. So whether they liked it or not, from then on the Kercher family had a vested financial interest in the guilty verdict being sustained. If Guede was the sole perpetrator they would receive nothing in civil damages, since he is penniless. The wealthy Perugian Caporali family, who had adopted him at the age of 16, had earlier disowned him.

So the pressures throughout were, quite naturally, for the victim's family to position itself as pro-prosecution. It was almost impossible to find any published comment remotely critical of them, or of the prosecution case they supported. Following their release, Knox and Sollecito both made heartfelt appeals to family to seek the truth, and to engage in some sort of joint closure; but confirmation bias and the other issues outlined above appear to have made this impossible. Misplaced sympathy is still being generated in the blogosphere as described in *Chapter 5*.

Lesley Molseed's family

In the case of Stefan Kiszko, after the trial was over members of the family of the murdered girl were vociferous in their condemnation of him; and her mother called for restoration of the death penalty for paedophile murderers. The family of at least one of the girls whose evidence had helped secure his conviction supported this call. To her great credit, however, when Kiszko was finally exonerated Lesley's mother April apologised to Stefan and to his mother Charlotte (see *Chapter 6*).

The family of Darlie Routier

In the case of Darlie Routier family divisions seem to have been exploited more subtly. Neither of the parents (Darlie and Darin) of the murdered boys were remotely credible as perpetrators of the murder by stabbing of their young two sons. Yet there were divisions between them, with Darin having already engaged in dubious actions strongly suggestive of fraud. He was in financial difficulties at the time of the murder, and his wife's lawyers who had initially represented Darin had an agreement not to pursue any defence that might instead implicate him. It is likely that, unknown to Darlie, he had discussed the possibility of a staged burglary on his own house, and news of this might have been fed to a murderer; so it seems that he may have indirectly contributed to the break-in and brutal attack on the boys and Darlie, and so, indirectly to Darlie's trial, conviction and death sentence.

The David Camm case

It is worth considering the conviction of former state Trooper David Camm for the murder of his wife and two children Brad and Jill on 28th September 2000. No less than his third trial took place in September 2013. Overwhelming evidence points to this crime having been the work of one man with a history of violent robbery, Chris Boney. Eleven people were playing basketball with David Camm at the time of the murders; but largely based on supposed blood spatter analysis (by Tom Bevel, who was not professionally qualified in this regard), Camm was found guilty of the cold-blooded murder of his family, a story his murdered wife Kim's parents accepted. David's story is that the fine blood marks on his shirt were from him leaning across his wife's body to pick up his daughter who he believed was still alive. This case illustrates many of the problems with injustice in the USA. For the purpose of the present discussion once again it illustrates how families can be exploited, in this case by pitching the wife's family against the falsely accused husband.

The murder of Anni Dewani

Another illustrative case was the improbable charge by prosecutors in South Africa against Shrien Dewani who was alleged to have hired contract killers to murder his new bride Anni on their honeymoon in Cape Town in 2010. An investigative BBC TV *Panorama* programme, screened in September 2013,[4] examined much evidence that had been selectively ignored by police and prosecutors. The investigation throws strong suspicion that the powers that be in Cape Town, fearful of the effect of the murder on tourism, decided to downplay the role of the taxi driver and his accomplices to that of bit-part players. So Shrien Dewani, Anni's husband and a foreigner, was charged as the instigator of his wife's murder, a seemingly absurd proposition and one that much CCTV footage from around the time of abduction showed was highly unlikely. The father of the dead girl, meanwhile, avowed a firm pro-guilt position against his former son-in-law, and accused *Panorama* of conducting trial by TV. Yet investigative journalism is an absolutely essential element to help counterbalance the position of a corrupt *polizio-judicial* system, when a trial is likely to be biased. It is a common observation that possessive fathers can be resentful of their daughters' lovers and partners, especially shortly after they have left the family nest, and this is something that can easily be exploited.

In 2014, Shrien was extradited back to South Africa and his case was heard before a single female judge. She found the prosecution witnesses to be totally unreliable and their fabricated stories unbelievable and threw out the case principally on these grounds. Dewani's late wife's family were devastated, but this decisive action by the judge does great credit to the integrity of the judiciary in South Africa. Such independence was also evident when Oscar Pistorius was tried in front of another female judge, following the shooting by him of his girlfriend, Reeva Steencamp, a decision which has since been overturned on appeal.[5]

The strange case of Dr Jeffrey MacDonald

Jeffrey MacDonald was a successful doctor and surgeon and a member of the Green Berets. His pregnant wife Colette and two daughters were brutally clubbed and stabbed to death in his home in Fort Bragg, Texas on the night of February 17th 1970. MacDonald, who was also injured,

---

4. https://en.wikipedia.org/wiki/Murder_of_Anni_Dewani
5. http://time.com/4297257/oscar-pistorius-sentence-murder-reeva-steenkamp/

maintained it was a Sharon Tate-style attack by drug-crazed hippies. Crime writer Joe McGinniss described the murders and attendant story in great detail in the book *Fatal Vision.* MacDonald approached McGinniss in 1978 and asked him to write his story. MacDonald initially had the strongest support from his murdered wife's stepfather, Freddie Kassab, who, however, later, from 1971, turned against him, and ultimately used the strange US relic of the Grand Jury to have him successfully indicted.

The ten-year saga that led to MacDonald's conviction for the murder of his family is grippingly told in *Fatal Vision,* and reading it I was gradually persuaded, as McGinniss had been, that MacDonald murdered his family. One thing that raised suspicion from the beginning is the clearly narcissistic nature of the doctor as he casually describes his extra-marital affairs, both before and after the crimes. Whether or not MacDonald is a full-blown CNE, is open to debate, especially as he was taking dexamphetamine prior to the murders, and these may have led to an argument followed by impulsive violence. Kassab, once convinced of MacDonald's guilt, worked tirelessly and finally got the trial process re-opened. Perhaps the most persuasive aspect of the case is that for fully a year after the murders Kassab had been MacDonald's most fervent supporter, before what appeared to be some strange lies by him made Kassab question the doctor's story. MacDonald eventually took McGinniss to court for fraud. The case was settled out of court in 1987 with the payment to MacDonald of $325,000. As of 2016 it should be stressed, MacDonald still protests his innocence, has a massive following of supporters, but is in prison serving three life sentences.[6]

Conclusions

None of us expect to find ourselves accused of a murder or other crimes of which we know we are innocent. Yet this is precisely what happened in the three main cases considered in this book. The psychopathology of unjust or even malicious prosecutions and its major problems lie, we believe, in the structural weakness of *polizio-judicial* systems. The

---

6. The similarities between the murders of the Routier children and attack on and apparent framing of Darlie, and the slaughter of the MacDonald family are striking. Once again the possibility exists that serial Killer Edwards, who knew Fort Bragg well, and killed there at least once, was the actual perpetrator.

secondary victim (someone at risk of being victimised by those within the justice system) contributes unknowingly, often through inaction or excessive trust, to such injustices. We have seen how important it is not to be over-trustworthy of the system, and to realise that CNE and sometimes frankly psychopathic individuals may be at work within it. They may even succeed in fashioning a corrupted system in their own image.

CNEs have a capacity and overwhelming need to control others, and if unchecked will take over any system or organization. Young people and those that are most trusting of others are probably most vulnerable to their wiles. It is vital, under such circumstances, that their nearest and dearest place themselves physically, with no delay, close to their son, daughter or spouse and immediately obtain the best local legal advice possible. They must not impede an investigation, but do need to protect those dear to them and the time to do this is at the outset.

It is important also to realise that not everyone who is being paid to work for justice is actually doing so. There are 'bad eggs' as well as good ones in any legal basket: although you, the potential innocent accused, know that you are innocent, not everyone else does. Your proximity to the crime scene and to the murder victim immediately makes you a suspect in the eyes of the law, and innocent behaviour such as a wiggle of the hips (as Amanda Knox found), or slip of the tongue, may set in train a series of events that leads you to become the prime suspect. At its worst, you may be being targeted by individuals within the legal system.

Police and prosecutors tend to be judged by the level of convictions they secure, rather than the number of perpetrators they catch. Once an individual has been convicted they are drawn into a black hole, and this process continues with the trial: a dangerous lottery, and it matters not a great deal under what system. Essentially justice becomes a game in which the stakes get higher the further on you go. It is also a game in which the prosecution holds all the high cards. A primary purpose of this book, however, is not to offer advice to individuals who find themselves under the microscope for reasons that are beyond their control. Nor is it to try to change human nature. We have seen in these cases just how unjust justice can be, in Italy the UK and the USA; but that is no surprise, since justice systems are designed and run by human beings.

Our serious purpose, by highlighting how things went wrong in these and other cases, is to try and suggest some general principles and changes that may help make justice more just: see the closing chapter.

Meanwhile, since we are talking here about sex crimes and crimes of physical aggression, we need in the next chapter to return to some basic physiology as it affects the sexes. We believe that these should be included in every curriculum of every course of law enforcement, because the accusations in all three of these cases made no biological sense.

CHAPTER NINE

Sex, Hormones, and Crimes of Physical Aggression

In two of the cases considered in detail in this book crimes of great violence were, according to the prosecution and agreed by the jury, supposedly perpetrated by women—one against another woman, the other by a mother against her own defenceless children. That is strange, because the most violent acts perpetrated by our species, acts of war, rape and pillage, are carried out by men and not women. This is linked to differences in biology between the sexes, and the effect of testicular hormones on the male body and brain. These are things that are simple to explain, but not widely understood outside the medical fields of human endocrinology and reproduction. So let us run over some simple sexual and reproductive facts that go back tens of millions of years to which it is hoped lawyers, judges, jurors and journalists might pay special attention.

Hormones

First, what is a hormone, and how is gender determined? Hormones are chemical messengers secreted into the blood stream by one set of cells in the body, that act by attaching themselves to receptors on the surface of or within specific 'target' cells at distant locations. Among the most important, as well as the best understood, are the sex hormones, which have a simple chicken-wire steroid structure and are concerned with the related processes of physical sexual behaviour, essential for the reproduction of the species.

Each of us has 46 chromosomes (two pairs of 23) in every cell of our body apart from the end-reproductive ('germ') cells, which contain 23. Individuals with 46 chromosomes of which both the sex chromosomes are X, are phenotypically (i.e. in their gross body structure) female; and 46

XY individuals are phenotypically male. This gender difference is determined by the presence or absence of a Y chromosome, which is uniquely specialised for the important function of imposing features that constitute male internal and external gender. Each and every female germ cell (egg or ovum) has 22 autosomes, and one of the two X chromosomes, while each and every spermatozoa has 22 autosomes and either an X or a Y chromosome. The X chromosomes code for a large number of genes and the much smaller Y chromosome many fewer. So in order to minimise imbalance between the sexes in other body functions, in all our ordinary (non-germ) cells one of the two X chromosomes (for a female) and the Y chromosome (for a male) is inactivated and does essentially nothing.

The critical role of the testes in determining gender

We have seen already that as well as the more obvious somatic differences between the sexes there are subtle but important gender differences in brain structure. These arise from the imposition of maleness by the testicular hormone testosterone on what is the default (female) pattern of development, *in utero* and during the first months after birth. This mirrors the physical differences in body structure, which are either imposed by testosterone or (in the case of the internal genitalia) by Mullerian Duct Inhibiting Hormone, which also comes from the foetal testis. The default body structure is female, which simply develops in the absence of testes; during development ovarian hormones are essentially inactive.

During the critical stage of physical sex differentiation, the main hormone to drive testosterone production from the fetal testes is the placental hormone called Human Chorionic Gonadotrophin (HCG), which acts on the testosterone-secreting interstitial cells of Leydig through cell surface receptors. Later in life these are acted upon by the pituitary gland's Luteinising Hormone (LH). HCG and LH are examples of peptide (i.e. small protein) hormones, which act upon receptors on the surface of their target cells. After birth in newborn boys there is a further brief testosterone surge, driven by LH from the pituitary, but thereafter this part of the pituitary gland, controlled by the brain and hypothalamus, switches off, and the levels of testosterone fall dramatically, and remain low until puberty. In both sexes reproductive function is put 'on hold' until physical growth has matured sufficiently. Puberty in both sexes is driven by the brain acting through the hypothalamus and thence the pituitary gland, and is advanced under conditions of plenty and consequent good nutrition (such as we have in the West); in any given population statistically it occurs two years earlier in girls than boys.

The differences in male and female gonadal function

Another simple but important difference between men and women depends on how the sex hormones are secreted into the bloodstream, and this in turn is linked to the processes of sperm and egg development. Sperm production is essentially a *production line process,* with more sperm produced in an average adult male in one hour than there are eggs produced in a woman's ovaries over a whole lifetime. Billions of wasted sperm are needed to look for the egg, which is much more improbable than finding a needle in a haystack. In contrast, egg production is a *batch process* and the production of the whole store of eggs for a lifetime, around a million or so, has occurred well before birth. Each month after puberty a few such eggs are called on to mature, and normally one is selected for release (ovulation).

This difference is also reflected in the secretion of the biologically active sex hormones, whose primary purpose is also the continuation of the species. Thus, in the male once puberty has occurred (a process which starts at night-time), men have a more or less continuous production of testosterone by the interstitial (Leydig) cells, at levels which are at near-maximum all the time. This testosterone not only stimulates sperm production (along with the pituitary hormone FSH), but is also a necessary stimulus to male sex drive and the physical processes of emission and ejaculation of semen. Testosterone (and its conversion product dihydrotestosterone) enhances a feeling of strength, wellbeing and aggression as well as of potency. It will stimulate whatever sexual urge the man is otherwise inclined to (be it homosexual or heterosexual), or, in a psychologically disturbed individual, other and aberrant sexual urges. An obvious example is the male who was sexually abused as a child, and may have been programmed by that experience to behave similarly as an adult; and in violent individuals, the process of sexual stimulation often becomes mixed with physical aggression.

In women, testosterone levels are low and there are two additional steroid sex hormones which come from the ovaries, and whose production is anything but continuous. These are the main oestrogen, oestradiol, whose level varies about ten-fold during the ovulatory cycle, and progesterone, whose level varies as much as 100-fold. Testosterone in women plays a small role in stimulating sex drive, but blood levels are 20-fold lower than they are in men. As already mentioned, egg production in women is a batch-wise process, and *the primary purpose of the ovarian hormones is to pave the way for and then to sustain pregnancy.* The normal ovarian cycle is obviously an essential prelude to this biological process; and any effect on wellbeing is of secondary consequence. So the rising blood levels of oestradiol as the (normally single) egg is selected, develops and matures, is followed by a surge of LH release from the pituitary into the bloodstream, which triggers egg release (ovulation). Once the egg is released it travels down the Fallopian tubes to the uterus, and on the way 'hopefully' is met by spermatozoa, one of which will fuse with it and insert its DNA (fertilisation). With cell division, development of the embryo, placenta and membranes begins.

The rise in LH that caused ovulation then stimulates the rest of the follicle to develop into the corpus luteum, which secretes large amounts of both oestradiol and progesterone, and these complete the preparation of the lining of the womb, which was started by oestradiol alone, for implantation of the fertilised egg. It is then a race against time, because only when implanted will the embryo start to produce its own driving hormone, human chorionic gonadotrophin (HCG) which will sustain the function of the corpus luteum throughout the rest of pregnancy. If that does not happen, or if it happens too late, the corpus luteum shrivels and dies, estradiol and progesterone levels decline, the surface lining of the womb is shed and the uterine lining bleeds. This extraordinarily turbulent cyclical female hormone activity produces lability in mood as well as body structure in many women, of a type neither experienced nor understood (but easily exploited) by men.

Another important difference in behaviour between adults of the two sexes can best be understood by considering the structure and function of ovaries and testes, their germ cells, how they are produced and nurtured. These are the cells that contribute roughly 50 per cent of the genetic material from each parent to the offspring (actually, because of the smaller size of the Y than the X chromosome, in males slightly more genetic material has come from the mother. But this doesn't show, because in the female one X is inactivated in every cell, as is the Y in male cells.) It is a simple fact that the ovaries produce eggs at one time, with all the cell division having occurred before birth. Subsequently small batches of a dozen or so are recruited each month, of which normally one is selected for release and possible fertilisation.

Sex hormone priorities in men and women compared

Everything about the female hormone cycle is directed towards optimising the chances, if that egg is fortunate enough to be fertilised, of carrying the resulting embryo to term. The resulting hormonal cycle is one of two halves, respectively before and after release of the egg. In the first half we see a progressive rise in levels of oestradiol up to ovulation (which is triggered by a surge of LH from the pituitary). This is followed by production of oestradiol with large amounts of progesterone from the residue of the follicle, the corpus luteum. These hormones together prepare the uterus (womb) for implantation; if conception has occurred, the corpus luteum is kept going by HCG from the fetal placenta. If not, both the ovum and the corpus luteum die, the lining of the womb is shed, menstruation occurs, and the process is re-initiated for the next batch of follicles. The over-riding biological purpose of this cycle is to achieve a successful pregnancy, during the course of which the mother is the sole source of nourishment and physical protection for the fetus. There is an enormous investment by the mother in sustaining the fetus throughout pregnancy.

This unique support by the mother then continues after birth, when nutrition becomes extra-uterine, from breast milk and suckling, driven by the important pituitary peptide hormones prolactin and oxytocin. Immediately after birth, there is a process of bonding between mother and baby, initiated and sustained by the processes of birth, suckling and nurture, and their attendant hormone changes. As the child matures, bonding works both ways and both changes and becomes reinforced. Normal women, especially coming from normal loving families, are extremely unlikely to be physically and impulsively violent towards their own children. Any case in which this is alleged, especially where there is no evidence of maternal psychosis (depression or schizophrenia) is immediately to be seen as highly suspect. Uncomfortable though this may be for lawyers, *biological truth normally trumps judicial truth*.

In considering crime and aggression we also need to take into consideration differences in physical strength between men and women, and how they arise. Again, the hormone testosterone is the body's main anabolic hormone, and accounts for the greater size and physical strength of men. This is not to say that women do not potentially have the same range of athletic ability (which depends on neuromuscular coordination) as men. But in terms of body strength they cannot compete. Women's brains are organized for a different biological function than those of men, since however much advocates of equality of the sexes argue it, they are the more natural care givers, whose biology designates them to be the predominant ones to raise and look after the next generation.

Mothers provide the body in which the baby grows for nine months, and the food during the early years of life; and they are the dominant home-builders. The male's role in sexual reproduction is transient, and simply confined to providing sperm on a continuous production-line basis; his role after intercourse is to provide food, defence and physical protection for the smaller and less muscular sex, and for her offspring. And in conditions under which our species has evolved, one role of the male is for potential physical aggression needed to protect and to fight enemies and kill prey. That is what the male body (including the brain) is much better designed for than the female.

Acts of physical aggression; gender differences

It is another simple fact of human nature that acts of physical aggression are the dominant preserve of adolescent and young adult males. Therefore we should be intrinsically more sceptical when crimes that are the normal province of men are asserted in court or elsewhere to have been carried out by a woman. This is reflected in prison populations where 90 percent of prisoners are men, most of whom are convicted and imprisoned in their late-teens or early-twenties. By and large the women in prisons have been convicted for activities such as theft, prostitution, fraud (or are there for non-payment of fines connected to offences) that are not explicitly violent. Public prosecutors, and others in law enforcement, on the other hand, are much more often men than women. There is a particular danger to women accused of a crime of violence, as seen with both Amanda Knox and Darlie Routier, when a police investigator or public prosecutor is free to let his or her untutored notions of the origins of human behaviour run roughshod over probabilities, human biology and even evidence and proof.

For Darlie Routier (*Chapter 7*) the intrinsic probability of a caring and highly empathic young mother who nurtured and bonded with her sons, turning mad one night, stabbing them to death, and then staging an attack on herself is vanishingly small. The fact that this was ever seriously considered or argued in that case is condemnation enough of a judicial system that allows male public prosecutors and others to even suggest such things; let alone for a jury to verify them and condemn the remaining victim to death herself. For the jury, there can be little doubt of the danger here of *schadenfreude*, delight in the misfortune of others.[1]

In two of the miscarriages of justice we have considered, young women were accused of heinous crimes of violence. In the third it was a very sick man with testicular failure, from a first generation immigrant family, and a bit of a misfit and mummy's boy, who was also recovering from severe illness; just the kind that school bullies target. In all three cases evidence appears to have been either tampered with, lost or created from nothing solid, principally by men in positions of power it might be argued who were living under the 'mask of sanity', and who were being paid to solve crimes and protect citizen, not to destroy innocent lives. In each case, the process of reversal and recompense proceeded at snails pace and/or was vigorously opposed by men and women within the system that had

---

1.   'Love...does not delight in the misfortune of others. It only delights in the truth,' St Paul writes
       in 1 Corinthians, Verse 13.

allowed bad things to happen. In each case events were aided and abetted by the general public, and encouraged by a press that thrives on salacious violence and horror stories and loves a witch-hunt. Those who felt their targets guilty painted them as psychopathic people, a common 'trick' that CNEs themselves sometimes routinely engage in (and of which of course they have perfect inside understanding). And remember that in any population something between one and five per cent of the population will have a primary defect in amygdala function of CNE that defines them as potentially psychopathic or sociopathic.

Gender differences in manifestations of psychopathy

Psychopathy is probably about as common in women as it is in men. However its manifestations are different, with the lack of empathy tending to be of a more spiteful and less physically violent nature in psychopathic women than men. Even when they engage in targeted aggression, female psychopaths are much less likely to do so using physical violence than are their male counterparts. Quite simply, their body structure and sexual biology are not adapted for it. There are rare documented cases of women engaged in violent crime, such as the infamous moors murderess Myra Hindley, and Rosemary West; but in both these cases and many others the driving force was a dominating CNE/psychopathic male. In the absence of the dominant male it is highly improbable that these violent crimes would have occurred at all.

So in the case of Amanda Knox, the story of a previously normal and happy young woman targeting her female flat-mate under any circumstances is highly improbable. Unfortunately, the alternative story that she was being set-up and set upon by ruthless professionals operating within a CNE system, was less appealing to newspaper editors (and more litigiously dangerous) for them. As we have discussed in the light of Joel Bakan's book, *The Corporation,*[2] the press, consisting of corporations, is itself intrinsically psychopathic. And in a system where state-funded litigation by the legal authorities is commonplace, the imbalance in power makes simple truth much more risky.

---

2. *The Corporation: The Pathological Pursuit of Profit and Power*, Constable & Robinson, 2004.

Darlie Routier and her improbable biology

With Darlie Routier, the case against her was if anything even more far-fetched. We are asked to believe that a normal mother whom all the evidence indicates adored her two oldest sons, awakes in the middle of the night and in a mad frenzy viciously stabs them, then tries to stage an attack on them as victims including by stabbing herself and impaling her necklace deep into a wound. She then draws upon potentially Oscar-winning acting abilities as she puts in a frantic call to the police for help, saying her babies have been stabbed. If one listens to her heart-rending appeal over the phone (available on the internet) it is clearly genuine and anyone with normal empathy would recognise it as such. So right from the beginning the story spun by officials who were supposed to be solving these crimes was impossible. And with John Cameron's recent uncovering of Edward Edwards the horrific serial killer in the USA, active all over the USA over 64 years, we easily begin to theorise, rightly or wrongly, how police under pressure (and conceivably compromised) might act.

Darlie had undoubtedly been suffering from a post-partum depression in the months before the murders, but seems to have been recovering. The hormone changes and swings we have seen in the normal menstrual cycle are as nothing compared with those that follow childbirth; and they sometimes lead to severe depression. To this is added the fact that babies are demanding, and wake at odd hours, so that is why she was sleeping downstairs away from the neonate, who was upstairs with her husband. In any case, depression would not lead a woman to kill her children, but rather to kill herself, something her writings suggest she had contemplated at the height of her depression, but had rejected mainly because she loved her boys. And that was weeks before, and she was on the mend, though still worried by financial problems.

What swayed the jury was suspect emotional evidence used to construct the myth of a cold and heartless woman. The judge not only allowed this, but actually let the detectives plead the Fifth Amendment, when asked questions about the circumstances of the filming of the silly string incident, without putting it into the context of two hours of filming of the service and burial which revealed the mother's true grief? This left a damning image in the minds of ten of the jurors.

Sex hormones and Stefan Kiszko

With Stefan Kiszko we also see that for reasons that are unclear, the investigating police confused the unusual with the criminal. Here was a man who had recently been extremely ill, from severe anaemia and the long-term consequences of severe testicular deficiency. He had been treated in hospital, and recently started on a lower dose of testosterone replacement than normal. His doctor (one of the authors) had repeatedly told the authorities that all this would do was arouse normal sex urges. This is because criminal behaviour depends on the structure of the brain, which develops *in utero* and childhood; it is not caused by testosterone, which is the natural hormone, acting on a normal brain. Testosterone, of course, may be a trigger for increased sexual activity, but does not, as was it seems also believed by defence barrister David Waddington, produce deviant and vicious behaviour against an innocent child.

Instead, Lesley Molseed had been abducted and murdered by a man engaging in criminal sexual behaviour, and we now know that targeting and assaulting small children was part of a pattern in his life. Yet the police, following leads from other small children, became convinced of Kiszko's guilt, and then set about extracting a false confession from him. Not only this, but they ignored and then suppressed evidence (sperm heads on the girl's clothing) which absolutely proved that Kiszko could not have murdered Lesley Molseed. They also ignored positive physical evidence from two witnesses (Mrs Tong and Mr Coverdale) that was incompatible with Kiszko. This problem was then compounded at Kiszko's trial, when his defence fell into the same trap.

Some conclusions

It is evident from these three cases that when considering crimes, much greater weight should be given in criminal investigations and in courts of law to the possibilities of normal and abnormal biology in relation to reproduction. The reasons for this lie in differences in hormones, physical strength and the reproductive roles of men and women. This has determined the different morphology of males and females, as seen during early fetal life, with a silent period during childhood, and then re-activation to prepare for reproduction at the time of puberty.

Not only are there obvious and dramatic physical differences related to the reproductive tracts of males and females. There are also major differences in how their brains function, and the principal factor that has determined these physical differences is exposure of the developing male brain to high concentrations of testosterone before and immediately after birth. It is exceptionally unusual for women to commit crimes of aggression, and almost unheard of against other women, as we were asked to believe in the murder of Meredith Kercher. In this context, official statistics almost certainly provide an overestimate of violence by women,[3] for the simple reason that many of the less probable ones will also have been mis-convictions. One exception may be women who are on hard or hallucinogenic drugs at the time the crime was committed (as for example in the case in Novi Ligure in Northern Italy when a couple aged 16 and 17 murdered the girl's mother, and her 12-year-old brother[4]).

On the other hand, burglars are normally male, and in a normal society this propensity to burgle defines an individual as anti-social and sometimes also as psychopathic. For Amanda Knox's recently acquired boyfriend Raffaele Sollecito to go along with a violent sexual crime against another woman because of a deep dissatisfaction with consensual sex, as was suggested, is a highly dubious hypothesis. And exposure of a male who has hitherto been deficient in testosterone to this hormone will not change his character, as we were asked to believe in the case of Kiszko. And for a mother to turn on her two beloved children in a fiendish act of violence, because she had concerns about sustaining her lifestyle, as we are asked to believe in the case of Darlie Routier, is vanishingly improbable.

So maybe we have to look elsewhere to understand how such official secondary crimes — that is to say false convictions and imprisonment in the name of the law — can come about. And it seems almost too obvious to have to point out that *they must arise from a combination of abnormalities within the systems that are supposed to protect us, and the people administering those systems.* After all, every person employed in

---

3.   In 2014 19.6 per cent of those arrested for violent crime in the USA were women (https://www.fbi.gov/about-us/cjis/ucr/crime-in-the-u.s/2014/crime-in-the-u.s.-2014/persons-arrested/main). And see Davis, Carol Anne, *Women Who Kill: Profiles of Female Serial Killers*, Alison and Busby, 2002.

4.   See Nerenberg, Ellen, *Murder Made in Italy: Homicide, Media, and Contemporary Italian Culture*, Indiana University Press, 2012.

the police and the law is either male or female, with a strong numerical bias in favour of men. They too are subject to normal human biology of body and brain, of sex and hormones. But the systems they administer may have changed fundamentally little in outlook since medieval times, when they were developed under the influence of religious beliefs most people no longer hold. In Italy during the course of the trial of Amanda Knox and Raffaele Sollecito, the courtroom emblem set high above the judges and jury, was the image of Christ on the cross, dying for our sins. And the chief public prosecutor is an intensely devout Catholic.

There seems to be precious little legal interest in what is actually biologically possible behind crimes of violence. There may also be strong influences resisting changes that are needed in order to re-establish some level of common sense. Unless justice is weighted in favour of the innocent there is little chance of catching the real criminals, and treating them in ways that make the rest of us safer. It is time for us to now examine the age-old time-honoured witch-hunt and its modern-day equivalent; a particularly vicious form of *schadenfreude* that may well enter into the equation when considering unjust prosecutions and convictions.

CHAPTER TEN

Witch-hunts Through the Ages

'Witchcraft is one of the most baseless, absurd, disgusting and silly of all the humbugs.'

P T Barnum, *The Humbugs of the World: An Account of Humbugs, Delusions, Impositions, Quackeries, Deceits and Deceivers Generally in All Ages* (1865).

From shamanism to monotheism and Christianity

Horrific practices of witch-hunting and burning were conducted over hundreds of years in Europe and the USA, including in the name of Christianity. Witchcraft and Shamanism are similar. Shamanism is man's widespread 'primitive' religious practice, and involves a practitioner ('shaman/priest') reaching altered states of consciousness in order to encounter and interact with the spirit world, and channel transcendental energies. A shaman is a person regarded as having access to, and influence in, the world of benevolent and malevolent spirits, who typically enters into a trance during a ritual, and practises divination and healing. Shamanism, doubtless in many forms, was the religion of the Neolithic period. It at least gave equal credit to the roles of men and women; it was not intrinsically misogynistic. Later monotheistic religions, including Christianity, by contrast emphasised the dominance of men and subservience of women. Shamanism was and is highly threatening to other religions.

More than 40 years ago, the academic ancient language researcher and expert on the Dead Sea Scrolls, John Allegro in *The Sacred Mushroom and the Cross* presented radical and controversial linguistic evidence about the origins of Christianity.[1] He reasoned that the many Christian gospels (of which four became accepted into Roman Catholicism) had been written in code so as safely to describe only for the initiated the rituals to be performed before attaining the heightened spiritual state obtained by taking the hallucinogenic mushroom. Allegro did not find favour with the church.

Heresies and the origins of witch-hunting

There is much to indicate that one dominant Christian sect, to the exclusion of the others, was elevated by Constantine to the official religion of Rome. Only four gospels were included, which came to be literally interpreted as historical events. Allegro contended that the mushroom was morphed into the sacrament. Meanwhile, especially in the countryside, the ancient local witchcraft practices continued in their various forms, and as they presented an obvious challenge to Church authority were of necessity ruthlessly suppressed.

Over time, as with all religions, the latter was also confronted with its own schisms, and with the Protestant Reformation and rebellion against the Pope as representative of St Peter and thus Christ on Earth. These and other heresies were dealt with severely. And conversely wherever Protestantism prevailed, believers became engaged in fighting the counter-heresy of Roman Catholicism. Such battles extended right across Europe. They may now seem as nothing compared with the revolution that followed the development of the scientific method, and the evolutionary theories of Charles Darwin that grew out of it. This came to threaten more and more all the known anthropocentric certainties about Man's special place in a Garden of Eden at the centre of the Universe.

The witch-burning epidemic

In 300 years over the fourteenth to seventeenth centuries, predominantly in the countries of North-Western Europe, it is estimated that more than 100,000 people, mostly women, were tried, tortured and put to death for

---

1. John M Allegro, *The Sacred Mushroom and The Cross: A Study of the Nature and Origins of Christianity Within the Fertility Cults of the Ancient Near East* (Anniversary edn. 2009), Gnostic Media Research and Publishing.

supposed witchcraft. In the succeeding half millennium we may be sure of one thing; human nature hasn't changed much, either for better or for worse. Culture has changed enormously, but as naked apes we have not evolved significantly beyond our ancestors who lived many thousands of years before modern civilisation came into being. Therefore it behoves us to look at the events and the people that drove the world's witch-burning craze, and draw any lessons that apply to this day. For example, why were three quarters of the witches who were burned women, and all of the witch-hunters men? And were there features of the witch-hunt in one or more of the three cases of unjust prosecutions we have chosen to examine here? Let us run briefly over the history of witch-hunting and burning in Europe and see what parallels we can find with the cases under consideration. Death by burning, that was so often the mode of execution, was doubtless symbolic of the fires of hell, since witches were supposed to consort with the malevolent world of Satan.

It is quite possible that the reader may not have been persuaded of the innocence of the four innocent people considered in these three murders. Of course, according to the law you (or rather the instrument of the law, the jury) do not have to find them to be innocent, but just *not guilty because there is a reasonable doubt as to their guilt*. You will, we hope, have at the very least accepted the certain innocence of Stefan Kiszko, since the real murderer of Lesley Molseed is now known. It is established beyond doubt that he was Ronald Castree, who has been locked away on the basis of exceptionally strong DNA and other evidence. And we can surely be certain that witchcraft was a figment of the imagination, and therefore that the hundreds of thousands of people convicted and usually killed for creating disasters by communing with the Devil were, to the last woman, innocent of such a charge.

The Black Death and two misogynistic psychopaths

The craze seems to have been started by a natural disaster, the Black Death (c.1343). This was the first and most severe pandemic to hit mankind and is estimated to have reduced the world's population from 450 million in 1343, in ten years to 300 million. We now know that it was caused by the bacterium Yersinia pestis, which is natural to the oriental rat flea, and was spread via the Silk Road and then on merchant ships, by the black rat. Theories of disease in the fourteenth century were primitive, and it was natural to look for scapegoats. It is said that the persecution of women as witches started in Talence in Aquitaine, in 1351; Sophia and her widow mistress Lady Elizabeth who had survived the plague were accused of consorting with the Devil to destroy the town. They were both tortured and then burnt at the stake.

The propensity to hunt witches in Europe thereafter can be laid firmly at the door of two men; the first was Nicholas Eymerich, the ultra-misogynistic Inquisitor General of Aragon, who linked the crimes of heresy and sorcery in his masterwork *Directorium Inquisitorum* (1376). This thesis was to be built upon more than 100 years later, by the likewise misogynistic and psychopathic Dominican priest Heinrich Kramer, who was appointed as Inquisitor for the German provinces just North of the Alps. He worked with, and gained some respectability from, the more moderate academic Jacob Springer of Cologne.

Together they recruited Pope Innocent VIII to issue an edict, which allowed Kramer a free hand to root out witches. In Innsbruck he overstepped his powers, and came to be regarded as a dangerous fanatic. However Kramer, over the next two years (1485–7), composed what was to become the new witch-hunting bible, called *Malleus Maleficarum* or *The Hammer of the Witches* (1486). The advent of the printing press meant that this malicious book achieved best-seller status. In it he explained that most witches are women because their insatiable carnal lust meant they consorted with the Devil. He claimed that they enjoyed the sexual act more than men and were more corruptible. His claim that disbelief in the existence of witches was itself heresy, would in future years be widely used to suppress dissent.

Heinrich Kramer's catch-all formulae

Kramer in *Malleus Maleficarum* itemises all the ways in which the Devil secured his converts, which included midwives who offer newborns to Satan. He poured out his theories in blunt sexual terms, venomously hateful of women. Witches had extensive powers and could raise damaging storms and render animals and humans sterile. They could transport themselves from place to place through the air. They could reveal the future and even remain silent under torture, perhaps the first example of Catch 22: you are guilty if you confess, more so if you don't.

Witches could make women barren and men impotent; and they could turn men into beasts. And Kramer created a veritable catalogue of false reasoning on how to catch witches. The names of witnesses were to be kept secret from the accused. And, in a rule reflected in Perugia (viz use of the charge of *calunnia* by prosecutors against Amanda's parents) any defender must be certain the accusation was unjust, for fear of being prosecuted themselves. And he was past master at describing the use of torture. Confession meant guilt, so anyone who would not confess must be tortured. In order to uncover hidden charms the accused should be stripped naked and then tortured until a confession had been extracted. Amanda and Raffaele were both stripped naked and examined by a doctor immediately after they had been arraigned.

If a charge was not legally proven, as laid down by Kramer, the accused might be released, but should not be declared innocent, so they might be later brought back to court. Do we see a close analogy to the repeated trials *ad infinitum,* possible in 21st century Italy? Even first offenders who abjured their heresy had to perform absolution in public and then be imprisoned for life. The book appeared just as the Protestant Reformation hit Europe, and was widely used as a tool to smash that heresy; but over time it was later adopted under the equally misogynistic Martin Luther as a tool to be used by Protestant clerics against Catholics. It was to become for many years a book that was invaluable to all religious extremists.

Let us consider a few examples that resonate with modern collective extremism. In 1581, the Archbishop of the German town of Trier initiated a campaign against Protestants, Jews and witches, which lasted a decade and decimated the city. It was only ended when the economy collapsed with deaths that included many farmers. We can see an analogy here with the excesses of Mao Tse Tung's 'Great Leap Forward' in the late-1950s when with disastrous consequences steel production was magically augmented by melting ploughshares and other farming implements, and in the process causing famine.

Ten years after the Trier campaign, under a Prince Bishop Balthazar von Dernbach, the city of Falda was subjected to another witch-hunting and burning campaign that led to the deaths of hundreds of people, most of them women. Then the city of Wurtzberg was for eight years, from 1623, subjected to a witch-hunting and burning campaign, by another Catholic Prince-Bishop, Adolf von Ehrenburg. This even included children who were convicted of having intercourse with demons. In a rare piece of enlightenment, one inquisitor, the Jesuit priest Friedrich Spee, who was sent to Wurtzburg, became convinced of the invalidity of confessions obtained under torture. He published a book in 1631, *Cautio Criminalis* or *Precautions for Prosecutors*. This book had some effect in leading to the reduction in witch burning in Europe.

In Tracy Borman's book *Witches: A Tale of Sorcery, Scandal and Seduction*[2] she tells of two sisters, Margaret and Phillipa Flower, who were hanged for witchcraft in Lincoln, England, in 1619. They had been interrogated and had made a full confession. Witchcraft confessions tended to follow a common pattern, because (as we saw in 1975 with Stefan Kiszko) inquisitors dictated what they wanted to hear and prisoners were too terrified not to assent. It is probable that the minority of burned witches who were men were ones who had the guts to defend innocent women, the primary target of CNE prosecutors.

The modern-day witch trial of Amanda Knox

On the night of November 5th/6th 2007, after her boyfriend and alibi had first been softened-up by tough questioning, Amanda Knox was interrogated for nine continuous hours overnight. Knox eventually told the police what they wanted to hear. In the words of chief investigator Edgardo Giobbi, 'She told us what we knew to be true' — in other words, she repeated the theory police had 'cobbled together' — that her boss Patrick Lumumba was the murderer. This confirms that interrogations produced the outcome that the interrogators desired, not the truth.

Prosecutor Mignini's initial preferred murder scenario appears to have been that Amanda had directed others to join with her and kill Meredith

---

2. Jonathan Cape, 2013.

Kercher in a satanic ritual. The murder, after all, happened the night after Halloween, and he postulated that the date slipped because of another appointment. How little times have changed! This theme guaranteed immediate and continuing worldwide media interest. We should not, however, forget the evidence that we have considered concerning the need to cover the role of Rudy Guede as sole perpetrator; and the police in failing to control activities they already knew about. As with medieval crimes and natural disasters, the witch is the natural default suspect. At the time of the Kercher murder Mignini was already under investigation for abuse of office, accused of orchestrating an illegal wiretapping operation as he attempted to pursue the 'Monster of Florence' (MOF)[3] — a serial killer who has never been caught. In a series of hastily targeted actions, multiple men had been repeatedly accused, convicted and released. Mignini came onto the scene with his Investigative Group for Serial Crimes (GIDES) collaborator Michele Giuttari in 2001, 16 years after the last of the seven double MOF murders.

From the outset he took his lead from an unusual source, one Gabriella Carlizzi, a 'psychic medium' blogger who shared a passion for conspiracy theories involving criminal and satanic Masonic sects. She had as her particularly reliable source, a priest who had died 25 years previously, but to whom she still talked! She told Mignini that the murders were part of a Masonic conspiracy to obtain female genital body parts during the act of sex, for black masses by the mythical Order of the Red Rose. The dead priest's vendetta extended to 21 of the good and the great of Perugia. The theory was that one Francesco Narducci, a young gastro-enterologist and son of a famous gynaecologist and prominent Freemason, had been murdered by drowning because he knew too much. His death was a few days after the last Monster of Florence murder. In fact a great deal of evidence points to suicide in a young man who had a pethidine addiction and marital problems, and had recently been transferred (really demoted) to work in Foligno.

---

3. This was the accusation. It should be stressed that he was only convicted of the lesser charge of exceeding the powers of his office (https://en.wikipedia.org/wiki/Giuliano_Mignini). This itself was later overturned in Florence on a technicality, and referred for retrial to Turin. Such is justice in Italy!

Narducci was an exact contemporary of Mignini. For a time they were in the same class at school. Accounts from that time show Narducci as a dashing young boy and man, sought after by the girls, and good at sports. It seems strange that this boyhood connection is never mentioned in the local press; yet our personal psychopathologies become well cemented during childhood. Convincing contemporary accounts by pharmacists, boatmen and others, indicate that Narducci had gone off on the fatal date with lethal amounts of pethidine and was alone in a boat when he fell in the water and drowned. Nevertheless, Mignini's theory seeks to present the death as a murder involving a powerful conspiracy. For more on this grim 'fairytale,' see Preston and Spezi's book *The Monster of Florence*.

Arthur Miller defines the witch-burning phenomenon

In 1952 Arthur Miller published his powerful play *The Crucible,* an exploration of the witch trials in Salem, Massachusetts in 1693. Comparisons were made with the activities of Senator Joseph McCarthy and his attacks on Communists in the USA in the Cold War, which similarly relied on accusations rather than evidence. Miller's point was not only that the phenomenon of the witch hunt can take different forms but also that it has never gone away, however 'civilised' we think we are.

Forty years after the age of McCarthy and Miller, witch-hunts returned to America and Europe in the form of child abuse scandals, this time, as with McCarthy, involving mainly men, rather than women. One of the largest of these was centred on Bryn Estyn, then a children's home in Wrexham, North Wales. A massive operation began in 1991 and continued for ten years. Thousands of people were accused and hundreds were arrested as the investigation eventually extended throughout the UK. Some of the accused were guilty and were rightly convicted, but once the crusade started, no one was safe. Police and prosecutors 'trawled' for new victims by advertising in newspapers, encouraging former residents to identify and accuse more perpetrators. The 'victims' were promised compensation if a prosecution succeeded. Understandably, there was no shortage of men coming forward. Some were awarded tens of thousands of pounds by criminal injuries tribunals, but their stories would later be exposed as bogus.

The reach of the Bryn Estyn saga was so wide and lengthy that over two decades later it even encompassed Conservative party grandee, Lord McAlpine, who was in 2012, falsely accused by the BBC of being involved in child abuse at the home. He successfully sued for libel. Richard Webster, a cultural historian, followed the scandal and proved that most of the allegations were false. His book, *The Secret of Bryn Estyn: The Making of a Modern Witch Hunt* was published in 2005.[4]

Webster not only debunked the scandal, he also explained how and why witch-hunts still happen, why they have an irresistible fascination for the public and how the media relies on them to fire-up readers and boost circulation.

Witch-hunts continue today

There remains a general assumption that witch-hunts are historical phenomena and that in the modern-age science and reason has consigned them to history. Nothing could be further from the truth as Webster explained in his book:

'The demonological anti-Semitism of the Christian middle ages or the great European witch-hunt of the sixteenth and seventeenth centuries were, according to this perspective, terrible aberrations from the path of progress; they belong to the childhood of humankind rather than to the state of rational maturity we have now reached. Witch-hunts are things that happen in other countries or other eras than our own. We have passed beyond them.'

He continued by explaining that such a view of human progress is 'not only mistaken but dangerous,' something that the history of twentieth-century Europe certainly offers no evidence to support it. Both modern European anti-Semitism and Stalin's purges involved the persecution or annihilation of entire groups of human beings imagined as "evil" or "unclean." Following an explanation of the origins of anti-Semitism, he

---

4. Extracts from *The Secret of Bryn Estyn* are used with the permission of the estate of Richard Webster. It is published by Orwell Press, see also http://www.richardwebster.net/secret.html

moved on to describe witchcraft more specifically in words that uncannily predict the treatment that was to be projected onto Amanda Knox:

'Projecting feelings we experience as alien onto those whom we define as alien is one of the ways in which we attempt to get rid of them. The process of demonising cultural enemies is, in this sense, entirely normal. It is also dangerous. Whenever we allow any group of human beings to be demonised, the anxieties associated with our dreams of purity throughout history will almost inevitably be brought into play; we will begin to imagine the group in question in the same terms which are found in other demonological fantasies.'

Webster also explained that witch-hunts were not the creation of the mob; on the contrary, they were often initiated and sustained by the actions of those at the top of society, for their own ends. We have already seen this with the works of Eyrich and of Kramer.

Belief fosters invention

So we see that what Webster describes (if the theory is correct) fits neatly the CNE prosecutorial mind-set and explains that the people we should fear the most are those who may be both deluded and also have the power to act by enslaving the innocent with the collusion of those they control. Delusions are especially effective when they have been constructed in the mind(s) of a person or persons totally lacking in empathy and working within a system created in their own image.

'By turns fascinated and horrified by its vivid sexual content, many of those who were called upon, some three centuries ago, to scrutinise evidence of witchcraft, suspended their critical judgment. They unsceptically accepted accounts of crimes which were unlikely or impossible and came to believe unreservedly that they had discovered solid evidence for an evil conspiracy which did not in fact exist.'

He explained that whenever demonological fantasies are allowed to develop in our midst, 'there is always a danger that the same process of self-delusion may take place over again and [we] may begin unwittingly to "create" the very evidence [needed] to intensify this fantasy.' Webster added that such individuals and groups come to believe their own lies. Thus, did he unknowingly set the scene for what we suggest was another modern witch-hunt, this time thousands of miles away in Italy, with fewer characters than the other examples we have cited, but with a world-wide audience greater than any since McCarthy. So Kramer's *Malleus Maleficarum*, is arguably alive and well, applied in spirit if not in word. As discussed earlier in this chapter, few would have difficulty now in recognising Kramer as a dangerous and intelligent primary psychopath, a religious fanatic, who exploited his particular Christian misogyny to create his own witch-burning precursor of *Mein Kampf.*

For this kind of phenomenon to take hold there are two requirements: an imaginative source and a willing and gullible means of transmission. The scenario we believe to have existed is that Mignini was the source; in control of the evidence and crime scene investigation and with his years of practice a master at working alongside and briefing a compliant media. Without lazy journalists and greedy media owners, theories such as this would never gain traction. Webster explained that it is in the personification of evil and its use by the medieval church that the seeds of witch-hunts were sown and it is a deeply held belief in the power of evil as a tangible force that motivates zealots to pursue their crusades, convincing, even deluding, themselves and others in the process.

The prosecutorial psyche revealed

Author Nina Burleigh lived in Perugia while she researched her book, *The Fatal Gift of Beauty*. The *New York Post* printed a summary on October 2nd 2011 that included the following points:

'The story of Amanda Knox in Italy is of media, misogyny, mistranslation, misbehaviour—but chiefly superstition. Kercher's death was a terrible but simple act of sexual aggression against a young woman in her home. Yet while a prosecutor in the United States might see only the forensic evidence, the motives and the opportunity—the small-town Italian prosecutor Giuliano Mignini saw something more. It was a Halloween crime, and that was one of the first clues to register with Mignini, called to the crime scene fresh from celebrating All Souls' Day, a day when proper Italian families visit their dead. And on {the] scene was a pale, light-eyed 20-year-old girl who, prosecutors said in their closing arguments last week, had the look of a "she-devil."'

According to Burleigh, as late as October 2008, a year after the murder, Mignini told a court that the murder 'was premeditated and was in addition a "rite" celebrated on the occasion of the night of Halloween. A sexual and sacrificial rite [that] in the intention of the organizers ... should have occurred 24 hours earlier'—on Halloween itself—'but on account of a dinner at the house of horrors, organized by Meredith and Amanda's Italian flatmates, it was postponed for one day. It is hard to see how his colleagues and fellow prosecutors and Judge Massei can in all seriousness have allowed such prejudicial matters to enter court records; yet they did.'

Burleigh continues that to understand Mignini's worldview, to get what he saw when he looked at the crime scene at Hallowtide, on a Thursday night, and to see what led him to think of a woman leading a sex game, we must dig far back into the history of the long battle of Catholicism versus alternative spirituality in Italy and know its signs and symbols as well as he does. She goes on to explain the influence of the Masons in Perugia, Mignini's ambivalence towards them and their habits of bizarre one-footed rituals:

> 'Mignini was very familiar with this Masonic ritual. At 7 Via della Pergola, the home of Meredith and Amanda, the track of single bloody shoe prints was evidence enough of their involvement.'

Evil as a force
Burleigh continues:

> 'Mignini was also comfortable with the notion that his Catholic Church still battles the forces of paganism, and chief among the church's traditional pagan foes was an old cult in Italy that revered the fertility goddess Diana. Italian women executed as witches in the 1300s said they followed a

"lady of the game" into the forest, where they practiced animal transforma-
tion, becoming beasts that could fly, and travelled long distances, entering
houses through windows and walls, drinking wine, leaving behind faeces,
and waking up in their own beds the next morning unsure of how they'd
gotten home.'

So whether Burleigh is right or wrong, she suggests that Mignini
didn't just use witchcraft legends, to bolster his case, he may actually
have believed that witches are abroad today, are a force in the world and
that evil is a power as real as electricity, exuded by the Devil, and that
people like Amanda Knox and Raffaele Sollecito are his agents. In his
own words, Amanda was 'a diabolical, satanic, demonic she-devil' who
'likes alcohol, drugs and hot, wild sex'. In 2008, *The Times* reported
that the prosecuting team believed Knox had killed Kercher as part of a
'perverse game of group sex' and 'some kind of satanic rite.'

In the *New York Post:*

'It was a Halloween crime, and that was one of the first clues to register
with Mignini, called to the crime scene fresh from celebrating All Souls'
Day, a day when proper Italian families visit their dead...Mignini always
included witch fear in his murder theory, and only reluctantly relinquished
it...the point is this: there is no grand conspiracy of Satan-worshippers.
It is a myth, created by a certain kind of highly active religious imagination. There are no Black Masses where human sacrifices or dark sexual
games on blood-soaked altars take place. There are a few sad fantasists who
daub pentagrams on things...Once you know that, you know that the case
against Amanda Knox could not be what it seemed.'

Evidence? 'Well, she was sexually active, they said and had a sex toy,'
reported Timothy Egan in the New York Times. 'I half-expected prosecutors to throw Knox in a tank of water to see if she sank or floated, *a
la* the Salem witch trials. If all the attention to the Knox episode makes
people take a second to look at other questionable cases,' said Egan, 'then
perhaps the tide from Perugia will lift other boats.'

The witchcraft delusion extends to others

Joan Smith in a *Guardian* 'Comment is Free' blog posted just before the 2011 acquittal, parodied a scenario that most would have thought beyond parody if the possible outcome had not been so serious. She pointed out the extent to which Mignini's colleagues had believed his fantasy:

> 'Here are the news headlines for 1486: in the fair city of Perugia, a she-devil hath falsely accused an inn-keeper of murder most vile ... Sorry, let me start again. This isn't the 15ᵗʰ century, when "witches" were being hunted all over Europe, tortured into confessing and burned at the stake. In 2011, no one seriously believes that women go mad with lust and sell their souls to the devil—or do they?...Astonishingly, exactly that accusation has been made in an Italian court this week by Patrick Lumumba's a lawyer called Carlo Pacelli. He used the occasion of an appeal by American student Amanda Knox against her conviction for the murder of a British student to call her an "enchanting witch" and attack her in terms that would be instantly recognisable to a mediaeval witch-finder.'

The sexist nature of the witchcraft fantasy

The idea that women are natural liars has a long pedigree. Kramer's *Malleus Maleficarum* unleashed a flood of irrational beliefs about women's 'dual' nature. 'A woman is beautiful to look upon, contaminating to the touch, and deadly to keep,' the authors warned. The book claimed that '[A]ll witchcraft comes from carnal lust, which is in women insatiable'.

> 'You might imagine that the crime for which Knox and her then boyfriend, Raffaele Sollecito, were convicted in 2009 was unpleasant enough without dragging in a lot of medieval mumbo-jumbo'...Pacelli's...outburst brought into the open a strain of irrationality and misogyny that exists as an undercurrent in many headline-grabbing criminal cases. Behind such insinuations—regardless of whether the woman in question is a victim or a perpetrator—lie irrational and indeed medieval assumptions about the untrustworthiness of women. The *Malleus* traces this "fault" all the way back to Adam and Eve, claiming that woman was created from a "bent" rib and

is therefore defective: And since through this defect she is an imperfect animal, she always deceives.'

Total control

In Italy the prosecutor is the leader of the investigation. He or she can direct the police as he or she wishes, direct the activities of the crime scene investigation team and supervise the press releases. He or she can start with a simple but tragic burglary and murder case, add on unrestrained accusations and conclude with a 'cartoon recreation.' In John Follain's pro-guilt book he records with no trace of irony:

> The film was (Assistant Prosecutor) Comodi's idea. When she realised the film's potential, she decided to show the entire reconstruction. For most people what you see on TV exists; what you don't see on TV doesn't exist.'

Four years later she was brought by the prosecutor of the Supreme Court before the Disciplinary Committee of the Judiciary (the CSM) for having created this film (made by a firm named *Nventa*, at a cost of 182,000 Euros). She was, however, judged to be not guilty of the charges (viz: irrelevance, prejudicing proceedings or wasting public funds). Even light sanctions, requested because of her excellent record, were rejected by the CSM.[5]

Almost all will agree that nobody should be tried as a witch, in a case defined by superstition, misogyny or fantasy. Attention-grabbing but misleading details can, as we have explained, become embedded and impossible to discount, except by trained professionals, no matter how many later retractions, corrections or assurances that such seeds should not have been planted earlier.

---

5. See http://www.lanazione.it/umbria/cronaca/2013/12/06/993004-meredith-processo-ccomodi-pm-assolta.shtml

CHAPTER ELEVEN

Witnesses, Evidence and Forensic Science

It is increasingly recognised that there is in all jurisdictions a crisis in how courts evaluate and use evidence; and that defects in the system lie behind many miscarriages of justice. Science has been responsible for the incredible advances in knowledge and technology over the past four centuries, so let us start by examining what is meant by 'the scientific method', and consider what this means when it comes to solving crimes.

The scientific method

The scientific method involves techniques for investigating phenomena, acquiring new knowledge, and integrating it with existing knowledge. It starts from a previous knowledge base with a new hypothesis about a particular phenomenon; then makes predictions that follow from that hypothesis; it then tests those predictions, and in the light of the results refines the hypothesis. It is a common sense method of getting to the truth, of which in most of our everyday actions we are unaware. But it is absolutely central to all forms of science.

An important element of any scientific hypothesis is that it must be falsifiable, that is, there must be a possible set of experimental results that if present will demonstrate that it is wrong. Scientists, being human, are susceptible to the same faults as others. Suppose that a scientist comes up with a brilliant idea; being human, he or she has thereafter a vested interest in that idea. He or she thought of it and if it turns out to be correct will bask in the glory of appreciative colleagues (and possibly make lots of money).

So the originator of a particular hypothesis now has a vested emotional interest in it being proved correct; the extent to which this colours his or her objective judgment varies from person to person. But he or she is inevitably subject to the pressures of confirmation bias; the strong temptation is to see only results that support the hypothesis and to ignore ones that oppose it. This means that *the scientist is professionally bound to follow the scientific method and construct experiments that are aimed at proving himself or herself wrong*. If as a result of these his or her hypothesis is confirmed, others in that field are then obliged to carry out further experiments designed to confirm whether or not this is the truth. And a vital element of all such experiments is that the observer must be blinded to the results, and that controls are carried out which will show whether or not the results are valid, and not due for example to chance, contamination or fraud.

Forensic science

The word 'forensic' refers to scientific tests or techniques used in connection with the detection of crime. It is, however, also quite differently defined as the presentation of argument, suitable for courts of justice to come to a judgment. Forensic science is the recognition, collection, identification, and interpretation of physical evidence, and its application for criminal and civil legal purposes among others.

It should go without saying that in a court of law the same rules need to be applied to the evaluation of scientific evidence that may incriminate or exonerate the accused. Since all other evidence received by the court is by definition soft (except physical exhibits), it is of particular importance that putative hard scientific evidence is what it claims to be. That means that the methods must have been validated and approved by the relevant body of scientists, and steps taken to ensure that the evidence so derived does not get distorted by prosecutorial (or defence) sleight of hand. The prosecutorial method is the very antithesis of the scientific method, as it seeks to verify the hypothesis at all costs, and not to falsify it. When we look at forensic methods in practice we can immediately see some major potential problems, of which there are highly illustrative examples in the three main cases examined in this book.

The vital importance of high quality, uncontaminated crime scene data

An essential starting point for solving a crime of violence must be the collection of reliable data, because if this is not carried out with meticulous care, any conclusions drawn from it will be worthless. At the start must be a rigorous scientific technique, and attendant documentation as applied to samples obtained from the crime scene must be comprehensive and accurate. To yield valid conclusions this evidence must be collected and then stored in a manner that should be demonstrably beyond reproach and free from confirmation bias.

This means that the initial evaluation of a crime scene has to be thorough, done by properly trained professionals; and shown to be so by objective recording. Rigorous internationally accepted protocols must be in place to establish that essential evidence is collected and documented with the maximum chance of allowing the crime itself to be reconstructed. This should ensure that the chances of the perpetrator(s) being caught are maximised, and the risk of pinning the crime on any innocent person minimised.

This can only be done once, at the beginning, after which *the crime scene must be officially and permanently closed*. It cannot subsequently be revisited on the whim of the prosecutor, as happened in the Kercher murder, in order to cherry-pick a sample that had been missed, or that had been judged by the same evaluators as insignificant in the first place unless the entire circumstances are fully explained.[1] It also follows that the evidence must be collected and then stored according to a pre-ordained protocol for that sort of crime (for example a rape or a particular murder), and done independently of any pet theory the collector of evidence has developed as to the identity of the perpetrator.

The job of the crime scene investigator is therefore to collect evidence, not to seek support for a policeman's or prosecutor's hunch. It therefore follows that the collection and evaluation of crime scene evidence should be independent of other aspects of the investigation. Otherwise there is

---

1. A number of serious crimes have in fact been solved by crime scene officers returning to the scene and locating DNA, in one murder case where specks of blood had been painted over. The point is that everyone needs to be assured that contamination has been not possible; DNA-testing may, e.g. disprove an alibi.. For an example see *The Cardiff Five*, Sekar S (2012), Waterside Press.

a risk that it will be contaminated, as we have seen happened in these three cases, as a direct or indirect result of someone higher up the chain of command wishing to achieve or confirm a particular result towards which he or she had an intrinsic or potential bias.

Anyone obstructing the collection of evidence (such as blocking measurement of the temperature of a corpse, as happened in the Perugia murder) should be subject to sanctions. It surely follows that the forensic science laboratory itself, and all those tasked with collecting evidence, should work independently of the police and the courts; and those working at all stages of the process need to be shielded from bias.

The role of science in the trial process itself

Let us consider first a trial following the adversarial system, as applies in the UK and the USA, and now notionally in Italy. The trial comes as the endgame of an investigative process, but even if evidence has been collected to the highest standard, we are no longer dealing with the world of objective scientists and the scientific method.

Rather we are facing untidy remnants of bygone judicial systems, more divining than scientific in nature, that have ostensibly been revamped to incorporate elements of modern science. Notionally the trial is supposed to come at the end of a system intended to find the truth, after an extensive filtration process has led to a particular individual being in dock. In England and Wales the test in practice is that the Crown Prosecution Service (CPS) proceeds only if there is evidence of every ingredient of the offence as legally defined and prosecution is in the public interest — the CPS works on the basis that there must be at least a 50 per cent chance of securing a conviction. The prosecutor then acts as an advocate on behalf of the prosecution, and so has a vested professional interest in securing a conviction of the person or persons on trial. Lawyers for the defence have a vested interest in the opposite outcome. Mixed in with the question of justice is therefore the professional question of the conflicting reputations of two sets of lawyers. The judge is supposed to act as an impartial administrator of the law, and (in a criminal case) the jury is the final arbiter. The jury's decision is crucial, since it represents the judicial black hole from which return is extremely difficult. Yet the jury is not an individual with individual responsibilities, but a collection of individuals, many of whom as we have suggested might rather be elsewhere.

What follows in court is the determination of 'judicial truth', which as we have seen may be far removed from real (scientific) truth. True, there are elements of scientific proof that enter the trial process, but these are inevitably contaminated not just by the atmosphere of the crime scene but by the procedures and formality of court. One particularly severe problem is the grossly variable levels of reliability of what can be presented to a judge and jury under the general mantle of evidence.

Intrinsic unreliability of certain forms of evidence

Much of what passes in court as intuitively credible evidence, is in fact highly unreliable. This includes eye-witness identification, evidence from prison snitches, and confessions, which separately and together featured high on the list of reasons for convicting people later shown to be innocent by DNA analysis as a result of the Innocence Project in the USA. We have considered these in *Chapter 8*, but it is worth touching on them again here.

Considering first the eyewitness; one would think that a woman who has been raped by a stranger should be able to recognise her attacker, but this assumption has been shown even at the best of times to be highly unreliable. Conventionally the witness is given a series of individuals (men obviously) or a series of photographic images and asked to make a choice. Of course with eight people on an identity parade (seven fillers and one the suspect) there is at least a one in eight chance of 'correct' identification. In fact it is likely to be much higher than this if there are some obviously irrelevant choices that do not fit the witness's description. And it is made more so if the person organizing the identification parade — be it photographic, or by the classic physical line-up — is aware who the suspected rapist on parade actually is. Non-verbal indication of the 'right' answer is easily transmitted by someone on purpose or inadvertently by subtle clues. Thereafter it is well-established that a woman who is initially uncertain about a man's identity, will become more certain with the passage of time and repetition. So what the court sees is the end-product of a process of reinforcement and finally perhaps even the implantation of false memories.

The prison snitch usually comes forward to say that a fellow prisoner has privately confessed to a crime, and that he or she has decided to do his or her duty and pass this information on to the authorities. Such a witness is obviously to be regarded as intrinsically suspect or unreliable. The fact that he or she is a convicted criminal casts doubt upon his or her honesty, and furthermore he or she has possible motives for cooperating with those in authority. In the discussion about Edward Wayne Edwards, America's recently identified most prolific serial killer (*Chapter 7*), we have seen that he was past master at this, and used it to falsely identify men to be convicted of murders he had carried out. In return he got his sentence reduced, which made him free to leave and kill again.

That is not to say that a 'prison snitch' may not on occasions actually be telling the truth about a fellow-inmate, but that the motive for doing so is intrinsically suspect, especially if in return he or she has been offered a more lenient sentence, or some other incentive to 'help' with an investigation. But the snitch in prison is not the only potentially suspect witness. There are plenty of dubious potential snitches outside prison; petty drug dealers and tramps on the fringes of criminality, willing to come forward to provide evidence against someone else if they see that it might help them; testimony in exchange, for example, for more lenient treatment by the police.

Antonio ('Toto') Curatolo, the bench-sleeping self-styled born again anarchic Christian heroin addict flaunted by the prosecutor as a key witness in *Caso Meredith* (*Chapter 2*), falls into this category. In his case he was 'found' by a trainee journalist who worked for the *Giornale dell'Umbria*, a newspaper that stood out among a guilt-leaning Italian press. Not only did it take six months for Curatolo to be 'found', but this was the third murder case in which his testimony was used to convict someone. By any normal criteria he was never remotely credible as a witness. A question mark hangs over the judges during the preliminary hearings and later, who repeatedly considered his testimony to be valid. Clearly there is something unjustly inflexible about the power the trial judge at each level of the process possesses.

Two other groups considered in our three illustrative cases fall into the category of 'suspect' witnesses. The first are the various children, who we saw used to provide evidence against Stefan Kiszko. In the immediate aftermath of Lesley Molseed's murder there was a state of 'moral panic', arising from the horror that there was a sexual predator and murderer of innocent children on the loose. The children who testified against Kiszko had been witnesses to what was perceived as the sort of behaviour (genital exposure) that was expected of a paedophile killer. Thus it was believed (without any evidence) that as a prelude to an abduction and attack such a man would have exposed himself to others — young girls — in the age group of the murdered girl. Children are in any case highly suggestible, and liable in a moral panic to try to be overly helpful. In this case there can be little doubt, from later admissions of these now ex-children, that one of them had invented the story in order to get a kick — and the others had made a story up 'just for a lark'. For them it was a game. In reality, whether it had been true or false, it had no conceivable relevance to the murder of Lesley Molseed. However to the police it fitted with their (incorrect) image of the sort of man they were looking for. This error was then compounded at the trial by Kiszko's half-hearted defence, whose counsel should have spotted that it was both irrelevant and highly prejudicial. Finally the judge regarded it as important and commended the children in court, supporting its role in Kiszko's false conviction.

The second type of unreliable witness is the person with an implanted false memory, such as the witnesses to the supposed scream made by Meredith Kercher at the moment when she was attacked. An elderly lady, living within a stone's throw of the murder house, awoke at around 11 pm to empty her bladder, and heard a scream through double glazed windows. She reported this to the authorities many months later; she became more certain with the passage of time. And because the prosecution put her forward as a reliable witness and she was obviously an honest person, this was accepted by the court as valid witness testimony as to the time of death.

Evidence of a scream in itself was largely irrelevant; since though it adds to the perceived drama it hardly matters whether during a violent attack the victim does or does not emit a scream. But we were told (it was not recorded) that Amanda had also imagined a scream when she was interrogated on the night of 5th/6th November five days after Meredith's murder. This construct by a girl under severe stress was used in a circular manner to argue that Meredith had in fact screamed. Then months later, a witness comes forward to testify that she heard such a scream, and this was used to pinpoint the time of death; this by the same professionals whose action had prevented the pathologist making temperature recordings necessary actually and forensically to pinpoint the time of death. There is real science behind the use of serial temperature readings on a corpse to back-extrapolate to the time of death.

Tampering with witnesses

Witnesses can be tampered with in many ways to influence the outcome of a murder trial. In the Routier case, it seems the recording of Darlie's distraught and obviously exculpatory telephone call to the police immediately after the attack was never played to the court. Instead, coaching of the hospital witnesses—nursing staff and doctors—appears to have occurred, from the disparity between written records in the notes (which also showed a highly distraught mother) and what was said in court. When interviewed by police, and supposedly calm and lacking in emotion, Darlie was under sedation with strong tranquillisers. Those staff members who stuck with the truth were not called to testify. And other forms of technical tampering can also occur. For example also in this case, all but one of the family members who would have testified as character witnesses for Darlie were cited by the prosecution as possible witnesses in the murder trial, and so were excluded from attending the trial. This included Darlie's mother, sister, and her in-laws. The prosecution who had blocked their attendance then failed to call them to give evidence. So the prosecution greatly reduced the direct and indirect support of important character witnesses.

We have seen in the case of Stefan Kiszko that the police were at best in error in failing to recognise the importance of calling Christopher Coverdale, the lorry driver who had seen Lesley Molseed being helped up a slope on a remote highway within minutes of her death by the real murderer. The existence of this witness was almost certainly withheld from the defence. A weak defence also meant that the girls whose witness statements were often contradictory were not cross-examined in court.

In the Perugia murder case, it seems to us to be clear from the official transcript of Rudy Guede's interrogation by the public prosecutor that he was being coached, and words put into his mouth; when he failed to give the 'right' answers there was a ten-minute break in the interrogation. It was a legal technicality, which allowed Guede's statements in a so-called fast-track trial, and later appeals, to be used against Knox and Sollecito, without allowing them to face their accuser. This in turn was reminiscent of the judge allowing two police officers in Darlie's case to plead the Fifth Amendment as if they themselves were on trial; and then to withhold this extraordinary fact, highly prejudicial to the police account, from the jury whose job was to decide between guilt and innocence, life and death.

Undue weight given to a confession, even if retracted

The natural human reaction on being told that a suspect has confessed to a crime is to accept it as the truth. And this is not changed in most people's minds by a later retraction, as we saw with Stefan Kiszko. Police and prosecutors know that juries hold confessions in high regard. It is a simple fact that normal people under normal circumstances cannot imagine any condition in which under pressure they would confess to something they had not done. We just don't believe we would ever buckle under psychological or even physical pressure. We believe that the only answers we would give for example under the notorious technique of 'water-boarding', and other forms of torture, are true ones. And everyone trusts professionals not to have fed the accused with information only the perpetrator would know. When that happens, as was the case with Stefan Kiszko, we know the police must have settled on an innocent person.

Every rule, of course, has its exceptions. Strangely, and in keeping with the concept of *dietrologia* (that is, that the obvious explanation that fits the facts is too simple to be true), it sometimes suits prosecutors in Italy not to accept a spontaneous confession at face value.

They will argue a confession both ways, reminiscent of the old Catch 22 test for witches. For example in the case of the murder in Puglia in 2010 of 15-year old Sarah Scazzi, months later her uncle took police to where he had 'found' Sarah's mobile phone. Shortly afterwards he took them to the well in which he had disposed of Sarah's remains by tying her body by the legs and suspending her far into the well. He then confessed to having murdered her himself. He is a man, and most murders of attractive young women are by men with a sexual motive. This highly probable sequence, however, was apparently too simple for the (female) prosecutor, and at the time of writing the court has instead found Sarah's Aunt and 22-year old female cousin (who both claim total ignorance and innocence) guilty of murder, and has condemned them to life imprisonment.

Instead of accepting the evidence backing the genuineness of the uncle's confession, they have now charged him with a strangely Italian crime of 'auto-calunnia'; that is to say slandering himself. This, they claim, was done to cover up for the murder of Sarah by two women with whom she apparently had a good rapport! Do they not know that the vast majority of sexually motivated crimes of violence against young women are by disturbed adult males? It seems that common sense is not a pre-requisite for Italian prosecutors, who if push comes to shove can, of course, always appeal to their own authority.

The question of the paid court expert

Of particular danger is the question of the self-proclaimed expert, whose opinion is often vested with an oracular authority before a judge and especially a lay jury. Just as we have seen with science, it is not sufficient for supposed experts to express opinions that masquerade as real scientific data. A particular danger derives from the recurrent court expert, since even if he sets out to be objective, at the back of his mind there is constant nagging pressure, from the financial motive, to please his paymaster. Forensics is swamped with self-defined experts, who are known and repeatedly used as prosecutorial hired guns to testify on techniques that have not been scientifically validated. A golden rule should be applied that experts should only be called upon to present evidence of techniques that have been shown to be valid by controlled scientific experiments, and are accepted as such by the relevant scientific community.

Unfortunately experts appointed by the prosecution almost always give a biased slant, and that is even when they are testifying on genuine scientific data, such as DNA profiles. But there are even more dubious techniques which do not even at their best fulfil these criteria; these include blood spatter analysts, handwriting analysis, lie detector tests, bite mark analysis, hair microscopic analysis, and all sorts of prints from ears down to feet and shoes. The blood spatter evidence by Tom Bevel that helped to convict Darlie Routier and David Camm is a case in point. Such witnesses are always helpful to the prosecution, and so will be called upon in the sure knowledge they will support the prosecution theory.

Filming all aspects of the collection of evidence

It can be argued that evidence, whatever its nature, is only valid if it can be shown to have been collected properly. Therefore objectivity must be brought into the process of gathering evidence. Digital cameras are now inexpensive, and easy to use, and provide a formal record that can also be assessed by others. So it seems obvious that it is critical to film any confession to a crime; first, this should be done as soon as possible after the event, with evidence presented that only the murderer would know. And any subsequent retraction should also be recorded in full. Such a policy is highly likely to reduce the risks of a false confession in the first place, since the use of any form of coercion should be evident from the film of the interrogation.

It is clearly also of great importance to film the collection of evidence at the crime scene. This was in fact done in the case of Meredith Kercher, and showed appallingly sloppy technique, consistent with a very poor level of forensic or scientific training. More worrying is that in Court this didn't seem to matter, at least to the prosecution. This speaks of a deeply ingrained level of arrogance, which was also evident by very little evidence of disciplining of the prosecution even in matters of simple courtesy and respect to the accused. In the case against Amanda Knox and Raffaele Sollecito it is claimed by the public prosecutor that their interrogation on the night of 5th/6th November 2007 was not recorded, and the reason given was shortage of funds! The spurious nature of this claim is further highlighted by the fact that the Public Prosecutor sees nothing wrong with bringing a *calunnia* charge against Knox (which was eventually thrown out by a judge in Florence in 2016) for saying that she was struck by a female police officer during the course of this same interrogation.

The official written Court Record (or transcript of the trial) is of great importance, because the jury will often need to refer to it in coming to their verdict. Furthermore, in any subsequent appeal this assumes a major importance. Normally the court stenographer uses shorthand notes, supplemented by a tape recording, to reconstruct an accurate record. In the case of Darlie Routier the court stenographer, who clearly had other things on her mind, made such a bad job of it that later no less than 30,000 substantive errors were found that subsequently had to be corrected. This undoubtedly influenced the result of Routier's appeals, which have to be based on the Court record.

Is DNA now the unassailable forensic flagship of scientific evidence? DNA profiling is without doubt an extremely powerful technique, especially when large amounts of DNA from a single individual are found in residues of an incriminatory body fluid such as blood or semen. Since many crimes of violence by men against women are of a violent sexual nature, DNA profiling is particularly useful where there is semen. Microscopy and specific biological tests will readily identify a stain as originating from a particular body fluid. But the use of the polymerase chain reaction allows for the amplification of miniscule amounts of discriminatory bits of DNA from just a handful of cells. We leave these small amounts in dust and on any surface we touch; so the problem with DNA is that it is easy for contamination, possible at any stage, to undermine its value. This becomes more risky as the technique is pushed to its limits. In a confrontational court of law, we have seen that DNA data is highly susceptible to abuse if not used in a strictly impartial scientific manner.

And where the laboratory is beholden to the prosecution, as we saw in the Kercher murder, impartiality goes out of the window. Detection of a person's DNA at a crime scene does not mean they are the murderer;

but such evidence can easily be distorted, even if the DNA has not been deliberately planted. And we have seen that Prosecutors and their paid witnesses are far from being impartial.

DNA testing of semen stains may demonstrate that a particular individual is innocent, since the semen emitted generally belongs to the murderer. This indeed has been the most powerful tool of the Innocence Project, with most of the more than 300 people released having been through DNA on rape kit specimens. But when using DNA profile to condemn someone, we have to be very careful not to be bamboozled by its very power, and to ignore other strong exculpatory evidence. In the cases in this book we have seen historical forensic freeze frames of the use and abuse of DNA and it is worth going over them here.

Stefan Kiszko was convicted in 1976, on the softest of circumstantial evidence, of having brutally murdered Lesley Molseed on October 5th 1975. Semen stains had been left on her clothing, but this was well before the era of forensic DNA testing. Because Kiszko had defective testes he did not produce sperm and the police knew this, but they had already targeted him. In order to convict him it was necessary for them to suppress the evidence that sperm heads were on the dead girl's clothing. As a result of this duplicity Kiszko served 16 years in prison before, essentially by chance, the lie was exposed and he was released. Meanwhile the real killer had been free to strike again, and had tried to do so at least twice. Thirty years after Lesley's murder, and after Stefan Kiszko's death, the power of DNA had come to the fore; enough sperm heads were present on scotch tape imprints from Lesley's clothes (miraculously still kept by the laboratory) to carry out a DNA profile, and the data went onto the UK's national DNA database. Five years later still Ronald Castree had a buccal sample taken after being accused by a prostitute of violence. A DNA profile was done, put on the matching part of the database, and this revealed a perfect match with that of the historic sample from the sperm on Lesley Molseed's clothing. The jury was convinced at his trial that other evidence was strong enough to back up the powerful nature of such a perfect match, and Castree was finally convicted of her murder.

In the Kercher case, by way of contrast, we saw an extraordinary phenomenon, which must be unique in modern murder cases, in which putative semen stains at the crime scene were not apparently subjected to any testing or a DNA profile! Repeated attempts by the defence at various stages to persuade the court to order such a test were to no avail. Consequently we still do not know for certain whether the sperm came from Rudy Guede or from an unknown male accomplice postulated by the prosecution. (Even Italian prosecutors recognise that a woman can't produce sperm). Yet the same courts spent millions of Euros of Italian taxpayers' money considering DNA profiles taken from a knife that had no rational connection with the murder, and a contaminated bra clasp that was recovered from the crime scene 46 days after the murder, during which time the cottage had been inadequately secured and had been vandalised.

Then finally, in the ongoing case of Darlie Routier, who has been on Death Row in Texas for 19 years, we see the power of the judicial black hole once a case is considered closed. In the USA it is extremely difficult to force the authorities to conduct DNA profiles, for example on the blood-stained sock recovered 75 yards from the crime scene, or a partial finger print left on the table top. The murderer had probably used the sock to clean blood from the two murdered boys off his hands as he escaped. It could provide obvious and powerful exculpatory evidence for Darlie Routier. But then as we have seen, there is much evidence to indicate that the police investigation was not directed at finding the perpetrator of this horrendous murder, but instead to pin it on the nearest available family member. To do this they used a range of bad forensic techniques, concealed exculpatory evidence, put pressure on witnesses, and used illegal filming, in order to deliberately ensnare an unsuspecting mother.

Conclusions

It is increasingly obvious that our legal systems are too often charging and convicting the wrong people for crimes of violence. Our purpose here is to suggest ways in which the system can be strengthened to become fit for purpose. There are several fundamental points to address, regardless of whether the system concerned is adversarial, inquisitorial, or a mixture of both.

First there obviously needs to be much greater recognition of the kinds of individual and collective psychopathology that lead to crimes of violence in the first place, and that may then influence adversely their resolution. We are talking of crimes of aggression, which as we have seen is either reactive or targeted. Only the psychopath, totally lacking in empathy, engages in targeted aggression. Almost all psychopaths in prison are men, for the simple reason that the young men are intrinsically more physically aggressive than women. Likewise anyone is capable, if provoked, of *reacting* aggressively, although thresholds vary and such aggression is more likely to be physically violent in men. Another important consideration is that *targeted* aggression is not necessarily physically violent; the purpose is to damage the other person, but it can take place in the context of the aggressor's area of expertise. Physically violent psychopaths are almost always male, while psychopaths of either sex engage in physically non-violent targeted aggression. This is where the danger lies for any profession, including the law.

So any system should acknowledge the possibility that some of those working within it may themselves be individuals who have grown up with Constitutional Negative Empathy. We refer here to the police, prosecutors, and others who are employed by the rest of us to maintain law and order. Such individuals live behind a mask of sanity and superficial charm, but lack conscience and have a strong propensity to create systems in their own image.

The press, as with all corporations, functions as a collective psychopath, and so is readily susceptible to exploitation. A major risk to justice is represented if intrinsically non-empathic investigators are allowed to feed the press with sensationalism that distorts the truth. Such people understand that fears of the public at large can easily amplify a moral panic, and they do not hesitate to exploit this. This happened in all three cases examined in this book. The media, especially tabloid newspapers and the relatively new phenomenon of news/chat/celebrity gossip websites are driven by sales and clicks. Any extravagant and exaggerated news programme about violent crime is welcomed and highlighted. The maxim of the Daily Mail's founder, Lord Northcliffe, 'get me a murder a day', has never been truer. The press should not be allowed to comment on suspects after they have been arraigned, and abuse of pre-trial detention should be censured.

To minimise the risks of abuse of power there needs therefore to be more formal discipline and a strict division of powers and responsibilities, starting with crime scene investigation. The people whose job is to analyse the crime scene need to be properly trained and monitored from outside, so that in the critical early stages evidence of high quality is collected. Trained individuals using established techniques should apply the scientific method at all stages. Witness evidence needs to be obtained early in an unbiased manner, taking recognition of the power of confirmation bias, and false memories. Detailed written notes need to be kept, and all interrogations of suspects need to be video-recorded. Such procedures should be monitored and subjected to audit by individuals outside the polizio-judicial system.

To reduce the risk of creating a psychopathic local justice system the prosecution service needs to be separate from the police, and also from the judiciary; Italy's system whereby the public prosecutor controls everything, beginning with the forensic investigation, is clearly vulnerable to deliberate or inadvertent abuse, since even the best prosecutors are also flawed human beings; some will have the same negatively empathic characteristics as full-blown primary psychopaths. The risks are compounded by role swapping; judges doubling up as prosecutors. Individuals at all levels need to be held accountable for mistakes, and sanctions need to be meaningful.

In the light of all this, trial procedures need to be overhauled, with much greater recognition of the imperfections of individual systems, and of the general imbalance in favour of the prosecution. Greater weight needs to be given for advocacy in favour of the accused, and to *establishing real, rather than merely judicial, truth*. Juries should be drawn from areas remote from the crime, and sequestered (i.e. kept away form outside influences) as happens in the UK.

Judges need to insist that assertions in court are supported by presentation of facts; and experts must be able to justify their claims by reference to verified data and studies. In addition, judges should be required to study forensic science to a level that enables them to demonstrate that they understand expert evidence and are able to challenge it with authority when appropriate. In recognition of the ever-present possibility of infiltration of psychopathic behaviour leading to injustice, this overhaul should extend beyond the trial, with independent systems of review that are fair and effective. Obviously those who made a contested decision, must not be able to block its review as happened with Darlie Routier. Expert witnesses, particularly those who are consulted on medical and quasi-medical matters, should have been approved for this role by a panel of their peers before they are allowed to embark on what, in some cases, can be a lucrative sideline that can include influencing juries towards convicting the innocent.

Finally, prison privatisation inevitably distorts the function of imprisonment away from justice and towards increasing profits. Where this happens as in the USA, profits equate to long prison sentences in stark prisons, while powerful prison corporations spend large sums lobbying politicians to approve the building of more facilities. There have even been cases of judges being bribed to increase sentences. These institutions are also engaged in what amounts to slave labour. This runs counter to the increasing recognition that overly punitive sentences achieve little except to destroy lives and provide more work for the prison systems.

CHAPTER TWELVE

Preventing Injustice: A New Psychopathological Approach

The central argument of this book is that all supposed justice systems have intrinsic weaknesses and that many arise from human psychopathology. If this is not recognised and addressed, innocent people will continue to be caught in the line of fire, convicted and punished. These systems operate in the *name* of justice, but as the cases described in this book show often merely pay lip-service to the scientific method or fail to adopt it correctly. There is no reason to do other than insist on having scientific proof that an individual has committed a particular crime.

We conclude that all too often the root cause of such cases may lie in individuals lacking sufficient emotional empathy, working within and further developing a psychopathic comfort zone that is ripe for targeting innocent soft targets as happened to Amanda Knox, Raffaele Sollecito, Stefan Kiszko and Darlie Routier. In order to address this, as we have argued, a less emotionally charged term than 'psychopathic' is needed. After all, what we need to address is the *potential* for harm unique to a particular kind of individual, acting under a professional umbrella that tends to encourage this.

A less pejorative term

One problem with discussing people with an intrinsic high propensity to abuse positions of power and responsibility comes from the fact that the terms 'psychopath' and 'sociopath' tends to be pejorative. It is not fair to condemn someone for what they might do. Both describe the worst *consequences* of a particular brain dysfunction, and not its root cause. We have suggested using the term constitutional negative empathy (CNE), with the affected individual being termed a constitutional negative empath.

This fits well for those normal people who lack this propensity, as noted by the writer and self-confessed sociopath M E Thomas in her insightful book *Confessions of a Sociopath* (*Chapter 1*).

The acronym CNE certainly shows more respect for many important people in our midst than categorising them all as primary psychopaths. It is less censorious, does not imply any *necessary* wrongdoing, and so should concern or upset fewer affected people. And it does not imply that nothing positive can be done about such individuals, especially when young, to prevent them from becoming full-blown psychopaths, and to help them to channel their particular qualities in positive directions.

Violent, sexual, and paedophilic CNEs are of course what most people understand by the word 'psychopath'. The late Sir Jimmy Savile, who was seemingly protected for years by people who for whatever reason failed to ask questions, was it seems from the available evidence, an active and dangerous *paedophilic CNE*. But such individuals can also be classified by occupation, as professional, financial, prosecutorial, medical, political, etc., referring simply to the given area within which the subject operates. The common factor is that all have the an inherent defect in amygdala function and in their core empathy circuit, that sets them apart from most people in society and who are therefore unable to socialise normally. This defect makes them all in specific ways difficult and potentially dangerous people. An important part of the danger they pose as adults comes from an unwillingness to recognise the danger signs in childhood and adolescence. One of the most dangerous propensities of people with CNE is that they may engage in *instrumental aggression*, which is easiest and most tempting within their chosen spheres of expertise.

The purpose of the criminal justice systems

Criminal justice systems have two essentially different functions. The first is to *detect and as far as possible to prevent* crimes, including crimes of violence. The second is to secure *appropriate punishment for the guilty, and arguably some retribution or reparation for victims*. There are variants on these purposes depending on the standpoint of individuals: some prefer a restorative or problem-solving approach rather others a retributive one (with CNEs arguably at the extreme punitive end of this scale), but all agree on the need to prevent crime in some way. The system itself has a responsibility not to actually make things worse. Thus, for example, we do not want to punish a criminal in such a way that, once his or her punishment is over, he or she is even more likely to commit further crimes. And there is a doubly important reason not to convict the wrong person; it is unjust, a miscarriage of justice and leaves the real perpetrator at large.

Can justice systems be improved?

No system can ever be perfect, but that is no argument against striving for perfection. The first step is to acknowledge that some people within any system will inevitably try to abuse it. This fundamental assumption results from the fact that all systems are run by human beings. We contend that the three cases in this book involved unjust prosecutions, within three jurisdictions from notionally civilised countries each with a background of a supposedly Christian ethic. Individually and together, they highlight many problems, and show that advances in forensic science offer no guarantee of justice unless properly deployed, and if they are themselves misused may instead lend a spurious validity to outcomes, including under the misplaced rules or due to *dietrologia*.

DNA-profiling is one advance, whose very sensitivity makes it easy to misuse; sensitivity and specificity are quite different things, but corrupt, failing, inadequate or misguided systems can obscure this. With low copy number DNA, as the sensitivity increases, the specificity decreases; and to ensure justice we require absolute specificity.

Now, for the first time, we have some objective scientific under-standing of the functioning of the human brain. One of its grossest pathological disturbances, CNE, disrupts the brain's complex empathy circuit. Magnetic resonance imaging (MRI) actually allows us to visu-alise different parts of the brain, working in real time, and to quantify the function in response to signals representing distress in others. And there is every reason to believe that such techniques will be refined in the coming years. For the first time the response to specific psycholog-ical stimuli can be measured objectively, and used to study the basis of specific types of potential criminal thinking. The same can of course also be applied to the judicial and prosecutorial mind. Such advances present a quantum leap forward, when compared with the subjective assessments by 20th-century psychologists such as Freud and Jung whose sometimes unclear theories can now be questioned and tested.

The need for a modern understanding of science

Our management of criminals and criminal investigations, and the relevant justice systems, would be expected to have changed for the better as a result of advances in science. Instead, the systems themselves seem often to be locked in a time warp, with strong suspect-centric tendencies and confirmation bias at all levels. Time-and-again we see that the rules of evidence are no guarantee of justice if the system itself is weighted against the truth; because people within it, as we have sought to demonstrate, must be assumed to show intrinsic bias, just as all other humans do.

Within our legal systems we need to fit a modern understanding of the scientific basis of the types of 'evil' mind that lie behind crimes of aggression. The biological basis of evil and good, of aggression and friendship, determine how human beings interact with and care for one another. Within societies there are two seemingly conflicting models of human interaction; one that depends on control, and one on the give and take of normal social interaction. For the latter to develop we have seen the need to see in the distress of another a mirror of one's own potential distress. What principally stops normal people from engaging in crimes is not prescribed rules or religious beliefs, but inherent brain biology. Empathy lies at the very base of morality and is essential for human socialisation. From early childhood this is a powerful force to restrain us from deliberately harming others. Unfortunately a specific defect in this circuitry lies at the root of CNE and so of psychopathy.

Recognising the empathy system and its defects

So if we are to improve our justice systems we need to understand our weaknesses, and how we and others exploit them. If we fail here, even the most empathic among us may miss the danger posed to ourselves and others by individuals who completely lack emotional empathy, and who abuse the power this gives them. Each and every structure and profession in our modern world needs to recognise the nature of such individuals and the harm they can do unchecked, through their inability to socialise and their capacity for instrumental (targeted) aggression. For effective prevention, they do need to be recognised at an early stage, and then understood. Then, given the right constraints, indeed, some may and do make positive contributions to the lives of others. Such people are thick-skinned and fearless, and so the best may be good as well as bad natural leaders; Winston Churchill it is said was a bully at school. They do not, however, lead their lives by the same rules as the rest of us.

The violent criminal

Looking first at violent criminals, there is no disagreement that the most dangerous of these score high on Robert Hare's Psychopathy Checklist Revised (PCL-R), especially for features related to lack of empathy and conscience (Group 1 features). These offenders, who are mostly men, need to be treated differently from other criminals. They are unlikely to improve with education, and it may not be possible to rehabilitate them into normal society, since studies have shown that with training they simply learn to be better at committing *instrumental* crimes and at escaping detection. On the other hand other criminals whose violence has come from *reactive* aggression are likely to improve and to become more responsible as they grow older. They may simply need appropriate psychological counselling and training, for example to cope with and manage anger, and to avoid circumstances (including drugs and alcohol) that make them more prone to violence. For them prolonged incarceration for its own sake is costly to society, at best pointless and at worst highly damaging. On the other hand for the serial psychopathic murderer who cannot be reformed, lifelong incarceration (life imprisonment with a 'whole life' but possibly a reviewable tariff) may indeed be necessary.

It is our contention that CNEs also exist on the 'robed side' of the legal divide. Punishment traditionally meets violence with violence, so it should come as no surprise that the same type of brain that can flout the law without guilt might under different circumstances comfortably work within the law risking injustice. This does, after all, have a certain symmetry. We just need to consider the violent nature of retribution — with its Old Testament teaching of 'an eye-for-an-eye and a tooth-for-a-tooth.' We saw this in the case of Stefan Kiszko, an innocent man who ended up being in the wrong place at the wrong time, and was fitted into a pre-existing decision that he was the culprit in a way that would not have occurred with a better understanding of CNE traits and confirmation bias. As a result, he was falsely convicted of a brutal paedophile murder that he could not possibly have committed. Once in prison and convicted, he too was brutalised by other prisoners as explained in *Chapter 6*. For the same reason, prison authorities although notionally condemning such actions, may, it is sometimes claimed, overlook homosexual rape of other prisoners.

The Meredith Kercher murder case illustrates what happens if the judicial system itself is placed in an Ivory Tower that allows for questionable logic: an institution designed to uphold the law may do so by re-confirming its own mistakes. Following the disaster of the Mussolini years and the Second World War in Italy, the justice system was separated completely from politics. But both should have been fully reformed and safeguards put in place. Politicians in an imperfect democratic system such as we believe Italy has, at least have to present themselves regularly for election. They are not therefore defined as being individuals so intrinsically perfect, *ex officio*, that their actions cannot be questioned. On paper, of course, it is made clear that police, prosecutors and judges just like everyone else need to abide by the law; but the ready (some would say ruthless) use of hard to defend charges of *calunnia* (slander) against public officials, or the threat of them, by public prosecutors at the exchequer's expense can be relied on effectively to silence criticism. Further, the Italian *magistratura* is set up as a locally pyramidal system, a *cosca* (or clan) with power concentrated in a few hands at the top, and little if any geographical mobility. This seems to be a recipe for infiltration by CNEs, who may then be free to create a 'local tyranny' including by appointing people in their own image below them. Unchecked, the same disease will spread laterally, to involve lawyers, and the police (who as we have argued are already well-recognised as being vulnerable).

A 306 page long submission to the Supreme Court by the lawyers of Raffaele Sollecito was considered on March 25th 2015. It is an extremely well-reasoned and forceful legal submission, and reason would say that it simply had to be accepted and Raffaele exonerated if there is any remnant of justice within the law. And fortunately, to the surprise of many, it was. But this depended in our view on reigning-in how advanced the cancer of CNE had by then become. There are even limits to what can be written in such a document for fear of judicial reprisal!

It could not be suggested in Italy, for example, that there had been a prosecution-mediated conspiracy, or that there was an attempt to cover up for a failed police investigation or police-led crime. The motivation report, released on September 7ᵗʰ 2015 however castigates those charged with investigating this crime within a crime, but lays the blame on the non-investigating police. Police, however, acted under the direction of the public prosecutor. Any official errors in this class of public servants are by definition made in good faith, even when it is argued that they have assumed epidemic proportions. This reluctance to call a spade a spade comes from powers given to the *magistratura*, on behalf of citizens and ordinary people, who pay for it through taxes. It therefore seems that a fundamental element of any new deal legal charter is *recognition that the legal system itself must be monitored and effectively controlled, from outside its own ranks, for the occurrence and elimination of CNE behaviour.*

Psychopathology of press and public

In addition to the legal system itself, we have seen a need to control what goes on in the press and the responses of the general public that it influences. Both play an important role in areas in which the brain's empathy circuit is normally involved. The flip side of empathy is hatred directed against those found to be, or painted as being, guilty of horrendous crimes. Intrinsically empathic people can themselves easily fall into this psychological trap. In a trial the jury is supposed to be impartial, and that can only happen if its members have not already made up their minds or made them up too soon, without properly considering all safe evidence. If they have erred, this belief is then compounded by the fact that the prosecution presents its case and evidence first. This allows confirmation bias to set in, and the defence may have an uphill task and an impossible job to shift the thinking of individual jury members, let alone secure a sufficient majority, back towards an unbiased and fair decision.

It is easy to be lulled into thinking that because a trial takes place in a courtroom, this insulates it from the outside; but with the best will and rules in the world that is never the case. This fact must be the single strongest argument against the jury system, and in favour of one that involves well-vetted and trained judges. It is why, notionally at least, in Britain and the USA, as soon as someone has been charged with a crime, there is supposed to be an information shutdown around it, certainly as regards prejudicial information concerning the suspect. This is in recognition of the presumption of innocence, which as we have seen helps counterbalance things that will always favour the prosecution, back towards the defendant. So control of the excesses of the media becomes of great importance. It is not just about a free press but responsibilities.

The English and USA media can sometimes be bad enough in this regard by using subtle modes of expression, but the Italian system, with its free and open press speculation and open discussion of prosecution evidence, is inimical to justice. It is not really supposed to happen like this, but it seems that almost routinely police and prosecutors act together to feed the press with tidbits and innuendo, preparing the public and potential jurors in turn for the sculpted evidence that will follow. Thus, as explained in *Chapter 2*, as early as two days after Meredith Kercher's murder the press was being fed with indications that this was a crime involving a woman, and someone who was close to the deceased victim. There we also considered the lies, half-truths and spin that went into first the character assassination and then the conviction of Amanda Knox. Hans Kramer, author of *Maleficus Maleficarum*, described in *Chapter 10* might well have felt at home here. Fortunately, again, the Supreme Court's motivation report is highly critical of the role and exploitation of a press hungry for sex and scandal. It does not, however, deal with impact of the blogosphere beloved of the likes of Harry Rag (*Chapter 5*).

Italian problems

In Italy there are several other indicators of a criminal justice system out of control. One is that prosecutors and judges come from the same nest, and operate interchangeably. In the appeal of Amanda and Rafaelle, the prosecutors to a man or woman were incensed that judges Hellmann and Zanetti had not been taken from the panel of *criminal* trial judges, in other words from what we will call the 'party of the prosecutors.' Doubtless Hellmann and Zanetti were not therefore vulnerable to the sort of behind the scenes activities that one close colleague can exert on another if they are from within the same *cosca*. In their opinion this made them unfit to consider the case, ostensibly because of inexperience but really for fear of their being too open-minded.

But wait a minute! Guilt or innocence are supposed to be determined by scientifically provable objective *facts,* not the kind of obtuse assertions that we see time-and-time again emanating in court from prosecutors in a system that seems to give more weight to the number of words used than to their meaning. In fact, even under Hellmann and Zanetti, and doubtless for the very reason that they were trying not to be tripped up, it was astonishing to witness how little discipline the judges exerted over the prosecution. And in the Nencini appeal against that appeal, it was evident to us that the judge was much less tolerant of the defence lawyers than of the prosecution. Is it possible to suggest that the prosecutors influenced matters behind the scenes, and that the judges in turn failed to discipline prosecutorial excesses in court? Such indiscipline is something seen time-and-again in Italian committee meetings, but in court it really matters if misrepresentations and factual errors are left unchallenged.

Another special problem in Italy is the dilution — or rather the swamping — of the *criminal* case with the *civil* case by both being run concurrently, so that much less protection is offered to the accused which we have also described fully in earlier chapters.

A third problem is that in Italy legal processes and trials proceed at snail's pace, during which time the accused tends to be treated as if he or she were guilty. The 'non-existent' bail system is such that individuals can, effectively, be punished in anticipation via the use of prolonged incarceration before trial. No court decision except the very last, is ever final, and every court's decision can be appealed in the Supreme Court by the prosecution as well as by the defence. The justice system is a stop-start process that can never get up to speed, and its slowness means that the lay members of the jury are free to discuss the evidence with the press and in public. So in the end the court's decision will only go against the prosecution if, as in the case of the Hellmann appeal, the judges themselves are actually not already siding with the prosecutor.

A final problem arises from prejudicial publicity and the fact that everyone holds an opinion, especially if the case involves the murder of a women or child. For anyone to get off on appeal it basically needs two trials—one in the official system, another in the court of public opinion.

American problems

The 51 states of the USA each have independent laws and legal systems; the federal courts are only involved for crimes that cross state borders, occur in or involve a federal jurisdiction (for example, US-registered ships at sea, crimes involving the mails), or towards the end of the tortuous appeals system. The single greatest problem in Texas, where Darlie Routier was tried and convicted is undoubtedly the existence of the death penalty. Of course, along with this comes a whole range of supposed checks to make sure it is not applied to innocent people such as in our opinion Darlie clearly is. A second major problem is the extreme politicisation of the legal system, of which a peculiar anomaly is that the general public elects its own prosecutors and, in some states, its judges. Prosecutors in turn see this as a step up the career ladder towards becoming a judge, some other political office, private legal practice, or other private sector position. And the President of the United States appoints, with approval by a majority of the US Senate, the judges of the USA Supreme Court and all other federal judges, to fill any vacancy.

A third major problem in the USA is that it is made extremely difficult for an individual once convicted to appeal, and this is the case even when new facts come to light to show that the evidence used to convict them was false, or that evidence was withheld from the jury. Once the trial has taken a person past the point of presumed innocence they are presumed guilty; this contrasts with Italy, where on paper at least you are presumed innocent right to the end of the whole legal game of chequers.

It is just that in Italy you are *treated* as if you are guilty, while in law you are still *presumed* to be innocent.

A fourth problem, which again stems from the politicisation of the legal system, is the number of people in prison and the enormous length of prison sentences. No politician can be seen at election time to be 'soft on crime.' Politically driven crackdowns on crime started at about the time of Ronald Reagan's presidency, with in some states such concepts as 'three strikes and you're out' (which spread to England and Wales) — that is incarceration for life (or automatically a longer sentence). Some of these strikes, which may be relatively trivial individually, can occur when you are still a minor. With anti-social crimes perpetrated by non-psychopaths this behaviour peaks in the late-teens and thereafter declines dramatically. So the per capita prison population in the USA is now the highest in the world, and has tripled to 2.3 million since 1980 including many people who should not really be there in justice terms.

In an attempt to manage this problem, two thirds of states sub-contract to independent prison companies, of which CCA, GSO and Cornell are listed on Wall Street. All are major contributors to the funds of the two main political parties, the Democrats and the Republicans. Federal and state prisons and private prison companies, under the umbrella of 109 UNICOR Prison Industries, paying as little as 23 cents an hour, use what is in effect slave labour. They manufacture most of the US armed forces' protective gear, and a host of everyday items; and since six times as high a percentage of black men as white men are in prison, one could argue that slavery was never in fact abolished, it just became state-sponsored.

British problems

The 'crime' behind the mis-conviction of Stefan Kiszko considered in *Chapter 6* took place in 1975, in contrast to 1996 for Darlie Routier, and 2007 for Amanda Knox and Raffaele Sollecito. So we are not comparing contemporaneous events. On the other hand, the conviction of Ronald Castree, the real murderer of Lesley Molseed for which crime Kiszko had been falsely convicted of, also took place in 2007. It depended principally on DNA evidence, which since it related to semen on the dead girl's clothing, was extremely strong evidence of guilt. Of the three cases in this book, Kiszko's is the only one in which the conviction was backed up by a false confession (immediately retracted) and it well illustrates the continuing power of the confession in the mind of the general public, and therefore of juries. The confession once made is not neutralised by a retraction (and the Kercher and Routier cases shows how a non-confession or inadequate denial can have a similar effect).

What we often do see in Britain is a willingness to introduce changes in the light of past injustices, even if these injustices are only righted slowly. There is probably less resistance to facing-up to institutional mistakes in Britain. Since the time of Kiszko's conviction, England has introduced the Crown Prosecution Service, which takes the power for deciding who to prosecute, out of the hands of the police. The false conviction of the Guildford Four and Birmingham Six took a great deal of effort and pressure from the public to overturn and it remains the case that righting any miscarriage of justice is frequently a long, painful, stressful and costly process.[1]

As we have seen in relation to the Kercher case, the controls such as they are on the British press concerning cases at home do not apply when writing or broadcasting about crimes by or against British citizens abroad. And in Italy, regardless of the truth, the press (and the blogosphere) can be as biased as they like, safe in the knowledge they will not be sued (unless, maybe, for attacking the system itself!).

Problems that affect all three jurisdictions

There is a qualitative as well as quantitative difference between different types of anti-social behaviour, and this is well recognised from studies on criminal offenders. The Hare Psychopathy Checklist Revised (PCL-R) considers and evaluates the emotional component and the anti-social component. The former depends on an inherent defect in part of the brain's empathy circuit, the amygdala, which is the fundamental basis of constitutional negative empathy (CNE). The anti-social components of the checklist, on the other hand, are influenced independently by

---

1. For further information, see e.g. *The First Miscarriage of Justice* by Jon Robins, (2015) Waterside Press which contains an explanation of the role and workings of the Criminal Cases Review Authority and its inter-action with the Court of Appeal.

environmental deprivation and emotional or physical abuse by others, especially during the brain's formative years. Both components of the checklist involve aggression; the one unique to Type 1 features (i.e. CNE) is termed *instrumental* aggression. The Type 2 (anti-social) features are associated with *reactive* aggression, which, although also increased in psychopaths, is a normal form of provoked aggression, mediated by connections within the frontal cortex. In anti-social individuals this reactive aggression is triggered at a much lower threshold than normal; it is also susceptible to behavioural management, which instrumental aggression is not. Returning to the Kercher murder, it seems that Rudy Guede scores high for both components.

Since the powerful technique of DNA profiling was developed in Great Britain in the 1980s by Peter Gill and Alec Jeffreys, it is worth listening to their cautions over its use, and specifically how the very power of the technique can swamp other more mundane, but completely exculpatory, evidence such as a watertight alibi. This swamping led to the false imprisonment in the UK of Adam Scott for six months for a violent crime of rape. Finally, and fortunately it was realised in that case that there had been a contamination event between his DNA sample and the crime sample, which was also analysed in the same laboratory.[2] Gill is especially cautious in his warnings about the dangers of expert witnesses, who are often used as instruments of the prosecution.

Should considerations regarding the empathy circuit influence selection for entry into the professions of law enforcement? It seems self-evident that CNE in a prosecutor or judge is likely to bias his or her decision-making; so should there be some restriction on people who are made that way from entering this profession? We do not, after all, allow people who are colour blind to drive public service vehicles or fly aircraft, because they cannot distinguish between red (for stop) and green (for go); so why should we allow the empathy-deficient to operate in an area where empathy recognition in others is important? And/or, should there be some form of ongoing checks through a person's career, to make sure the individual has not been changed adversely by experience, to the extent

---

2. See http://www.independent.co.uk/news/uk/crime/rape-accused-adam-scott-was-victim-of-forensics-error-regulator-finds-8193163.html

that he or she is losing his or her judgement, and any inborn tendency to CNE is being hardened by practice?

Selection for entry into a profession such as the law usually occurs when the individual is still not fully mature; but we know that CNE is largely inherent, is evident in young children and adolescents by for example a tendency towards bullying behaviour and cruelty to animals, and that it is determined by neurotransmitter problems in the central amygdala relay station. For the first time in history if we set our minds to it we should be able to detect the presence of CNE in young people, using objective scientific criteria, and then look for ways of stopping it from getting worse or harming others, and helping to integrate them in society without damaging others. This forms a major part of the argument proposed by lawyer M E Thomas in her book *Confessions of a Sociopath*.

'Cloning'

There seem to be problems with like people selecting like, especially in terms of CNE. The existing peer-driven selection process for professions is likely to exclude youngsters with gross behavioural disorders revealed in childhood or adolescence; however the main criteria used are always academic accomplishment and knowledge.

The systems we have described are, as we have argued earlier, suscep- tible to CNE traits and practitioners of a similar mind-set. The latter lack a normal aggression inhibition mechanism whereby they feel the distress of another as their own, and so they have failed to socialise normally. The consequence is that they tend to engage in instrumental aggression especially against the vulnerable, and that may include the innocent and the accused, a fact that is intrinsically inimical to justice itself. As part of the syndrome they are fearless, will cover up, show superficial charm, even lie and come to believe their own falsehoods. As they move upwards in any profession, CNEs will tend to appoint those below them who are similar, or will at least keep quiet or comply, and will exclude people who question their authority or actions. There are few better ways of ensuring compliance than threatening a person's job or future career prospects. This tends to distort the system itself, a process that will get worse with time. We would argue that to a high degree in all three cases described in this book there is evidence of collective or institutional empathic failure, which in turn has been set in place through the effect of a defective system or one or more CNEs in critical positions of power within the justice system.

If this sounds an extreme argument, it is necessary to reflect that some professions select specifically *in favour* of such factors. It is, for example, obvious that the special armed forces are drawn from members of those who lie at the extremes of deficient empathy. They are kept in check (supposedly) by strict rules of discipline, and it may be argued that extreme psychopaths tend to be eliminated because their fearlessness may put special operations at risk. But these fighters are undoubtedly selected for a range of skills and traits, among which are fearlessness and the capacity to switch off empathy. We have already pointed out that within the medical profession, the least empathic tend to move into areas where patient contact is lower (such for example as pathology), rather than physicians who need to communicate with all sorts of people. And certainly surgeons need to develop a thick skin and not dwell too much on their inevitable past mistakes.

Intrinsic problems

Our justice systems evolved in the medieval period, when the individual meant little in comparison to maintaining order in society as a whole. This in turn involved the use of superstitious and religious beliefs for the purpose of control. Whatever the system of order, individuals with CNE tend to work their way into positions of authority. In the words of Lord Acton, power corrupts, and absolute power corrupts absolutely. The concept of 'guilty beyond reasonable doubt' led to rules of evidence, which have been refined progressively as new techniques such as finger-print analysis and in modern times DNA profiling were developed, but these very techniques hold dangers, since they can easily be abused.

What can and should we learn

How can the deficiencies in current justice systems be countered, and what are the lowest common denominators for *polizio-judicial* reform? We suggest a basic minimum procedure and practice to be shared by the civilised world, which the United Nations and all signatories should accept. These should be designed to:

- minimise the risk that individuals with CNE get into and then retain positions of power at all levels within and in all arms of the country's *polizio-judicial* system;
- prevent the inadvertent or intentional targeting of innocent people at all levels of the system;
- define basic forensic good practice, especially in cases of murder, rape and crimes of violence;
- detect and neutralise as rapidly as possible rogues within the system;
- monitor and audit all cases of unjust prosecution, and learn from the 'near miss', as for example explained by Peter Gill in the UK 'DNA near miss' case of Adam Scott.
- prevent practitioners and juries from engaging in confirmation bias; and
- prevent and hold authorities and individuals accountable for abuses of human rights, such as prolonged and unnecessary pre-trial detention.

Some of our tentative suggestions summarised

1. The inclusion in the forces of law and order, notably the police, prosecutors and judiciary, of individuals with CNE presents a grave risk for the innocent. It may never be possible to exclude such individuals completely, but measures should be in place to minimise their potential for harm. We believe that abuse of power by such people may well lie at the heart of many miscarriages of justice. We are not picking specifically on these professions, except that they hold the responsibility for solving crimes and administering justice. As we have discussed, finding the truly guilty provides the opportunity for preventing further crimes, while convicting an innocent person protects the guilty and may even give the actual perpetrator a false sense of bravura.

2. There is evidence that over more than half a century one sadistic psychopath in the USA (Edward Wayne Edwards) single-handedly exploited others within the police and justice systems to pin his own murders on dozens of innocent people (arguably including on Darlie Routier: *Chapter 7*). We think that there is an urgent need to profile individuals entering the police and the legal profession for such elements as empathy as well as honesty and intelligence. Re-evaluations should be undertaken at regular intervals, and when an individual is promoted within or across professions.

3. There should be much better continuing education within all professions that are concerned with justice on modern concepts of psychology and the psychopathology of violence, as well as about the biology of men and women: *Chapter 9*.

4. In Italy, there is a national obsession with crimes of violence, as revealed in such popular programmes as *Chi l'ha visto?* and *Porta a Porta*. Thus within ten days of the horrific murder of eight-year-old Loris Stival, the public prosecutor had provided the media with many stories indicating the unreliability or supposed downright lying of Loris' mother, who herself denies having had anything to do with her son's death. Salacious comments on blogs reinforce this. We saw the same thing within four days with Amanda Knox. This included detailed discussion of taped phone conversations between various friends and relatives, information that was promptly and inaccurately leaked to the press. This all leads to a presumption of guilt, and public condemnation, which makes a later fair trial virtually impossible. It provides the public prosecutor with even more power than is already provided *ex officio*. Such actions should be forbidden, and the subject of sanctions, with individuals held responsible for their actions; all officials in positions of power should be required to take out malpractice insurance against affecting the outcome of trials. This needs to be attended with a much more effective sanctioning system. For example the commissioning of the cartoon in the Perugia trial, recognised to

be at best irrelevant, should have been charged to the responsible prosecutors, or their insurers.

5. We have seen that confirmation bias means that once individuals have formed a view they have a natural tendency to see only evidence that supports it, and to discount or blot out anything that refutes it. Even the most objective of us are imbalanced in this context. If you add this to a poor understanding of science, and of the evaluation of evidence, you have a recipe for convicting solely because the prosecutor is pushing for it. We therefore propose that there needs to be a marked tightening up of regulations concerning what the press can and cannot write, and what prosecutors and police may or may not say. At least in the UK there are stricter regulations once an individual has been charged; but this does not apply to cases that are being tried abroad, which it should. There are doubtless other important details to be included in this regard in a public prosecutor's code of practice.

6. At the present time successful prosecutions do not necessarily have anything to do with a finding the truth, and much to do with one-sided arguments that paint a picture of guilt. In Italy this is enhanced by two major aberrations. The first of these is that there is no career separation between judges and public prosecutors. There is little attempt to move prosecutors and judges between different jurisdictions and much too much power is placed in the hands of the public prosecutor. This needs to be addressed, by arrangements to monitor for behind the scenes deals or briefing of any kind and rules to deal with the situation.

7. In a jury trial, a group of supposedly normal individuals with no formal training in the evaluation of evidence is called upon to adjudicate between two opposing versions of the truth; that of the prosecutor and defendant. There should be much greater education of jurors, and attention paid to the opinions of dissenting voices within the jury. It is extremely doubtful whether juries as seen in

Italy where there is a mixture of professional judges and lay jurors, can function as anything other than rubber stamps. Therefore there should be removal of the judges from the jury, and restoration of judges to a position *super partes,* such as is seen in England. We believe that there is a case for criminal cases in all jurisdictions to be tried by trained judges rather than a non-expert lay jury: see especially problems discussed in *Chapters 8* and *9.*

8. There is a need in our view to minimise elements of retribution within the justice system, and to be prepared to review especially anomalous cases, and the cases of individuals who continuously protest their innocence. Also for the development of formal scientific review of the psychology of individuals who have been convicted of horrendous crimes, in an environment that is separated from that leading to their conviction. This also means that the death penalty (where applicable) should be seen as impeding justice, and declared by the UN to be a violation of human rights. For example, in the case of Darlie Routier, an independent federal review system should be able to override the local Texas bureaucracy by recognising and negating obvious injustice. The black hole of conviction needs to be weakened in favour of the innocent person who has been trapped by it. Modern concepts of psychopathology need to enter the justice system at all levels.

9. The use of one trial to bias another trial, as we saw in the case of the fast track Rudy Guede verdict influencing that of Amanda Knox and Raffaele Sollecito is highly prejudicial. Within Europe, the power of the European Court of Human Rights to monitor trials as they are in progress should be increased, especially when there is common knowledge of abuses of procedure. The European Court of Human Rights needs to be made much more proactive, and do much more to force the more flagrant violating countries to step into line, and reform their procedures.

10. The capacity for opinionated individuals (such as the notorious Harry Rag: *Chapter 5*), to hide behind pseudonyms on the internet, blogs and social media, is highly prejudicial to justice. This is not a trivial matter and has led to a phenomenon closely resembling the witch trials of the past. There can surely be no justification for allowing comments in the press and the blogosphere to be made by persons whose identity is concealed. This is surely a matter demanding urgent consideration by the European Court of Human Rights and those responsible for policing the internet.

Conclusion

We have attempted to examine the means by which justice is delivered in the 21st-century in three prominent western democracies and we believe we have learned lessons and made recommendations that, if implemented, might reduce the possibility of miscarriages of justice in the future. The law is administered in a similar way and doubtless with similar flaws in most other countries that have their roots in western European civilisation, so there ought to be wider implications.

The origins of criminal justice lie in the need for those in power to control society, maintain the status quo, keep order and (if need be) subjugate the population, as Michel Foucault and others have argued. Religion and superstition played a part and punishment was deployed to enforce obedience and to act as a deterrent to criminals, *pour encourager les autres*. Offenders were often identified in arbitrary ways, confessions were forced and closure may have been more important than true justice. Times have moved on and the law has evolved to the point where genuine justice is sought for the benefit of society as a whole, not merely in the interest of an elite. Unfortunately this does not mean that scientific discoveries have always been properly deployed and our growing understanding of brain function and personality development has yet to be adequately recognised in the legal sphere.

If we were designing a justice system from scratch, it might look very different to what we have today. In the words of the individual who was asked for directions, 'Well, if I were you, I wouldn't start from here.' Nevertheless, we are here and reform is likely to be incremental rather than sweeping. The three false convictions we have written about provide examples of many of the challenges facing defendants in the often random, sometimes unfair (and even sometimes it might be argued) malicious contemporary criminal courts around the world. We believe that they contain many lessons and demonstrate flaws that are universal—and which may feature in countless miscarriages of justice. It is well past the time for changes in procedure and practice to be implemented.

Our recommendations are a start. There may be other ways in which improvements to justice might be brought about. We hope to see a growing debate on reform and that we have nudged justice a little way down this track. Every innocent person in jail represents a life damaged, a blemish on society and possibly an active criminal who is still at large and free to commit more crimes. This state of affairs is in nobody's interest. It represents a waste for society and an absence of the true justice that should be the aim of everyone. Justice is like a shark. To remain alive, it must keep moving.

Select Bibliography

Bakan, Joel, *The Corporation: The Pathological Pursuit of Profit and Power*, Constable & Robinson, 2004, ISBN 978-1-84529174-7

Baron-Cohen, Simon, *The Essential Difference: Men, Women and the Extreme Brain*, Penguin Books, 2004, ISBN 978-0-241-96135-3

Baron-Cohen, Simon, *Zero Degrees of Empathy: A New Theory of Human Cruelty*, Allen Lane, 2011, ISBN 978-0-713-99791-0

Berlins, Marcel and Dyer, Claire, *The Law Machine*, Fifth Edn., Penguin ISBN 978-0-14-028756-1

Blair, James, Mitchell, Derek and Blair, Karina, *The Psychopath, Emotion and the Brain*, Blackwell Publishing, 2005 ISBN 978-0-631233-36-7

Borman, Tracy, *Witches: A Tale of Sorcery, Scandal and Seduction*, Jonathan Cape, 2013. ISBN-13: 978-0224090568

Borchard, Edwin M, *Convicting the Innocent: Sixty-five Actual Errors of Criminal Justice* (1933), Forgotten Books, 2012, PIBN 1000464649

Burleigh, Nina, *The Fatal Gift of Beauty: The Trials of Amanda Knox*, Broadway Books, 2011, ISBN 978-0-307-58856-6

Cameron, John A, *IT'S ME Edward Wayne Edwards: The Serial Killer You NEVER Heard Of*, Golden Door Press, California, 2014, ISBN 978-1-885793-03-4

Cleckley, Hervey, *The Mask of Sanity: An Attempt to Clarify Some of the Issues About the So-called Psychopathic Personality*, C V Mosby, 3rd edn, 1955, ISBN 978-1-258-0-589-13

Committee on Identifying the Needs of the Forensic Sciences Community, 'Strengthening Forensic Science in the United States: A Step Forward,' 2009, National, Research Council, ISBN 0-309-13131-6, 352 pages, 6 x 9. PDF is available from the National Academies Press at: http://www.nap.edu/catalog/12589.html

Cruz, Kathy, *Dateline: Purgatory: Examining the Case that Sentenced Darlie Routier to Death*, Texas Christian University Press, Fort Worth Texas, 2015, ISBN 978-0-87565-610-6

Davis, Carol Anne, *Women Who Kill: Profiles of Female Serial Killers,* Alison and Busby, 2002, ISBN 978-0-7490-0572-6

Dayan, Colin, *The Law is a White Dog. How Legal Rituals Make and Unmake Persons,* Princeton, University Press, 2011, ISBN 978-0-691-15787-0

D'Elia, Maria, *Il Delitto di Perugia: L'altra Verita* [The Crime of Perugia: The Other Truth], Libro-inchiesta di Oggi, 2010

Dempsey, Candace, *Murder In Italy: The Shocking Slaying of a British Student, The Accused American Girl, and An International Scandal.* A Berkley Book, 2010, ISBN 978-0-425-28283-2

Douglas, John and Olshaker, Mark, *Law and Disorder. The Legendary FBI Profiler's Relentless Pursuit of Justice,* Kensington Books, 2013, ISBN 978-0-7582-7312-3

Dutton, Kevin, *The Wisdom of Psychopaths: Lessons in Life from Saints, Spies, and Serial Killers,* William Heinemann, London, 2012, ISBN 978-0-434-02067-6

Echols, Damien, *Life After Death,* Blue Rider Press, 2012, ISBN 978-0-399-16020-2

Fisher, Bruce, *Injustice in Perugia: A Book Detailing the Wrongful Conviction of Amanda Knox and Raffaele Sollecito,* 2011, ISBN 978-1-453736692

Follain, John, *Death in Perugia: The Definitive Account of the Meredith Kercher Case From Her Murder to the Acquittal of Raffaele Sollecito and Amanda Knox,* Hodder & Stoughton, 2011, ISBN 978-1-444-70655-0

Garrett, Brandon L, *Convicting the Innocent: Where Criminal Prosecutions Go Wrong,* Harvard University Press, 2011, ISBN 978-0-674-06611-3

Gill, Peter, *Misleading DNA Evidence: Reasons for Miscarriages of Justice,* Kindle Edn, 2014, ASIN B00LBXYKT2

Gilmour, David, *The Pursuit of Italy: A History of a Land, Its Regions and Their Peoples,* Allen Lane, 2011, ISBN 978-1-846-14251-2

Ginsborg, Paul, *Italy and Its Discontents. Family, Civil Society, State: 1980-2001,* Allen Lane, 2003, ISBN 1-4039-6152-2

Halttunen, Karen, *Murder Most Foul: The Killer and the American Gothic Imagination,* Harvard University Press, 1998 ISBN 978-0-674-00384-2

Hare, Robert D, *Without Conscience: The Disturbing World of the Psychopaths Amongst Us,* Guilford Press, 1999, ISBN 978-1-57230-451-2

Harris, David A, *Failed Evidence: Why Law Enforcement Resists Science,* New York University Press, 2012, ISBN 978-0-8147-9055-7

Hendry, Ron, *Single Attacker Theory of the Murder of Meredith Kercher,* Kindle Edn., 2013, ASIN B00EAQT2VS

Hendry, Ron, *When Innocence Doesn't Matter: How Flawed Police and Prosecution Methods Led to the Ordeals of Amanda Knox and Raffaele Sollecito*, Kindle Edn, 2015, ASIN B00UTPQSPC

Jarrett, Christian, *The Rough Guide to Psychology: An Introduction to Human Behaviour and the Mind*, Rough Guides Limited, 2011, ISBN 978-1-84836-460-8

Jones, Tobias, *The Dark Heart of Italy*, Faber & Faber, 2003, ISBN 978-0-571-22593-3

Kafka, Franz, *The Trial*, Vintage Books, 2009, ISBN 978-0-099-42864-0

Kahneman, Daniel, *Thinking, Fast and Slow*, Penguin, 2012, ISBN 978-0-141-03357-0. Reprinted by Farrar, Straus and Giroux, 2013, ISBN-10: 0374533555.

Kennedy, Helena, *Just Law: The Changing Face of Justice—And Why it Matters to Us All*, Vintage Books, 2005 ISBN 978-0-099-45833-3

Kercher, John, *Meredith: Our Daughter's Murder, and the Heartbreaking Quest for the Truth*, Hodder & Stoughton 2012, ISBN 978-1-444-74276-3

Kinsey A, C., Pomeroy W. B. and Martin C. E. (1948), *Sexual Behaviour in the Human Male*, Indiana University Press. ('Kinsey Report') ISBN 978-0-253-33412-1

Knox, Amanda, *Waiting to be Heard: A Memoir*, Harper Collins, 2013, ISBN 978-0-06-221720-2

Lynch, Timothy (Ed.), *In The Name of Justice: Leading Experts Re-examine the Classic Article 'The Aims of the Criminal Law'*, Cato Institute Washington DC 2009 ISBN 978-1-933995-22-9

O'Hara, Kieron, *Trust: From Socrates to Spin*, Icon Books 2004, ISBN 1-84046-531-X

Machievelli, Nicholo, *The Prince*, Oxford University Press 1979, ISBN 0-19-283397-9

Mansfield, Michael, *Memoirs of a Radical Lawyer*, Bloomsbury Publishing, 2009, ISBN 978-1-4088-0129-1

Mathieson, Thomas, *Prison on Trial*, Waterside Press, 3rd Edn, 2006, ISBN 978-1-904380-22-1

Medwed, Daniel S, *Prosecution Complex: America's Race to Convict, and its Impact on the Innocent*, Kindle Edn., 2012, ASIN B007FA38KW

Moir, Anne and Jessell, David, *Brain Sex: The Real Difference Between Men and Women*, Mandarin, 1989, ISBN 0-7493-0525-8

Nadeau, Barbie Latza, *Angel Face: The True Story of Student Killer Amanda Knox*, Beast Books, 2010, ISBN 978-0-9842951-3-5

Nerenberg, Ellen, *Murder Made in Italy: Homicide, Media, and Contemporary Italian Culture*, Indiana University Press, 2012, ISBN 978-0-253-22309-8

Patrick, Christopher J (Ed.), *Handbook of Psychopathy*, Guilford Press, New York, 2006, ISBN 978-1-5385-591-8

Petro, Jim and Petro, Nancy, *False Justice: Eight Myths that Convict the Innocent*, Kaplan Publishing, 2010, ISBN 978-1-60714-467-0

Pietras, David, *A Texas-style Witch Hunt 'Justice Denied': The Darlie Routier Story*, David J Pietras 2013, ISBN 978-1-49478-090-6

Preston, Douglas, *The Forgotten Killer: Rudy Guede*, A Kindle Single, 2013, ASIN B00CDU1H98

Preston, Douglas, *Trial By Fury: Internet Savagery and the Amanda Knox Case*, A Kindle Single, 2013, ASIN B00CDU1H98

Preston, Douglas and Spezi, Mario, *The Monster of Florence: A True Story*, Virgin Books, 2008, ISBN 978-0-7535-1704-8

Ramachandran, V. S., *The Tell-tale Brain: Unlocking the Mystery of Human Nature*, Windmill Books, 2012, ISBN 978-0-099-53759-5

Ronson, Jon, *The Psychopath Test: A Journey Through the Madness Industry*, Riverhead Books, New York 2011, ISBN 978-1-59448-575-6

Rose, Justin, Painter, Steve and Wilkinson, Trevor, *Innocents: How Justice Failed Stefan Kiszko and Lesley Molseed*, Fourth Estate, 1997, ISBN 1-85702-402-8

Russell, Paul, Johnson, Graham and Garofano, Luciano, *Darkness Descending: The Murder of Meredith Kercher*, Pocket Books, 2010, ISBN 978-1-84739-862-8

Simon, Dan, *In Doubt: The Psychology of the Criminal Justice Process*, Harvard University Press, 2012, ISBN 978-0-674-04615-3

Sollecito, Raffaele with Gumbel, Andrew, *Honor Bound: My Journey to Hell and Back with Amanda Knox*, Simon & Schuster, 2012, ISBN 978-1-4516-9639-4

Stafford Smith, Clifford, *Injustice: Life and Death in the Courtrooms of America*, Harvill Secker, 2012 ISBN 978-1-846-55625-8

Stout, Martha, *The Sociopath Next Door: The Ruthless Versus the Rest of Us*, Broadway Books, New York 2005, ISBN 0-7679-1582-8

Thomas, M E, *Confessions of a Sociopath*, Pan Macmillan, 2013, ISBN 978-1-4472-4273-4

Vollen, Lola and Eggars, Dave (Eds.), *Surviving Justice: America's Wrongfully Convicted and Exonerated*, McSweeney's, SF, 2008, 3rd Edn. ISBN 978-1-934781-25-8

Vronsky, Peter, *Female Serial Killers: How and Why Women Become Monsters*, Penguin Books, 2007, ISBN 978-0-425-21390-2

Wacks, Raymond, *Philosophy of Law: A Very Short Introduction*, Oxford University Press, 2006, ISBN 0-19-280691-2

Waterbury, Mark C, *The Monster of Perugia: The Framing of Amanda Knox,* A Perception
Development Publication, 2011. ISBN 978-0983-277415

Webster, Richard, *The Secret of Bryn Estyn: The Making of a Modern Witch Hunt,* 2005,
Orwell Press, (revised edn. 2009), ISBN 978-0951-59226-7

Wood, Rocky, Morton, Lisa and Craig Chapman, *Witch Hunts: A Graphic History of the
Burning Times,* Kindle Edn., 2012, ASIN B00ALQDVLI

Index

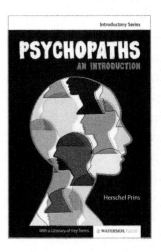

**Danger, Development and
Adaptation: Seminal Papers on
the Dynamic-Maturational Model
of Attachment and Adaptation**
by Patricia McKinsey Crittenden
Edited by Andrea Landini, Martha
Hart, Clark Baim and Sophie Landa.
With a Foreword by Rodolfo de Bernart.

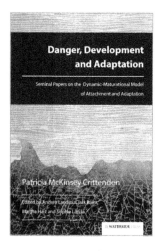

Invaluable to psychologists, psychothera-
pists, psychiatrists, social workers, criminal
justice professionals, mental health and
child protection workers, counsellors, educa-
tors, and people in the helping professions generally. It is also relevant to
people working in the fields of learning disabilities, older adults, fostering
and adoption.

 This volume contains a selection of the seminal works of Patricia
Crittenden, one of the most creative and innovative thinkers
in the history of attachment theory. Crittenden integrates the
fields of developmental psychology and developmental psychopathology in her thought-provoking and insightful research on
attachment in normal and atypical development. Her ground-
breaking work on attachment and child maltreatment stimulated
the field to embark on translational research to prevent attachment insecurity and to promote resilient functioning'
*Dante Cicchetti, PhD., McKnight Presidential Chair, William
Harris Professor and Professor of Child Psychology and Psychiatry,
Institute of Child Development, University of Minnesota*

Hardback & Paperback | ISBN 978-1-909976-27-6 | 2015 | 592 pages

Three Cases that Shook the Law
by Ronald Bartle

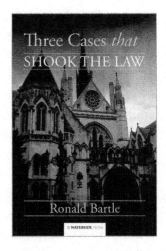

There are cases in the annals of English criminal law that forever resonate. In Three Cases that Shook the Law former district judge Ronald Bartle has selected three for close scrutiny: cases where the defendants paid the ultimate penalty even though demonstrably the victims of injustice. They are those of Edith Thompson who suffered due to her romantic mind-set, a young lover and the prevailing moral climate; William Joyce (Lord 'Haw Haw') where the law was stretched to its limits to accommodate treason; and Timothy Evans who died due to the lies of the principal prosecution witness Reginald John Halliday Christie who it later transpired was both a serial killer and likely perpetrator. Weaving narrative, transcripts and original court records the author presents the reader with a captivating book in which his long experience as a lawyer and magistrate is brought fully to bear.

> A cautionary tale which explores each case in fascinating detail via letters as well as transcripts and original court records. Criminal lawyers especially, as well as magistrates and judges will find it an illuminating read'
>
> *Phillip Taylor MBE and Elizabeth Taylor*
> *of Richmond Green Chambers*

Paperback & ebook | ISBN 978-1-909976-30-6 | 2016 | 240 pages

www.WatersidePress.co.uk

The First Miscarriage of Justice: The 'Unreported and Amazing' Case of Tony Stock
by Jon Robins
With a Foreword by Michael Mansfield QC.

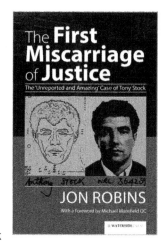

'I would have been the first miscarriage of justice ... There was this spate of cases: the Birmingham Six, Guildford Four and Cardiff Three. Each one was another nail in my coffin': Tony Stock, 2008. The story of Tony Stock is astonishing: deeply disturbing it sent out ripples of disquiet when he was sentenced to ten years for robbery at Leeds Assizes in 1970. Over the next 40 years the case went to the Court of Appeal four times and has the distinction of being the first to have been referred to that court twice by the Criminal Cases Review Commission. Tony Stock died in 2012 still fighting to clear his name: spending from his meagre savings to hire private investigators and hoping beyond hope to see justice.

The story of Tony Stock should be mandatory reading for everyone, not merely those involved with the laws. It concerns the quality of our criminal justice system and its serious reluctance and unwillingness to root out injustice'

Michael Mansfield QC

One of the most outrageous miscarriages of justice of modern times'

Barry Sheerman, Labour MP for Huddersfield

Paperback & ebook | ISBN 978-1-909976-12-2 | 2014 | 256 pages

Lightning Source UK Ltd.
Milton Keynes UK
UKOW05f1250160916

283153UK00004BA/110/P